THE CHURCH OF
SCIENTOLOGY

THE CHURCH OF
SCIENTOLOGY

A HISTORY OF A NEW RELIGION

HUGH B. URBAN

PRINCETON UNIVERSITY PRESS   PRINCETON AND OXFORD

Library of Congress Cataloging-in-Publication Data

Urban, Hugh B.
The church of scientology : a history of a new religion / Hugh B. Urban.
    p.   cm.
Includes bibliographical references and index.
ISBN 978-0-691-14608-9 (hardcover : alk. paper)   1. Scientology—History.
I. Title.
BP605.S2U73   2011
299′.93609—dc23   2011018694

British Library Cataloging-in-Publication Data is available

This book has been composed in Minion Pro

Printed on acid-free paper. ∞

Printed in the United States of America

1 3 5 7 9 10 8 6 4 2

- CONTENTS -

- ILLUSTRATIONS -

- ACKNOWLEDGMENTS -

Scientology is not an easy topic to write about. Indeed, for the reasons that I recount in this book—ranging from the intense secrecy of the church to its history of aggressive litigation against its critics—Scientology is arguably among the most difficult, contentious, and legally fraught topics one might choose to write about. The research for this book has led me on a rather remarkable journey, from the pulp novels of the golden era of science fiction to the occult circles of 1940s California, from L. Ron Hubbard's voluminous books, lectures, and bulletins to the FBI's extensive cold war files on the church, from secret CIA research on psychic abilities to the IRS's twenty-six-year battle with Scientology, from decentralized groups of Internet activists to Scientology's new wars of information in cyberspace.

Therefore, I need to thank a great number of individuals and organizations for their tremendous help with the writing of this challenging book. First, the Church of Scientology's Bridge Publications and Golden Era Productions were generous enough to send me three large boxes of Hubbard's books and audio recordings of his very early lectures from the 1950s. Several Ohio organizations, such as the Churches of Scientology in Cincinnati and Columbus, also graciously provided a great deal of information and insights into contemporary services and auditing.

Second, I am also indebted to a number of former Scientologists who agreed to be interviewed for this book and provided invaluable historical materials. Foremost among these is Gerry Armstrong, a truly generous individual who provided a tremendous amount of personal narrative, historical insight, primary research materials, and critical feedback on my work. Caroline Letkemen was also incredibly helpful whenever I asked for any advice or needed to track down a specific piece of material. And Hubbard's former personal physician, Jim Dincalci, generously offered his time to recount some fascinating stories from his years in Scientology and his current work with the Forgiveness Foundation.

Numerous current and former Scientologists also agreed to be interviewed for this book but asked to remain anonymous. One of them sent me over fifty pounds of primary materials from his years in the church as well as hours of fascinating interviews. Others recounted tales so remarkable as to be worthy of a cold war spy novel but asked that I not include any details that might trace the story back to them. Out of respect for their anonymity, I have necessarily left out some of the most astonishing material gathered during the research for this book.

Fourth, I would like to thank many members of the anti-Scientology collective known as "Anonymous" for their help in understanding the role of both cyberspace and physical space in their protests against the church. Foremost among them are Chef Xenu, who provided me with a tremendous amount of Scientology materials and fascinating insight into Anonymous, and Xenubarb, who helped me understand the role of new technologies in their physical and cyber protests against the church.

Finally, several editors, colleagues, and students have given me excellent advice and assistance with this project. Foremost among them are Fred Appel, who first suggested this project and whose diligent guidance helped me see it through to completion; the librarians at the University of California, Los Angeles, who were extremely helpful in accessing and sorting through their large special collection on Scientology; Jeffrey Kripal, an inspiring scholar and the only human being to have read almost every one of Hugh Urban's publications; Tanya Erzen, a brilliant ethnographer who really helped me think through the question of how to handle the interview material for this book; Ivan Strenski, whose sharp, critical intellect helped me think carefully about the category of "religion" itself; Catherine Wessinger, Rebecca Moore, Douglas Cowan, and the other editors at *Nova Religio*, who provided excellent feedback on some of my research on Scientology; and Kelly Schultz, an excellent young research assistant who helped me catalog and comb through a large swath of Scientology materials.

THE CHURCH OF
SCIENTOLOGY

- INTRODUCTION -

THE WORLD'S MOST CONTROVERSIAL NEW RELIGION AND WHY NO ONE WRITES ABOUT IT

> We have a practical religion. And before you say, "Religion, grrrr," think
> of that—it is a practical religion and religion is the oldest heritage that
> Man has. . . . We can only exist in the field of religion. Of course, it would
> be up to us to make religion a much better thing than it has been.
> —L. Ron Hubbard, "The Hope of Man" (1955)[1]

> Strange things seem to happen to people who write about Scientology.
> —Richard Behar, "The Scientologists and Me," *Time* (1991)[2]

Surely few new religious movements have been the subject of more scandal, controversy, media attention, or misunderstanding than the Church of Scientology. Well known for its high-profile celebrity patrons such as John Travolta, Kirstie Alley, and Tom Cruise, while boasting over seven hundred centers in sixty-five countries, Scientology has also been attacked by government agencies, anticult groups, and the media as a swindling business and a brainwashing cult. Its founder, L. Ron Hubbard (1911–1986), has been described variously as the man who "solved the riddle of the human mind" (by the Church of Scientology),[3] as "a mental case" (by the FBI),[4] and as "hopelessly insane" (by his former wife).[5] Since the 1950s, Scientology has come into a series of conflicts with various branches of the U.S. government, particularly the FBI, FDA, and IRS, regarding its status as a religious organization and its involvement in an array of alleged crimes. Dubbed the "Cult of Greed" by *Time* magazine, Scientology has been singled out by the media and anticult groups as the most rapacious and dangerous new religious movement today.[6] Among the most withering critiques was one that appeared in a June 2009 series in the *St. Petersburg Times*, which focused on Scientology's current head, David Miscavige. Using interviews from former high-ranking executives, the *Times* recounts an array of alleged abuse, violence, and humiliation at the very top of the church's hierarchy that ranges from the shocking to the downright bizarre.[7]

In response, Scientologists have long argued that this is a legitimate religious movement that has been misrepresented, maligned, and persecuted by media witch-hunters and McCarthy-style government attacks.[8] According to the church's *Freedom* magazine, the religion of Scientology has been consistently pounded by the media, government agencies, and anticult groups with "vituperative rumor, innuendo and allegation, all of which resulted in a hostile environment for the Church" and undermine the very ideal of religious freedom.[9] As such, Scientology raises some of the most profound legal, ethical, and political questions that lie at the very heart of the study of religion in the twenty-first century.

Yet remarkably, despite the tantalizing scandal that surrounds it in popular culture, Scientology has received little serious attention by scholars of religions. Apart from Roy Wallis's early study in 1976, J. Gordon Melton's slim overview, and James Lewis's recent edited volume, Scientology has rarely been submitted to a careful, critical study by historians of religion.[10] While some important scholarship appears in German and other European languages, surprisingly little remains available to English readers.[11]

The reasons for this neglect, however, are not far to seek. First, from its origins, the Church of Scientology and its founder have been shrouded in complex layers of secrecy. With a tight system of security and a complex, esoteric hierarchy of teachings, Scientology is surely one of the most impenetrable and least understood new religions. Second, the church has also tended to respond very aggressively to its critics, mounting numerous lawsuits and at times using extralegal means to respond to those who threaten it. A long list of scholars, journalists, former members, and even ordinary college students have reported being harassed and threatened for writing critically about Scientology.[12]

A History of Scientology as a Reflection on the History of "Religion" in Modern America

In this book, I will by no means attempt to write a new exposé of Scientology, nor do I claim to have infiltrated its inner secrets—something

I consider both fundamentally unethical and deeply problematic from an epistemological point of view. Many such exposés by critics and ex-members already exist, with varying degrees of credibility, and the print and television media appear to be generating ever more as we speak.[13] Instead, I approach Scientology primarily as a historian of religions.[14] My aim is not to unveil yet another secret of Scientology but rather to trace the complex, tangled, and often tortuous history of how this controversial movement came to *describe itself* and eventually *become recognized as* a "religion" in the United States—at least in the eyes of the Internal Revenue Service and the State Department—though, notably, not in the eyes of many other governments. And I want to use this specific case as a way to think more broadly about the complex, shifting, and contested category of "religion" itself in the twentieth and twenty-first centuries.

When L. Ron Hubbard unveiled his "revolutionary new science of the human mind" called Dianetics in 1950, he initially made no particular claims that it had anything to do with religion. If anything, he was quite critical of institutional forms of religion in his early lectures.[15] This position changed rapidly in the early 1950s, however, as Dianetics evolved into the Church of Scientology, first incorporated in December 1953. From the 1950s onward, Scientology began to adopt ever more elements drawn from Eastern religions, alternative spiritualities, and science fiction, such as the notion of an eternal spirit, reincarnation, past-life memories, supernatural powers, and a vast "space opera" history of the universe. Correspondingly, as the church quickly grew in wealth and numbers, it also began to face ever more scrutiny, investigation, and attack by the media and government agencies, particularly the IRS, FBI, and FDA. After an incredibly complex twenty-six-year battle with the Internal Revenue Service and a $12.5 million settlement, Scientology was in fact awarded tax-exempt status as a nonprofit organization by the IRS in 1993 and soon after recognized by the U.S. State Department in its annual report on religious freedom.[16] But the debate has not ended there. Indeed, the church faces a new war of information in the twenty-first century, as decentralized groups such as "Anonymous" challenge its legitimacy as a religion and mount ever more sophisticated forms of technological warfare in cyberspace.

As such, the case of Scientology is a striking example of the complex, shifting, and contested nature of religion in the late twentieth and twenty-first centuries. As the respected historian of religion Jonathan Z. Smith famously observed, our abstract category of religion is itself not a universal, monolithic, or homogeneous entity but rather an "imagined" category, a product of second-order reflection and generalization based on a vast array of diverse texts, myths, rituals, and traditions. As Smith put it, "Religion is solely the creation of the scholar's study. It is created for the scholar's analytic purposes, by his imaginative acts of comparison and generalization. Religion has no independent existence apart from the academy."[17] More recently, Russell McCutcheon has argued that religion is a "manufactured" category, that is, "a scholarly representation that operates within . . . a very specific set of discursive practices" and institutional structures.[18]

While I agree with Smith and McCutcheon that the abstract category of religion is largely an imagined one, I will, however, also argue that the case of Scientology reveals that the imagining of religion is by no means solely a product of scholars or academic institutions. On the contrary, the imagining of Scientology as "religion" has been an extremely complex historical process that spanned six decades and involved fierce debate among a wide range of different actors, only a few of whom are scholars. These include the movement's founder, his followers and ex-followers, the psychoanalytic and medical professions, the media, high-profile celebrity spokespersons, various government agencies such as the FBI, FDA, and IRS, foreign governments, lawyers, judges, anticult activists, and ordinary citizens posting on the Internet, in addition to a small number of academic observers. As David Chidester comments in his study of religion and American popular culture, "[T]he very term 'religion,' including its definition, application and extension does not, in fact belong solely to the academy but is constantly at stake in the interchanges of cultural discourses and practices."[19] And the debate over Scientology continues to this day, both on the streets of major cities and in the networks of cyberspace, as new generations of critics continue to contest the church's legitimacy as a "real" religion. In this sense, a critical history of Scientology gives us profound insights into what Talal Asad calls the "genealogies of religion"—that is, the complex historical construction of the phenomena that we now label "religion."[20]

Although this book focuses on the history of the church in the United States, it will also deal briefly with similar issues raised in the United Kingdom, Germany, Australia, and Russia for a comparative context. Scientology, I will suggest, is a critically important test case for thinking about much larger legal and theoretical issues in the study of religion as whole. Not only does it raise basic questions such as what gets to count as religion and who gets to decide; more important, it also raises profound issues of privacy and freedom of religious expression in a post-9/11 context of religious violence and rapidly expanding government surveillance.[21] Finally, it also forces us to rethink the role of the academic study of religion in the interpretation of controversial groups such as Scientology. How do we balance a truly serious, critical analysis of problematic groups like these while at the same time countering sensationalistic media attacks and respecting basic rights to privacy and freedom of religious expression?

Methodology and Sources: Balancing a Hermeneutics of Respect and a Hermeneutics of Suspicion

Because Scientology is such a ferociously controversial topic, I should first say a few words about myself and my own reasons for writing this book. I am not, have never been, and probably will never be a Scientologist. At the same time, I am also not an anti-Scientologist and have no particular axe to grind with this movement. My own interests in the church are twofold. First, most of my research to date has focused on the role of secrecy in religion—that is, the complex question of why some religious groups choose to keep certain aspects of their beliefs and practices hidden from outsiders, and, in turn, what are the larger social, political, and cultural effects of that secrecy.[22] With its highly confidential levels of advanced training, its intense control of information, and its long history of surveillance and espionage against the U.S. government, Scientology is among the most extreme examples of secrecy in a religious organization. And it raises some of the most challenging ethical and methodological questions involved in trying to understand something that is, to a large degree, closed to outsiders.

Second, I am primarily a historian of religions, and, as such, one of the central questions that interests me is the history of our category of "religion" itself—that is, the ways in which we have debated, defined, and redefined this complex term in relation to shifting historical and cultural contexts. Which groups do we privilege with the label "religion," and which do we exclude? More important, *what are the stakes*—legal, financial, and political—*in laying claim to the status of religion*? And what is at risk when government agencies, media, or academics *deny* a given group such status? Again, with its incredibly complex history of struggle with the IRS, anticult groups, and the media over its "religious" status, Scientology is an ideal test case for this question. In fact, when I teach our Introduction to Comparative Religion course at Ohio State, I often begin with the example of Scientology to force students to think hard about what is and is not a religion, who gets to decide, and what are the deeper investments in the way that we define religion in a complex, pluralistic, democratic society.

Much of the journalistic, academic, and popular literature on Scientology, it seems to me, is highly polarized and tends to fall into one of two rather extreme views. On the one side, we find numerous exposés by ex-members, journalists, and critics, who attack the church as either a cynical, money-driven business or a dangerous cult of mind control and power. Thus, Andrew Morton's best-selling book on Tom Cruise describes Scientology as "a paranoid movement reflecting the schizophrenic personality of the founder, a dogmatic cult dedicated to world domination."[23] Among the more scathing exposés of the church was the 2009 series by the *St. Petersburg Times,* which claims to reveal a "culture of violence of intimidation" that pervades the very highest levels of the church's hierarchy. The material presented in the *Times* report ranges from the disturbing to the surreal, including allegations that current head David Miscavige physically beat his senior executives and—in what would be among the most astonishing incidents in the history of American religions—forced executives to play a brutal, all-night game of musical chairs to the tune of Queen's "Bohemian Rhapsody."[24]

On the other side, many academics writing about Scientology (particularly in the United States) have gone almost to the other extreme, by trying so hard to counter the sensationalistic popular attacks that they at times seem to bend over backward to present the church in a positive light.[25] While the anti-Scientology literature relies almost exclusively on ex-Scientologists and anticult spokespersons, pro-Scientology literature tends to rely primarily on church spokespersons and scholars sympathetic to new religions.

Thus, in my approach to Scientology—and to all religions, old or new—I have tried to adopt a more balanced perspective, using a delicate combination of what I call a hermeneutics of respect and a hermeneutics of suspicion.[26] By a hermeneutics of respect, I mean that I am a firm believer in the First Amendment, religious freedom, and the wonderful diversity of religious worldviews that make the United States such a rich and vibrantly pluralistic democracy. As such, I approach Scientology, like all religious groups, with an attitude of sympathetic respect and a genuine effort to take its claims seriously. By a hermeneutics of suspicion, however, I mean that we should also not be afraid to ask difficult, critical questions of groups such as Scientology (as well as "mainstream" religions). How have they *used* their claims to religious status? What have been the *effects* of this movement on its members and others? What are the social, historical, and political contexts in which this movement emerged, and how did it interact with government, media, and other forces? As we will see in the pages of this book, Scientology has a documented history of extremely problematic behavior ranging from espionage against government agencies to shocking attacks on critics of the church and abuse of its own members. A serious, respectful history of the church does not mean that we should ignore or belittle these aspects of the church—any more than a serious history of the Catholic Church would belittle the Inquisition or sexual abuse by contemporary priests. On the contrary, it demands that we look at these traits as closely, fairly, and critically as the more admirable aspects of the church.

While I am not claiming to expose any new secret information about Scientology in this book, I have drawn upon a great deal of published and unpublished materials that have never before been examined. Among them are Hubbard's first Dianetics and Scientology lectures from the early 1950s, which the church's own Bridge Publications and Golden Era Productions were generous enough to send me in large numbers. I have also made extensive use of UCLA's invaluable special collection on Scientology, which contains thousands of documents, including letters, magazines, flyers, pamphlets, posters, and other ephemera. And I have been fortunate enough to have a very generous former Scientologist send me a vast number of documents from his years in the church, which includes hundreds of magazines, auditing materials, and copies of Hubbard's letters and bulletins. Finally, I have drawn upon the FBI's extensive files on Hubbard and Scientology, obtained through the Freedom of Information Act, and evidence produced during the church's thousands of court cases, many of which give key insights into its pursuit of religious status.

Although this book is primarily a historical study and not an ethnography, I have also done a number of face-to-face, phone, and email interviews with a wide range of both current and former Scientologists. Again, most of the existing literature on Scientology is quite polarized in its use of interview material: while most academic sources rely almost exclusively on official church spokespersons, virtually all of the journalistic exposés rely primarily on highly critical ex-members. In this book, I have striven for a more balanced approach by using interviews with both current and ex-Scientologists to supplement arguments based on the printed material. In so doing, of course, I am fully aware that both current and former Scientologists have their own biases, agendas, and axes to grind; and both kinds of sources therefore need to be read critically and contextually.

Despite these important qualifications, however, I have found the interview material to be some of the most insightful for understanding *both* the powerful appeal of Scientology to many individuals *and* the many controversial, problematic, and at times shocking aspects of this movement. On one side, I have spoken to numerous practicing Scientologists who offer glowing testimonials about the ways in which the church has changed their lives and empowered them to go out and help others. Many church members whom I have met in central Ohio credit their success both in their business careers and in their personal relationships largely to Scientology. Another enthusiastic member I interviewed in Cincinnati worked with Scientology's Volunteer Ministers program in order to lead a team of rescuers to New Orleans in the wake of Hurricane Katrina.

On the other side, however, I have interviewed numerous former Scientologists who had rather darker tales to tell. Among them is Gerald Armstrong, who had been authorized to help write the official church biography of L. Ron Hubbard and then left the church when he discovered that most of what Hubbard had said about his life was untrue. Armstrong has truly stunning tales to tell of his ordeals after leaving the church, claiming that he was not only bombarded with myriad lawsuits but also physically assaulted, driven off the LA freeway, and threatened with assassination by a private investigator.[27] I also had a chance to interview Jim Dincalci, who was Hubbard's personal physician and close confidant during the 1970s; after leaving the church, Dincalci went on to found an organization called the Forgiveness Foundation, designed to help individuals (including numerous ex-Scientologists) deal with traumatic life experiences.[28] Finally, several former Scientologists agreed to speak with me only on the condition that their identity be kept absolutely anonymous. One former high-level Scientologist told me she was so fearful about talking and possibly being identified by the church that she had anxiety attacks for an entire week prior to our conversation. When we finally did talk, however, she let loose for over three hours in one sitting to recount her years in the church, her reflections on Hubbard, and her final decision to leave Scientology. Indeed, although it will not be central to this book, the interview material I've gathered from former Scientologists could probably serve as the basis for a spy novel or a thriller film.

No doubt, despite my best efforts, some readers will probably not be satisfied with my approach in this book. Many critics will likely find my account too generous to Scientology; and many defenders of the church will probably find it too critical. Moreover, this is a short book about just one aspect of a huge, complex, and multifaceted movement with an extremely tangled history. There are innumerable pieces of this story I have not told and countless, fascinating rabbit holes I have not gone down in this account. But this only leaves plenty of room for others to continue writing the history of the world's most controversial new religion.

Secrecy, Surveillance, and Censorship: Ethical and Epistemological Problems in the Study of Religion

With its complex layers of secrecy and its problematic history of relations with the U.S. government, Scientology raises some of the most
profound moral and hermeneutical questions that lie at the heart of the
study of religion. Indeed, it raises the fundamental question of how—
and *if*—one should go about studying a religious movement that chooses
to keep much of its teachings private and closed to outsiders. While
I have written a good bit about esoteric traditions and new religious
movements, ranging from Hindu Tantra to American Freemasonry and
British occultism, I would have to say that Scientology is in many ways
the most secretive religious community I have ever encountered. While
it is true that the church offers free Sunday services and other public
activities to non-Scientologists, the upper levels or "advanced tech" are
reserved for the most dedicated and well-trained members; and the
church has been extremely aggressive in enforcing its rights to the information contained in its higher grades.[29] As Ann Brill and Ashley Packard observe in their study of Scientology's war of information on the
Internet: "What makes the Church of Scientology controversial is not so
much Hubbard's teachings, but the church's tenacious secrecy and the
extremes to which it is willing to go to protect itself."[30]

From its origins, secrecy has surrounded much of the movement, beginning with its founder. Hubbard's own life story is something of a
mystery, since most of the official biography provided by the church has
proven to be less a factual account than a kind of "hagiographic mythology."[31] Hubbard in fact spent the last years of his life from 1980 to 1986
in hiding, having been named an unindicted coconspirator following
the FBI raids on Scientology headquarters and the arrest of his wife,
Mary Sue. Since his death, secrecy has continued to shroud much of the
church, from its heavily protected headquarters or "Gold Base" in River-
side County, California, to its intensive disciplinary program, the "Rehabilitation Project Force," which has been frequently criticized for its
alleged human rights abuses.[32]

As such, Scientology raises in the most acute way what I call the "ethical and epistemological double bind" that is inherent in the attempt to

study any highly secretive religious movement.[33] This double bind can be formulated as follows: first, how can one say anything meaningful about a group that is extremely private and regards portions of its teachings as off-limits to outsiders? Second, is it ethical to even attempt to penetrate the inner secrets of a religious community of which one is not a member—particularly one that sees itself as attacked and persecuted by media, government, and other critics? As Jeffrey K. Hadden argues, "To deny a religious group the right to protect its esoteric knowledge, indeed its most sacred texts, runs contrary to history and the American experience. It constitutes a denial to that group the protection of the Free Exercise clause of the First Amendment of the Constitution."[34] The Church of Scientology itself has argued that it should be given the same respect and protections given to any other religious community, citing examples such as indigenous traditions that have esoteric knowledge reserved only for initiates. As Mikael Rothstein comments in his analysis of Scientology's esoteric grades, Scientology officials "find it offensive whenever esoteric texts are published, and . . . they expect the scholarly community to abide by certain standards. . . . Scientology, in this respect, argues along the same lines as, for instance, Aboriginal Australians who have claimed the right not to have their sacred, esoteric songs or iconographic *churingas* published or otherwise shown to the public by anthropologists."[35]

To make matters even more complex, however, the Church of Scientology also has a long and well-documented history of aggressively confronting scholars, journalists, and ex-members who write critically about it. As Hubbard infamously wrote in his *Manual of Justice* in 1959: "People attack Scientology; I never forget it, always even the score."[36] In the late 1960s, this aggressive strategy toward critics was known as "fair game," meaning that opponents of Scientology could be confronted by any and all means at the church's disposal. Although the "fair game" doctrine was officially dropped after the 1960s, the church has continued to launch literally thousands of lawsuits against journalists, scholars, and others who have spoken critically about it. As various scholars have observed, Scientology's record of litigation "must surely be without parallel in the modern world."[37] This fact has been recognized not only by sociologists and historians of religions but also by legal scholars such as J. P. Kumar: "In the arena of religious litigation, the past twenty years have shown no litigant more fearsome or intimidating than the Church of Scientology. Whether defending against claims of abuse and fraud, pursuing individuals for defamation or copyright infringement, or even litigating against government agencies, the Church has acquired a well-deserved reputation for extremely aggressive litigation tactics."[38]

But the church has been known to resort not simply to legal measures but to extralegal tactics as well. For example, the first serious academic work on Scientology was Roy Wallis's *The Road to Total Freedom*, published in 1976. As Wallis recounts, he was visited by a Scientologist posing as an interested university student, who allegedly tried to make him confess to drug use. Shortly thereafter, letters were sent to his friends and colleagues suggesting that he was a homosexual.[39] Even more aggressive tactics have confronted journalists who have written critically of the church. As Richard Behar recounted his experience while researching his article for *Time* magazine in 1991, "[A]t least 10 attorneys and six private detectives were unleashed by Scientology and its followers in an effort to threaten, harass and discredit me. . . . A copy of my personal credit report—with detailed information about my bank accounts, home mortgage, credit-card payments, home address and Social Security number—had been illegally retrieved."[40] Thus, John Richardson of *Premiere* magazine offered the following advice to fellow journalists who write about Scientology: they should expect from the outset that anything they say about the church will meet legal challenge and perhaps extralegal intimidation: "[A]ct from the start as if you are already in a lawsuit. . . . There will be attempts to . . . lay groundwork for a case against you. So watch what you say."[41] In sum, anyone who writes about a movement as litigious and defensive as Scientology faces a basic dilemma. Does the writer "tell the truth, and damn the consequences," or does he or she "reflect that in over a hundred thousand words of text, anyone can make a mistake? There is a powerful tension between the threat of censorship and the possibility of enormous cost in time, effort and money for a single error."[42]

Ironically, in the course of my own research on Scientology, I not only had to think carefully about how the church might react to my work and the suspicions it might generate; conversely, I *also* met with suspicion from some ex-Scientologists I interviewed, who worried that I myself might be a covert Scientologist gathering information on them (!). For example, in 2009, I contacted Hubbard's former personal physician, Jim Dincalci, for an interview. He agreed, but added the following caveat: "Knowing the ways of [Scientology] informs any of us that you are very possibly a scientologist just gathering information for them, whether you are a professor, lawyer, doctor, politician or a movie star."[43] In a bizarre turnabout, I myself was suspected of not being just an enemy infiltrator of Scientology but a *possible covert Scientologist* conducting surveillance on ex-members.

Finally, both of these ethical and epistemological problems are rendered infinitely more complicated by the dawn of the information age and new communications technologies, particularly the Internet. Ironically, most of Scientology's esoteric materials have been made widely available on various websites since the mid-1990s. Despite the church's aggressive legal actions against an array of websites, the most confidential grades of Scientology continue to spread freely in cyberspace. So this raises another rather bizarre ethical and epistemological question, surely one unique to our own peculiar information age: Should we now simply ignore the fact that these "esoteric" Scientology materials are widely available online, in order to protect this church's rights to privacy? Or should we frankly acknowledge that, in the Internet age, little if anything can realistically remain "esoteric" for long and that Scientology's advanced tech should be analyzed freely like any other publicly available religious material? As Mikael Rothstein argues, "With the breakthrough of the Internet an entirely new situation has been created. . . . Pretending that the texts are *not* there is ridiculous, and acting as if anyone with potential interest in the subject is unaware of this material equally meaningless."[44] As such, the advent of the Internet has raised a number of profound new legal and ethical issues for both religious groups and those who would study or interpret them. For both sides want to invoke the First Amendment to their advantage—the Scientologists for their right to protect esoteric religious materials, and scholars and critics for their right to free speech, including free discussion of the more problematic aspects of the church. As Mark Fearer concludes in his discussion of Scientology's war of information on the Internet, "Both sides see the case as a First Amendment issue, but for entirely different reasons."[45]

In sum, the case of Scientology raises the "ethical and epistemological double bind" of secrecy in an especially acute and complex way. Indeed, it raises some of the most difficult questions at the heart of the attempt to understand *any* controversial new religion, and perhaps even at the heart of the attempt to understand religion itself. Do we have not just a right but perhaps an obligation to write openly about movements as controversial as Scientology, including the secret, confidential, and esoteric aspects of the movement? Or, conversely, is that itself an act of intellectual violence and an invasion of privacy?

I do not pretend to have an ideal solution to this extremely complex moral, intellectual, and methodological conundrum. For the sake of this book, however, I will offer my own alternative approach to the ethical-epistemological double bind. Here I will suggest that we may never truly be able to penetrate the "inner secrets" of Scientology; but we *can* still engage in a rich and complex history of the movement and its more visible interactions with other social, political, and legal structures over the last sixty years. Moreover, we can also use the case of Scientology to reflect on larger questions surrounding the meaning of religion itself—that is, how the term has come to be used in academic, popular, and legal discourse, who gets to define it, and what the stakes are in laying claim to "religious" status. These are questions that have become increasingly complex in the post–World War II era, amidst the rapidly expanding terrain of American religions in the late twentieth and twenty-first centuries.

Scientology and the Changing Spiritual Marketplace of Postwar America

The decades during which Scientology was born and initially flourished—the 1950s and 60s—were a period of tremendous growth, change, and experimentation in the American religious landscape. As historians of American religion such as Robert S. Ellwood and Wade Clark Roof have suggested, the United States of the post–World War II decades is best described as a thriving "spiritual marketplace," teeming not just with

a wide assortment of Christian denominations but also with newly imported forms of Eastern religions, UFO religions, and various forms of
occultism, magic, and neo-paganism.[46] These decades also saw the birth
of eclectic new centers of alternative spirituality, such as the Esalen Institute and what Jeffrey Kripal calls its "religion of no religion."[47] Already
promoting itself as the "Philosophy of a New Age" in 1957, Scientology
was an important and influential new spiritual offering within this complex, dynamic, rapidly growing religious marketplace.[48] As Hubbard's
former personal physician, Jim Dincalci, explained in an interview with
me, many young spiritual seekers in the 1960s were just beginning to be
interested in nonconventional religious ideas such as reincarnation, psychic phenomena, and alternative medicine. For him, Scientology was
one of the first movements he encountered that offered all of these ideas
in a persuasive, attractive, and seemingly "scientific" package.[49]

At the same time, like the popular American religious landscape, the
academic study of religion in the United States was also rapidly changing
during these decades. As Ninian Smart observes, although there had
been various fields in the United States during the first half of the twentieth century such as "sociology of religion," "psychology of religion," and
so on, the field of religious studies in the English-speaking world "basically dates from the 1960s."[50] Thus in 1963, the "National Association of
Biblical Instructors"—whose name clearly indicates its roots in Jewish
and Christian theology—changed its name to the "American Academy of
Religion," signaling a shift toward a comparative, pluralistic, and inclu-
sive approach. During the same decade, new departments of religious
studies were founded across the country, and influential journals of religious studies were established. In sum, the conventional view of American religiosity as comprising "Protestant, Catholic, Jew" (the title of Will
Herberg's influential 1955 book) was rapidly giving way to a much richer
understanding of the rapidly proliferating diversity of the American
spiritual marketplace.[51]

The study of religion in the American university was thus very much
a product of these decades, amidst the new interest in Eastern religions
and alternative spirituality. "It is no accident," Kripal notes, ". . . that the
explosion of 'comparative religion' in American universities coincided
exactly with the counterculture and its famous turn to the East."[52] But

the rise of the academic study of religion was also tied to larger historical and political forces during these decades, such as cold war anxieties
about godless Communism, new immigration patterns, and geopolitical
relations with Asia: "In the late 1960s and early 1970s colleges and universities established departments of religious studies as part of larger
cultural trends. The 'red scare' and anticommunist political mood en-
couraged interest in and defense of religion as a defining feature of the
democratic cultures. . . . The 1960s counterculture was fascinated with
so-called esoteric traditions, such as Buddhism and yoga, and also anti-
traditional explorations of occultism."[53]

Scientology was a key part of the redefinition of religion in contemporary America. As we will see in the pages that follow, Scientology reflects every one of these new cultural trends: anti-Communism, interest
in Asian religions, and fascination with the occult. And yet, interestingly
enough, its recognition as "religion" was quite slow in coming. The complex, tangled, often excruciating debates over Scientology's status as a
"cult," a "business," a "pyramid scheme," or a legitimate "religion" reflect
in microcosmic form the larger debates surrounding religion itself in
the postwar decades. Similar debates, of course, surrounded other new
spiritual offerings of this period, such as the Hare Krishnas (ISKCON—
International Society for Krishna Consciousness), the Unification Church,
Transcendental Meditation, and the Peoples Temple as well as more recent movements such as Heaven's Gate, the Branch Davidians, the Rae-
lians, and countless others. However, Scientology is arguably the best
documented of these controversial new movements, producing not just
thousands of pages of Hubbard's own technical bulletins and lectures,
but myriad court cases, FBI investigations, testimonies of hundreds
of current and former members, and countless websites proliferating
across the Internet—in sum, a veritable mountain of materials that reveal the history of this complex movement and its long road to recognition as a religion in the United States. Moreover, Scientology is also
unique in that we can clearly trace the genealogy of its *self-conscious attempt to make itself appear more like a religion and to fit more closely into
the accepted definitions of religion in modern America.* As such, many
critics have argued that Scientology is better understood not as a "religion" in the traditional sense; rather—as a colleague of mine put it

during an argument with me at a conference at Ohio State—it might be better described as a "simulacrum of a religion," that is, a self-conscious mimicry of the outward trappings of religion in order to obtain the legal benefits, privileges, and protections that come along with that status.[54]

Scientology is thus an ideal case for thinking about religion—that is, for thinking about how religion is defined, who gets to define it, and what the stakes are in laying claim to or being denied such status. Scientology has in fact fought long legal and political battles in many countries over precisely this question, with varying degrees of success: the church is today recognized as a religious institution in some countries, such as Spain and Australia (though in the latter only after being banned in three states up until the 1980s); in other countries such as Ireland and the United Kingdom the church is still not recognized as a religious or charitable entity; in some countries such as Germany, the church continues to be regarded with deep suspicion as an antidemocratic, even totalitarian organization; and in others such as France, it has been dubbed a dangerous *secte* (cult) and convicted of fraud as recently as 2009.[55]

But arguably the church's longest and most convoluted journey to recognition as a religion took place in the United States. Indeed, the pages of this book will trace a sixty-year ordeal that began with an unexpectedly popular form of therapy first published in a small science fiction magazine and culminated in one of the world's largest, most powerful, and wealthiest religious organizations that continues to generate controversy to this day. In short, a genealogy of Scientology, we will see, is in many ways also a genealogy of "religion" itself in the United States from the late 1940s to the present.

As anthropologist Talal Asad suggests, any definition of religion we might come up with is always and inevitably tied to "a particular history of knowledge and power."[56] That is to say, any definition is limited by the biases of its own time and place, its historical context and cultural prejudices. And any definition will necessarily include certain groups and exclude others, thus inevitably granting certain status, privileges, and rights to some while denying them to others. An obvious example is the case of the peyote movement and the Native American Church's long battle for religious recognition in the United States. Although peyote had been consumed as a sacrament by Native American tribes for at least seven thousand years, peyote use was banned and suppressed by the U.S. government in the late nineteenth century. The peyote movement was first formally recognized as a legitimate "religion" only in 1918 with the founding of the Native American Church, which, significantly, now described itself as a "church" and claimed to be "dedicated to teach the Christian religion with morality, sobriety . . . and right living."[57] Yet even so, its members would continue fighting a complex tangle of legal battles for the right to consume peyote up until the 1990s, and its legality still varies widely by from state to state.[58]

To cite another obvious example, when Joseph Smith and the early Mormon Church emerged in the mid-nineteenth century, they were widely ridiculed, attacked, and persecuted as a dangerous and subversive group. Yet today the Church of Jesus Christ of Latter-day Saints is recognized as the fourth largest Christian denomination in the world and by some even as a new "world religion."[59]

Finally, as many scholars of new religious movements have argued, the term "cult" has long been used to delegitimate, dismiss, and in some cases attack groups that do not fit the mainstream ideal of religion. Perhaps the most poignant example is the Branch Davidian church. Widely branded as a dangerous cult by the media, government, and anticult groups, the Branch Davidian compound in Waco, Texas, became the target of an aggressive raid by the Bureau of Alcohol, Tobacco, and Firearms in 1993, which ended in the tragic death of over seventy men, women, and children. As scholars such as Catherine Wessinger, James Tabor, and Eugene Gallagher have argued, the disaster at Waco might well have been avoided if the Branch Davidians were approached first as a *religion* that needed to be understood sympathetically on its own terms rather than as a dangerous *cult* that need to be confronted by overwhelming force.[60]

In sum, our definition of religion is at once historically contingent, widely varied over time, and inevitably linked to real relations of power. As Jonathan Z. Smith aptly observes, "The moral . . . is not that religion cannot be defined, but that it can be defined, with greater or lesser success, more than fifty ways."[61] L. Ron Hubbard himself, we might note, said almost exactly the same thing decades before in 1955, during his own attempt to assert the religiosity of Scientology: "You know that religion has a great many meanings. . . . It can mean an enormous number of things."[62] And any definitions we come up with will inevitably include and exclude particular groups, thus granting certain benefits and privileges to some while denying them to others.

While I would not presume to offer a final definition of religion of my own here, I find Bruce Lincoln's recent approach very helpful. While acknowledging the historical contingency of any particular definition and the impossibility of coming up with one that is universally applicable, Lincoln suggests that we can still use a kind of flexible, provisional, working concept of religion. Rather than a singular thing or essence, he argues, religion is better understood as a form of discourse that makes a claim to a particular kind of *authority*. Specifically, religious sorts of discourse make a claim to an authority that is believed to "transcend the human, temporary and contingent, and claims for itself a similarly transcendent status." Thus,

> Discourse becomes religious not simply by virtue of its content, but also
> from its claims to authority. Astrophysicists, for instance, do not engage
> in religious speech when they discuss cosmogony, so long as they frame
> their statements as hypotheses and provisional conclusions based on ex-
> perimentation, calculation and human reason. . . . But should they
> ground their views in Scripture, revelation or immutable ancestral tradi-
> tions, in that moment their discourse becomes religious because of its
> claim to transcendent authority.[63]

In this sense, we can view much of Scientology history from the early 1950s to the present as precisely an *increasing attempt to define itself in religious terms*—that is, a self-conscious effort to invoke a particular kind of transcendent status and authority. In the early phase of Dianetics, Hubbard made no attempt to define his new science of the mind as anything having to do with religion. Yet throughout the 1950s, 60s, and 70s, in response to a variety of internal and external pressures, Hubbard began to increasingly pursue what he called the "religion angle." Foremost among these were Hubbard's wars with the FDA, over his claims to heal physical illness, and his intense battles with the IRS, over his claims to tax-exempt status. Finally, by the 1990s, as we see in promotional films made by the church, Scientology was proudly declaring its authentic "religious" status as supported by courts in many nations: "Since Scientology is relatively new, you may hear the question asked: 'Is Scientology a bona fide religion?' Let me assure you it is, according to more than sixty-five court decisions around the world."[64] In sum, the pages of this book will trace the complex historical process by which a penny-a-word science fiction writer first established one of the first and most popular self-help therapies and then went on to found one of the world's most powerful and wealthiest but also controversial new religions.

Outline of the Book: Six Decades of Religious Controversy

Each of the chapters of this book will focus on one particular historical period, from the 1940s to the present, following Scientology's complex journey from an obscure self-help movement to a recognized religion with global reach and massive financial resources. Moving roughly decade by decade, I will show that Scientology actually lay at the center of a series of complex debates surrounding religion in the United States from the postwar era to the present, highlighting the contested boundaries between psychology, science fiction, occultism, Eastern spirituality, and cults that have shaped the discourse of religion in the modern world.

Chapter 1, "L. Ron Hubbard: American Entrepreneur, Spiritual *Bricoleur*," will suggest that Scientology's founder is best understood neither as a philosopher-saint (as the church portrays him) nor as a charlatan-madman (as most of the media portray him). Rather, if we place Hubbard in the context of other authors and science fiction writers of the 1940s and 50s, he begins to look more like a unique combination of an American entrepreneur and a cultural *bricoleur*, who blended together a wide array of psychological, spiritual, and occult ideas into a surprisingly successful new synthesis. While Hubbard was primarily known as a prolific author of science fiction and fantasy novels during the 1930s and 40s, he dabbled in a wide array of popular ideas and practices, ranging from psychoanalysis to occultism and magic. His first great breakthrough, however, was his new science of mind called "Dianetics" (1950). First published in the popular magazine *Astounding Science Fiction*, Dianetics made no particular claims to "religious status" but instead drew heavily on the work of Sigmund Freud, Otto Rank, and popularized versions of psychoanalysis available in the late 1940s. Remarkably, however, Hubbard was able to market his new science in a way that was hugely successful and reached a massive popular audience. In short, Hubbard was from the beginning an ingenious entrepreneur who straddled the ambiguous lines between spirituality and popular culture, occultism and science fiction, pop psychology and mass marketing.

In chapter 2, "Scientology, Inc.," I will examine the formation of the Church of Scientology, which was incorporated in late 1953 and began to advertise itself much more explicitly as a "religious" organization. Hubbard's shift toward a more recognizably religious entity seems to have been inspired not just by his further investigations into the human condition, but also by political fractures within the Dianetics movement and pressures from a growing number of critics in the media and the medical profession. While Hubbard's early system of Dianetics promised to offer optimal well-being in this lifetime, Scientology began to promote ideas drawn from a wide range of materials then available in the spiritual marketplace of 1950s America, such as a belief in reincarnation, a complex history of the universe, and many elements drawn from recently imported forms of Hinduism and Buddhism (including Hubbard's remarkable claim to be the future Buddha, Maitreya). Hubbard's pursuit of the "religion angle" as he called it, however, was by no means an immediate or smooth one, but rather one that happened in fits and starts throughout the 1950s and was driven as much by political and legal expedience as by spiritual concerns. But it appears to have worked remarkably well, as Scientology "franchises" rapidly spread amidst the thriving spiritual marketplace of 1950s America.

Chapter 3, "A Cold War Religion," will place Scientology in the context of the United States of the 1950s and early 1960s, amidst the discourse surrounding nuclear war, secrecy, and surveillance that pervaded much of these decades. From the very beginning, Hubbard marketed Dianetics as the ultimate solution to the nuclear era and as a discovery as important as the atomic bomb. But at the same time, his movement also displayed an intense preoccupation with secrecy and surveillance that mirrors larger concerns with information control in cold war America. Hubbard himself wrote numerous letters to J. Edgar Hoover and the FBI naming Communist sympathizers and offering Dianetics as a means to combat socialism. Meanwhile, the FBI, FDA, and other agencies also began to aggressively investigate Scientology for its potential subversive threat, leading to an escalating game of espionage and counterespionage throughout the cold war era. Not only did the FBI launch massive raids on Scientology centers in Los Angeles and Washington, DC, but the church responded in turn by its principle of "fair game," meaning that the church could respond to its enemies by any and all means necessary. Thus the church formed its own intelligence agency, the Guardian's Office, and began to run "security checks" on its own members in a growing obsession with information control both within and without the movement—an obsession that only reflected a similar obsession with secrecy and information control in 1960s America.

In chapter 4, "The 'Cult of All Cults'?" I will place Scientology amidst the intense debates surrounding "cults" and "brainwashing" that spread throughout the 1970s and 80s. Even more so than the many other new religions of this period, such as the Unification Church, ISKCON, or Peoples Temple, Scientology was regularly singled out by both the media and anticult groups as the most dangerous, litigious, and rapacious of all cults. In turn, Scientology has responded with aggressive tactics of its own. Perhaps the most extreme example was its barrage of lawsuits against the Cult Awareness Network (CAN), by which it first helped drive CAN into bankruptcy and then bought the rights to CAN's name, help line number, and service mark. Remarkably, the movement once branded the "cult of greed" now owns and operates the "New Cult Awareness Network" and advocates religious tolerance. As such, Scientology has been at the center of much larger debates about fundamental questions such as: How do certain groups become labeled in popular discourse as "cults," and what are the larger legal and political implications of such labeling? More important, how do we engage in a critical interrogation of highly problematic groups—including groups such as Scientology that have at times engaged in criminal activities—while at the same time respecting rights to privacy and freedom of religious expression?

Chapter 5, "'The War' and the Triumph of Scientology," will then explore the complex process through which Scientology actually did win tax-exempt status in the eyes of the IRS in the 1990s. The church's "triumph" was by no means a simple story, but rather the result of the longest IRS investigation in history, labyrinthine legal debates, and allegations of extralegal pressure that finally led to its status as a tax-exempt organization in 1993. Indeed, the details of the church's conflict with the IRS read like an espionage novel, complete with Scientologists breaking into IRS offices to steal mountains of documents, hiring private investigators to follow senior officials, and filing thousands of lawsuits. In fact, the details of the church's controversial settlement with the IRS were kept secret, despite Freedom of Information Act requests, until 1997 when they were leaked to the *Wall Street Journal*. Meanwhile, outside the United States, many other major governments have still not recognized Scientology as a legitimate religion, but regard it variously as a business, a "cultish psycho-group," or a "pyramid scheme." In an ironic historical twist, the U.S. State Department now criticizes the governments of Germany and other countries for their failure to respect Scientology's rights to religious freedom. As such, Scientology is truly an emblematic test case for thinking about the most basic questions of what constitutes a religion, who gets to decide, and what are the real stakes (legal, economic, political, spiritual) in being acknowledged as such.

In chapter 6, "Secrets, Security, and Cyberspace," I will examine the most recent wars of information surrounding Scientology in the rapidly expanding terrain of the Internet. If Scientology was attacked as a cult and a commercial enterprise in the 1970s, these attacks have grown exponentially with the proliferation of hundreds of anti-Scientology websites, Usenet newsgroups, and online communities dedicated to unmasking the church. And if Scientology was concerned with information control during the cold war era, that concern has become even more intense in the world of cyberspace, where the alleged "inner secrets" of Scientology can be instantly disseminated to a global audience. The church has in fact established its own "Religious Technology Center," dedicated to the control of Scientology copyrights and information, and has filed numerous lawsuits against individuals who have posted confidential church materials online. At the same time, however, Scientology has also become the target of a new and more challenging enemy, the decentralized Internet group known as "Anonymous," which has dedicated itself to exposing the church's deceitful tactics and spreading its version of the truth to a global Internet audience. One of my own former students actually joined the Anonymous protests and is now an active anti-Scientologist. After he posted some confidential Scientology materials online, he was threatened by church lawyers and had his Internet and email service terminated.[65] He then decided to join forces with Anonymous, adopting the ironic title "Chef Xenu" and working to disseminate as much information on Scientology throughout the Internet as possible. In short, the new "wars of religion" extend not just to multinational corporations but even to ordinary college students and to the innumerable tiny nodes of information that compose the Internet.

Finally, in the conclusion, I will argue that Scientology is a critically important case for thinking about much larger issues in the study of religion in the twenty-first century. First, it shows in a very striking way that our "imagining of religion" is hardly just a scholarly exercise but rather an intensely contested debate that has very real legal, economic, and political consequences. A critical rethinking of religion today, I will argue, would mean not just seeing religion as a complex phenomenon that is deeply entwined with the "secular" domains of law, media, popular culture, historical change, and political struggle. More important, as Bruce Lincoln suggests, it would also mean rethinking religion as a form of discourse that makes a claim to a particular kind of privileged status and authority—and specifically, a status that is believed to be transcendent, suprahuman, and/or eternal.[66] In the case of Scientology, the claim to such status has brought with it a number of tangible benefits, tax-exempt status not least among them. But with Scientology, as with any religion, the claim to such status is also always subject to challenge and contestation.

Second, the case of Scientology also raises profound questions about religious freedom and privacy in the twenty-first century, particularly amidst new forms of religious terrorism and new technologies of surveillance. How do we best undertake a respectful yet critical study of religions, an approach that interrogates the more problematic aspects of such groups while at the same time respecting rights to religious freedom and privacy? As authors such as James Tabor and Eugene Gallagher have shown in the case of the Waco disaster, the academic study of religion has a crucial role to play in these debates. Above all, it can provide critical analysis of *both* controversial religious groups *and* the media, anticult, and governmental agencies that confront them.[67] In my view, these are among the most important debates of the twenty-first century, amidst the rise of ever more complex networks of information and technologies of surveillance. These are debates in which I expect historians of religions to have an increasingly vital role to play.

- ONE -

L. RON HUBBARD
American Entrepreneur, Spiritual *Bricoleur*

L. Ron Hubbard is not an easy man to categorize and certainly does not
fit popular misconceptions of a "religious founder" as an aloof and
contemplative figure.
—Friends of Ron, *L. Ron Hubbard: A Profile* (1995)[1]

Dianetics is important politically. It indicates ways of controling [*sic*]
people or de-controling [*sic*] them and of handling groups which is good
technology. It is an American science.
—L. Ron Hubbard, letter to the U.S. attorney general
(May 14, 1951)[2]

At the heart of the mystery, controversy, and scandal that surrounds Scientology is its enigmatic founder, L. Ron Hubbard. Portrayed in the
church's literature as a rugged explorer, world traveler, and engineer,
equally accomplished as a "humanitarian, educator, administrator, artist
and philosopher,"[3] Hubbard has also been described by his critics as a
liar, charlatan, and madman.[4] Indeed, writing the story of Hubbard's life
is extremely difficult, since there are at least two very different versions
of that narrative. On the one hand, there is the church's official biography of Hubbard, which tells of his extensive travels throughout the Far
East, his successful academic career, and his heroic military service; on
the other hand, there is the counternarrative provided by critics and ex-
Scientologists, who claim that most of the official biography is fictitious.
As Hubbard's own son, L. Ron Hubbard Jr., put it, "Better than 90 percent of what my father has written about himself is untrue."[5] Former
Scientologist Gerald Armstrong has testified that he was assigned to
help write the biography of Hubbard for the church, but during the

L. Ron Hubbard applying the E-meter to a tomato plant, 1968. Getty Images

course of his research he discovered that virtually everything Hubbard had said about his life was false.[6]

Here I will not attempt to expose the "true story" of L. Ron Hubbard, an extremely tangled and legally harrowing endeavor (as Armstrong discovered). The official narrative of Hubbard's life provided by the church, I would argue, is best regarded not as historical fact; rather, as Dorthe Refslund Christensen suggests, Hubbard's biography is better understood as a kind of "hagiographic mythology"—that is, an idealized narrative composed quite self-consciously of mythic themes.[7] As such, it is neither more "true" nor more "fictitious" than the recorded biographies of other new religious leaders such as Madame Blavatsky, Elijah Muhammad, or Joseph Smith. Rather than try to prove the truth or falsehood of his biography, then, I think it is more productive to place Hubbard and his narrative very concretely within the context of American culture of the 1940s, in the immediate wake of World War II and the complex new religious landscape of the postwar era.

As historians of American religion such as Robert S. Ellwood and Wade Clark Roof have argued, the United States after World War II was a thriving "spiritual marketplace" in which new and old forms of spirituality were available in "plenteous diversity."[8] The dramatic postwar boom in American religions, Ellwood suggests, reflects a kind of "supply-side phenomenon," as religious organizations had the resources to offer a wide new array of spiritual possibilities, even as ordinary religious consumers had the means to partake of them eagerly: "[S]upply was better supplied in the Fifties than ever before, as . . . unprecedented prosperity meant that all denominations could put up the parish halls and skyline sanctuaries about which they had long dreamed. . . . [C]onsumers . . . had the means and the interest in the fifties to answer enthusiastically."[9] L. Ron Hubbard and his early Dianetics movement are perhaps the epitome of this thriving spiritual marketplace of postwar America. Combining elements of popular culture such as science fiction and fantasy tales with psychoanalysis, occultism, and Eastern religions, Hubbard created a unique new product with a growing niche market.

It is in this sense that Hubbard can be seen as a uniquely American combination of an entrepreneur and a *bricoleur*. Indeed, his new science of the mind and the movement it inspired was in many ways very well attuned to the shifting social and religious trends of American culture. Like other science fiction writers of the day, Hubbard dabbled in the occult and magical circles of the 1940s, even participating in the ritual magic of the twentieth century's most infamous occultist, Aleister Crowley. And like later science fiction writers such as Philip K. Dick, Hubbard claimed to have had an intense mystical experience, in which all the world's religious and philosophical mysteries were revealed to him.[10]

By his own account, Hubbard had explored the "countless odds and ends" of the world's spiritual traditions, from Sioux medicine men to Eastern mystics, from psychoanalysis to hypnosis, from magic and faith healing to experimentation in drugs: "[A]ttempts were made to discover what school or system was workable. Freud did occasionally. So did Chinese acupuncture. So did magic healing crystals in Australia and miracle shrines in South America. Faith healing, voodoo, narcosynthesis . . . "[11] And the results of his eclectic research became Dianetics, his "revolutionary new science of the human mind."[12] While *Dianetics* may seem implausible to many readers today, it shared the same *New York Times* best-seller list with other self-help manuals such as Norman Vincent Peale's *True Art of Happiness* and Henry Overstreet's *The Mature Mind*, not to mention best-selling books about UFOs such as Aimé Michel's *The Truth about Flying Saucers*.[13] In this sense, Hubbard seems not only surprisingly "mainstream" but perhaps even a trendsetter. Yet Hubbard was also a shrewd businessman who was able to identify and cater to an emerging new audience of spiritual consumers in the late 1940s and early 1950s. Though short-lived, his surprisingly popular new science of Dianetics was a bold example of his remarkable entrepreneurial skills.

As such, Hubbard is perhaps best understood as a *bricoleur* in the sense of the term used by Claude Lévi-Strauss and Wendy Doniger— that is, a creative recycler of cultural wares who "appropriate[s] another range of commodities by placing them in a symbolic ensemble."[14] An eclectic and ingenious cultural entrepreneur, Hubbard assembled a wide array of diverse philosophical, psychological, occult, scientific, and science fiction elements, cobbling them together into a unique, new, and surprisingly successful synthesis. Although his early *bricolage* called Dianetics made no pretense of being a "religion," we will see in chapter 2 that it soon morphed into something much larger with more ambitious "spiritual" aspirations.

"He Told One Hell of a Good Story": Hubbard's Hagiographic Mythology

While there is little agreement on the precise details of Hubbard's life before founding Dianetics and Scientology, there is general agreement

on one aspect of his character: he "told one hell of a good story."[15] Alva
Rogers, who knew Hubbard in the 1940s, remembers him as follows: he
"had a tremendously engaging personality . . . he dominated the scene
with his wit and inexhaustible fund of anecdotes . . . Ron's reputation for
spinning tall tales (both off and on the printed page) made for a certain
degree of skepticism in the minds of his audience . . . Ron was a persuasive and unscrupulous charmer, not only in a social group, but with the
ladies."[16] With striking red hair, a wide mouth, and a plump face, Hubbard was described by those who knew him as a personality that "either
charmed or repulsed immediately," dominating conversations with en-
chanting anecdotes and lively wit: "When he spoke . . . no one could steal
the floor from him."[17] To those who disliked him, such as Nieson Himmel, who knew him in the late 1940s, Hubbard was a "real con-man"
and "obviously a phoney. But he was not a dummy. He could charm the
shit out of anybody."[18] Novelist Gore Vidal also recounts meeting Hubbard in the 1950s, when Scientology was in its infancy: "He exuded evil,
malice, and stupidity," Vidal recalls, "but perfectly amiable to talk to."[19]

In an interview with me in 2009, Hubbard's former personal physician Jim Dincalci offered an intimate and complex picture of Scientology's founder. Dincalci described Hubbard as a man of "amazing charisma" who was always the center of any party, "wooing women and
playing the ukulele"; but he was also, Dincalci recalls, capable of bouts
of vicious raging, screaming, and yelling, and in his later years, bizarre
phobias about dust and germs.[20] But no one, admirer or critic, could
deny that Hubbard was a great storyteller.

Perhaps the greatest story Hubbard told was the story of his own life.
According to his own various autobiographical accounts and official
church biographies, Hubbard appears to be a larger-than-life figure, an
adventurer who set out to explore not just the farthest ends of earth but
also the infinite reaches of the mind in pursuit of the human dilemma.
He is, in short, as much "a daredevil barnstormer, a master mariner,
[and] a Far East explorer" as the founder of a revolutionary new philosophy.[21] As recorded in Hubbard's various published works and on the
church's current website, the story goes as follows.

Lafayette Ron Hubbard was born in Tilden, Nebraska, in 1911, the
son of Harry Ross Hubbard, an officer in the U.S. Navy. After moving to

Montana as a young boy, Ron received his first introduction to the spiritual world of the Native Americans, studying with a Blackfoot shaman at the mere age of six, even being "initiated into the various secrets of the tribe" and becoming "a blood brother of the Blackfeet, an honor bestowed on few white men."[22]

An avid outdoorsman, adventurer, and scouting enthusiast from his earliest years, Hubbard claimed to have become the nation's youngest Eagle Scout in March 1924.[23] In the late 1920s, young Ron began to travel widely, including journeys through Asia, where he learned the most intimate secrets of the Eastern sages. "Among the first westerners . . . admitted into traditionally forbidden lamaseries," he delved into the "dread mysteries of India," studied with Buddhist priests, and met "the last remaining magician from the line of Kublai Khan's court."[24] Back in the United States, Hubbard then mastered the sciences, studying engineering and atomic physics at George Washington University. In the 1930s, he turned his skills to writing. Under his own name and various pseudonyms, he published hundreds of novels and short stories and emerged as one of the most prolific writers of the golden era of science fiction. In the 1940s, Hubbard's restless spirit led him to the high seas once again, as he was elected a member of the prestigious Explorers Club and undertook a range of daring expeditions around the world. In the course of his travels, he also studied various exotic native cultures, including the Tlingit and Aleutian Island natives. During World War II, Hubbard served as a naval lieutenant, commanding several vessels in various theaters. Indeed, he claimed to have been crippled and blinded during the war, but later to have fully healed himself in 1944, using a synthesis of the various psychological techniques learned during his travels.[25] Finally, after his many adventures overseas, Hubbard sat down to write the groundbreaking new work that was the fruit of all his many travels, research, and investigation of the human condition—namely, "Dianetics," which in turn became the foundation of the new religion of Scientology.

Virtually every detail of Hubbard's life narrative, however, has been the subject of debate, and many critics argue that most if not all of his official biography is a fabrication—indeed, as much a work of fantasy as his own wildly imaginative pulp fiction tales. Skeptics have pointed out, for example, that most or all of Hubbard's academic credentials are fictional; Hubbard, the alleged "nuclear physicist" and "engineer," had enrolled in only one introductory course on molecular and nuclear physics at George Washington University, receiving a grade of F, while his courses in mathematics earned nothing higher than a D. His claim to a Doctor of Philosophy degree turned out to have been the product of a sham diploma mill called Sequoia University (which was never recognized by the state of California).[26] Far from a war hero, moreover, Hubbard was actually investigated for firing on an uninhabited island in Mexican waters and was judged by Rear Admiral F. A. Braisted to be "not qualified for command or promotion."[27] During the course of the *Church of Scientology of California v. Gerald Armstrong* suit in 1984, the court was presented with a vast amount of evidence concerning the details of Hubbard's life excavated by his would-be biographer, Armstrong. At the end of the proceedings, Judge Paul Breckenridge delivered the following, quite damning decision on Hubbard:

> The evidence portrays a man who has been virtually a pathological liar when it comes to his history, background, and achievements. The writings and documents in evidence additionally reflect his egoism, greed, avarice, lust for power, and vindictiveness and aggressiveness against persons perceived by him to be disloyal or hostile. At the same time it appears that he is charismatic and highly capable of motivating, organizing, controlling, manipulating, and inspiring his adherents.[28]

And yet, if we accept the Hubbard story not as an accurate historical document but as an intentionally constructed "hagiographic mythology," it then begins to resemble the familiar contours of the "hero's journey" so frequently encountered in other mythological traditions: the young boy departs from his mundane life, travels widely to encounter strange new worlds and confront danger, then returns home with profound wisdom and a new hope for humankind. In this sense, Hubbard's narrative is not so different from that of other new religious leaders, such as Madame Blavatsky's story of journeying to mystic Tibet or Joseph Smith's story of digging up golden plates in the wilderness. Perhaps the one truly unique feature of Hubbard's biography is that *he was himself a prolific author of science fiction and fantasy tales and thus had an unusually creative hand in the elaboration of his own narrative.* Indeed, he effectively fashioned the story of a hero—even a superhero. As a former member of Hubbard's staff, Cyril Vosper, put it, "He told so many stories of his exploits, in South America, the West Indies and places, that he would have to have been at least 483 years old to have had time to have done all those things, but that doesn't really matter. I mean it was just very entertaining really, except that he turned it into a religion."[29]

Space Opera and Soldiers of Light: Hubbard's Early Science Fiction and the Seeds of Scientology

Before his career as the founder of the world's most controversial new religion, L. Ron Hubbard was best known as a wildly prolific author of pulp fiction. Beginning in the early 1930s, Hubbard penned a truly astonishing number of science fiction, fantasy, mystery, and adventure tales, becoming one of the key figures in the "golden age" of pulp fiction. In the words of Jack Williamson, a fellow writer and contemporary of Hubbard, science fiction had finally burst into book form in the 1930s and 40s as almost the pop-cultural counterpart to the atom bomb: "Not quite as violently as the bomb, science fiction had been exploding. It had burst into book print."[30] Moreover, there was also a clear affinity between occultism and science fiction, from the golden age down to the 1970s, and fans of science fiction also tended to be interested in the supernatural realms of magic, psychic phenomena, and paranormal abilities. All of these are themes that appear both in Hubbard's fiction and in early Scientology.[31] According to John Campbell—the influential editor of *Astounding Science Fiction* and an early supporter of Hubbard's Dianetics—science fiction was exploring new terrains and new powers of the human mind that seemed as remarkable, frightening, and awesome as the bomb itself: "The atomic bomb seems powerful and impressive—but remember that it is merely an expression of human will and thought . . . human thought, not atomic energy, is the most powerful force for either construction or destruction in the known universe. It is this aspect that science fiction is exploring today—the most dangerous and most magnificent of all *terra incognita* still lies a half inch back of your own forehead."[32]

Averaging up to seventy thousand to one hundred thousand words a month, Hubbard was among the most prolific writers of the pulp fiction era. He could write on seemingly any subject and in any genre, from "jungle explorers to deep-sea divers, from G-men and gangsters, cowboys and flying aces to mountain climbers, hard-boiled detectives and spies."[33] Not only did he write in many different styles, Hubbard also wrote under the pseudonyms of many different identities, revealing a literary multiple personality that assumed the various names of Winchester Remington Colt, Lt. Jonathan Daly, Capt. Charles Gordon, Bernard Hubbel, Michael Keith, Legionnaire 148, René Lafayette, Ken Martin, B. A. Northrup, Scott Morgan, Kurt von Rachen, Barry Randolph, Lt. Scott Morgan, Legionnaire 14830, and Capt. Humbert Reynolds, among others.[34] Many who knew him commented on Hubbard's unbelievable literary productivity, both during his pulp fiction days and during the early years of Scientology. As his former physician Dincalci told me, Hubbard almost seemed to be engaged in a form of "channeling" or "automatic writing" in his extraordinary literary output: "I would watch him writing—he was channeling—automatic writing—his arm would just fly. I swear that all of Scientology came from channeling."[35]

Interestingly enough, Hubbard also served as the basis for a fictional character himself in Anthony Boucher's *Rocket to the Morgue*, a mystery novel that centers on the science fiction milieu of the 1940s. Here Hubbard appears in the guise of D. Vance Wimpole, a charismatic but not entirely trustworthy figure whose "unbelievable saga" made him "one of the damnedest and most fabulous figures in the whole pulp field." At once an adventurer, womanizer, and writer, Wimpole used "an especially geared electric typewriter because he composes faster than any ordinary machine can go. He only works six months out of the year and spends the other six hunting anything from polar bears to blonds."[36]

Among Hubbard's myriad titles from the period are "The Battle of Wizards," "The Dangerous Dimension," "Man-Killers of the Air," "Tomb of the Ten Thousand Dead," "Cargo of Coffins," and "Death Waits at Sundown." As fellow writer Robert Silverberg put it: "Space pirates, land barons, vindictive Graustarkian queens . . . nothing is too wild, too implausible, for the protean Hubbard."[37] At least two of Hubbard's early works are still considered classics of the genre: his pulp horror tale, *Fear*, and his postapocalyptic novel, *Final Blackout*.

However, even in Hubbard's early tales in magazines such as *Unknown*, we can see his interest in the paranormal powers of the mind and the higher potential of human consciousness. His stories often attribute exceptional powers to the mind, including "the power to heal or kill by thought alone."[38] As Hubbard asks in his 1940 classic, *Fear*: "If we could but see, for ever so brief a period, the supernatural, would we then begin to understand the complexities which beset man? . . . Are there not men in this world today who have converse with the supernatural, but who cannot demonstrate or explain and be believed because of the lack in others of that peculiar sense?"[39] Many of Hubbard's characters are also men obsessed with esoteric knowledge, roaming the universe and sacrificing everything to find "the Great Secret." Thus, the intrepid explorer Fanner Marston seeks the lost ancient city of Parva, a place of knowledge and power, possessing "the most advanced science in the Universe" that would make a man master of all. This Great Secret "had made a dead race rule the Universe! . . . And Fanner Marston would be the ruler, the new ruler, the arbiter of the destiny for all the Universe!"[40]

Some of the most interesting of Hubbard's early science fiction—and perhaps the most relevant for his later Church of Scientology—appears in his series of tales about a character named "Ole Doc Methuselah." Published in *Astounding Science Fiction* from 1947 to 1950 under the pseudonym René Lafayette, the "Ole Doc Methuselah" tales center on a boldly adventurous space hero and physician who is also a member of "the most elite organization of the cosmos," the Soldiers of Light: "But he was no soldier in the military sense, for the enemies he fought were disease, old age and the warped psychology that spawned only in the isolation of mankind's lost planetary colonies."[41] The Soldiers of Light are an organization of six hundred selfless heroes who have dedicated themselves to the "ultimate preservation of mankind" and take as their identifying mark the symbol of two crossed rods. On his spaceship christened "the Hound of Heaven," Ole Doc embarks on an "unending journey through the trackless galaxy" enjoying a "series of astonishing adventures on many worlds."[42]

As we will see later in chapter 2, these imaginative tales contain more than a few seeds of Hubbard's religious movement, the Church of

Scientology, which was founded just three years later. Like the Soldiers of Light who work under the symbol of the crossed ray rods to fight disease and save humankind, the Church of Scientology would work under the symbol of the eight-pointed cross to fight both physical and spiritual disease for all humankind. Like this elite group of Soldiers, Hubbard's Sea Org would later serve as the elite, inner core of his church, sworn by billion-year contracts to help save the entire planet. And like Doc Methuselah himself, who roams on an endless journey through the trackless galaxy on his ship with adventures on many worlds, Hubbard would also spend years roaming the earth's oceans on his ship, exploring ever-new spiritual universes. Indeed, the goal of Scientology itself is the state of Operating Thetan, in which the spiritual self or thetan is liberated from the bonds of the physical universe and is free—like Methuselah— to travel to any corner of the universe. As William Bainbridge points out, there is an obvious continuity between the superman figure of science fiction tales and the superman figure imagined by new religions such as Scientology: "Science fiction is filled with supermen—including comic book characters explicitly named Superman and created by science fiction fans. Some like Superman himself, are born superior."[43] Hence it is no accident that in 1951 Hubbard would publish an essay on Dianetics entitled "Homo Superior, Here We Come!" in the science fiction magazine *Marvel Science Stories*.[44]

However, perhaps the most striking element in Hubbard's early fiction that reappears in his later Scientology writings is his emphasis on the unlimited, even godlike power of the writer himself. For the writer has the all-creative power to generate entire universes out of his own imagination, to populate them, and to destroy them. The clearest example of this divine power of the author appears in "Typewriter in the Sky" (1940), a fantasy tale in which the pulp fiction author, Horace Hackett, has the power to create entire universes and then to insert his actual human friends into the stories, where they suffer the fate of his fictional characters. As Hackett himself says, this is a truly godlike power to fashion worlds and control people's lives:

the way you feel about stories sometimes. It's—well, sort of divine, some-
how. Here we are able to make and break characters and tangle up their

lives and all, and sometimes the characters get so big for us that they sort
of write themselves. . . .

When I go knocking out the wordage and really get interested in my
characters it almost makes me feel like—a god or something.[45]

As we will see in chapter 2, this godlike power to create and manipulate
new universes is the ultimate goal of Scientology itself—the goal of a
liberated spirit or "Operating Thetan," which is not only free of the limitations of the physical universe but also free to *create its own new
universe.*

Through the Curtain: Hubbard's First Glimpse of "the Secret"

Hubbard's first encounter with the spiritual realm is described in an unpublished manuscript entitled "Excalibur," said to have been composed
in 1938. A great deal of mystery surrounds this strange manuscript, and
Hubbard himself allegedly claimed that those who first read its powerful
secrets went mad or jumped out of windows. The church's own website
claims that the manuscript was hotly sought after by foreign secret services: "two copies were actually stolen by agents of foreign intelligence
services who wished to appropriate those ideas for political ends and
only sections remain."[46] However, the church has revealed the first few
tantalizing pages of the manuscript online.

Interestingly enough, according to the "Excalibur" narrative, Hubbard's breakthrough to the spiritual realm actually began with an operation and a kind of near-death experience induced by anesthetic. While
under the gas, Hubbard's heart allegedly stopped and he was given a rare
glimpse into the secrets of the afterlife. Yet after much struggle, he was
able to remember these great secrets and bring them back with him to
this mortal realm:

> It began with an operation—I took gas as an anesthetic and while under
> the influence of it my heart must have stopped beating, as in my terror I
> knew I was slipping through the Curtain and into the land of shades. It was
> like sliding helter-skelter down into a vortex of scarlet and it was knowing
> that one was dying and that the process of dying was far from pleasant.

For a long time after I knew that "Death is eight inches below life."

It was terrible work, climbing up out of the cone again, for something did not want to let me back through the wall, and then, when I willed my going, I determined it against all opposition.

And something began to cry out, "Don't let him know!" . . .

Though badly shaken I was quite rational when I was restored. The people around me looked frightened—more frightened than I. I was not thinking about what I had been through nearly so much as what I knew. I had not yet fully returned to life. I was still in contact with something. And in that state I remained for some days, all the while puzzling over what I knew. It was clear that if I could but remember I would have the secret of life. This in itself was enough to drive one mad, so illusive [sic] was that just-beyond-reach information. And then one morning, just as I awoke, it came to me. I climbed out of my tall ship's bunk and made my way to my typewriter. I began to hammer out that secret and when I had written ten thousand words, then I knew even more clearly.[47]

His literary agent at the time, Forrest Ackerman, also recounted this narrative as told to him by Hubbard. In Ackerman's version, we can see classic themes such as the acquisition of esoteric knowledge and the idea of separating from the physical body, which both became central to later Scientology. In this version, Hubbard also adds the warning that the knowledge he obtained is so profound and dangerous that it could destroy anyone who reads it:

He said that he had died on the operating table, and that he rose in spirit form, and he looked at the body he had previously inhabited and . . . he thought "where do we go from here?" In the distance he saw a great ornate gate . . . and the gate, as they do in supernatural films, just opened without any human assistance. He floated through and on the other side he saw an intellectual smorgasbord of everything that had ever puzzled the mind of man, you know, how did it all begin, where do we go from here, are there past lives, and like a sponge he was just absorbing all this esoteric information and all of a sudden there was a kind of swishing in the air and he heard a voice, "no, not yet, he's not ready" and like a long umbilical cord he felt himself being pulled back, back, back and he lay down in his body and he opened his eyes, and he said to the nurse, "I was dead, wasn't I?" Then he bounded off the operating table . . . he got two reams of paper, and a gallon of scalding black coffee, and at the end of two days he had a manuscript called "Excalibur" or "The Dark Sword." And he told me that whoever read it either went insane or committed suicide.[48]

The secret that Hubbard brought back to this world from his experience was ultimately boiled down to a single idea and a single word—the command to "SURVIVE," which he saw as the most fundamental driving force behind all existence. This would in turn become one of the key ideas in Dianetics and the foundation for much of later Scientology.

In this brief narrative we really find most of the classic elements of a narrative of mystical experience: an encounter with death or loss of self, a profound spiritual insight into ultimate reality and the nature of the universe, and a rebirth into the familiar world with a new sense of purpose. We might note that Hubbard's narrative is also reminiscent of accounts of astral projection, out-of-body experience, and the "astral cord" that, as we will see in chapter 2, were popular in the early twentieth century and appear in a modified form in Hubbard's early version of Scientology. Finally, Hubbard's nitrous oxide–induced vision is reminiscent of at least one other science fiction writer who recounted an equally intense mystical experience. In March 1974, Philip K. Dick recounted a remarkable series of visions (probably also associated with drug use), when he was lifted "from the limitations of the space-time matrix" and saw "what really existed." These experiences would be formative for the fiction of the last eight years of his life.[49]

The Occult Roots of Scientology? Hubbard, Jack Parsons, and the "Great Beast 666"

One of the most bizarre, tangled, and much-debated periods in Hubbard's early life took place shortly after his discharge from the navy in 1946 and his involvement in ritual magic and occultism in California. This story is far too complex and controversial to do justice here, so interested readers may read some of my and others' works where this bizarre series of incidents is treated in more detail.[50] What follows here is a much-abbreviated version of the story.

Moving to Pasadena after the war, Hubbard befriended the enigmatic rocket scientist and closet occultist John Whiteside (Jack) Parsons and became a resident in his rooming house known as "the Parsonage." In addition to being one of the most prominent rocket scientists of his day (with a crater on the moon named after him), Parsons was also an avid disciple of the infamous British occultist, Aleister Crowley (1875–1947)—the self-styled "Great Beast 666"—who is arguably the most important figure in the revival of magic, neo-paganism, and occultism in the twentieth century. Parsons was an initiate in Crowley's highly esoteric group, the Ordo Templi Orientis, and immersed in its most secret and most dangerous rituals. Sharing his interest in science fiction and magic, Hubbard soon became Parsons's close friend and a partner in his most esoteric magical rites.[51]

According to Parsons's detailed record of this period entitled "The Book of Babalon," he was engaged in a series of esoteric rituals based on Crowley's magic and the concept of the "moonchild." The aim of Parsons's "Babalon Working" was first to identify a female partner who would serve as his partner in esoteric sexual rituals; the partner would then become the vessel for the "magickal child" or "moonchild," a supernatural offspring that would be the embodiment of ultimate power: indeed, "this child would be 'mightier than all the kings of the Earth.'"[52] Apparently impressed by Hubbard's natural magical abilities, despite his lack of any formal training, Parsons made Hubbard an intimate participant in the Babalon Working and even his "Scribe" who served as the voice for Babalon herself during the rites. According to Parsons's account of March 2–3, 1946, Hubbard channeled the voice of Babalon, speaking as the beautiful but terrible lady who is "flame of life, power of darkness, she destroys with a glance, she may take thy soul. She feeds upon the death of men. Beautiful—Horrible."[53]

Apparently, Parsons believed that the rituals had been successful. Thus on March 6, he wrote excitedly to Crowley: "I have been in direct touch with One who is most Holy and Beautiful. . . . First, instructions were received direct through Ron, the seer . . . I am to act as instructor guardian guide for nine months; then it will be loosed on the world."[54] In short, Parsons believed that he had successfully "conceived" a supernatural being, who would then "gestate" for nine months before being born into the world. Ironically, however, Crowley himself was by no means approving when he learned of Parsons's and Hubbard's ritual activities. On the contrary, he seems to have been quite upset, writing to Karl Germer in April 1946: "Apparently Parsons or Hubbard or somebody is producing a Moonchild. I get fairly frantic when I contemplate the idiocy of these goats."[55]

The magical collaboration between Parsons and Hubbard was short-lived, however, and Parsons would never see his dream of the moonchild fulfilled. In 1946, Hubbard, Parsons, and Parsons's former girlfriend, Betty, formed a partnership called Allied Enterprises. Their scheme was to purchase yachts on the East Coast, sail them to California, and then sell them for a profit. Parsons put up $20,970.80, almost the entirety of his life's savings, while Hubbard put up a mere $1,183.91. Upon hearing of the scheme, Crowley himself suspected that Hubbard was playing Parsons for a fool and planning to betray him. In a cable to Germer, he wrote: "Suspect Ron playing confidence trick—Jack Parsons weak fool—obvious victim prowling swindlers."[56] Finally, Parsons concluded that Hubbard had stolen not just his girlfriend but all his money and so chased him down in Miami. As Hubbard and Betty attempted to flee on one of the yachts, Parsons performed a ritual curse involving the "invocation of Bartzabel," the spirit of Mars. Curiously enough, a sudden squall came up and forced Hubbard's ship back to port.[57]

Perhaps the most remarkable part of this whole story about Hubbard, Parsons, and secret sexual rites is that the Church of Scientology admits that most of these events really did happen. In October 1969, the London *Sunday Times* published an article that documented Hubbard's links to Parsons and Crowley; the church promptly threatened legal action and forced the *Times* to a pay an out-of-court settlement. Scientology then published a statement in the *Times* in December 1969, asserting that these rites *did* indeed take place but that Hubbard was sent on a special military mission to break up this black magic group. This he successfully did, the church claimed, "rescuing" the girl (Betty) and shutting down the occult operation:

> Hubbard broke up black magic in America. . . . [H]e was sent in to handle the situation. He went to live at the house and investigated the black

magic rites and the general situation and found them very bad. . . . Hubbard's mission was successful far beyond anyone's expectations. . . . Hubbard rescued a girl they were using. The black magic group was dispersed
and destroyed.[58]

It is worth noting, however, that neither the Church of Scientology nor
any independent researcher has ever produced any evidence for this claim.

Not surprisingly, there has been tremendous debate over Hubbard's involvement with Parsons and the influence of Crowley on later Scientology.
On one side, critics of the church such as Hubbard's own son, L. Ron Jr.,
have suggested that Hubbard was "deeply involved in the occult" and that
he even saw himself as the modern successor to the Great Beast.[59] Other
ex-members and critics of the church such as Jon Atack have alleged that
Crowley's magic lies at the inner core of Scientology.[60] On the other side,
the Church of Scientology itself has adamantly denied any connection
between Crowley's magic and Hubbard's religious ideas; indeed, it forced
the London *Sunday Times* to pay a settlement for suggesting that there
might be such a connection.[61] Meanwhile, many scholars such as Roy
Wallis and J. Gordon Melton have largely dismissed Hubbard's connection to Crowley, arguing that "there is no evidence that Hubbard's system
of Scientology owes any great debt to that of Crowley."[62]

Here I will not attempt to resolve this complex debate, other than to
suggest that Hubbard's involvement in ritual magic is perfectly in keeping with his character as an eclectic spiritual *bricoleur*.[63] While I would
by no means suggest that Crowley's magic lies at the inner core of Scientology, I do think it represents one of the many, many elements that
Hubbard explored and incorporated into the rich *bricolage* of Scientology. As we will see in chapter 2, many Crowleyian elements *do* reappear
in early Scientology, such as the idea of "exteriorizing" the spirit from
the body and acquiring a variety of paranormal abilities. But these elements are also mixed together with those drawn from science fiction,
Eastern religions, and various other sources.

The Birth of Dianetics: Liberating the "Superman" Within

Whatever the true nature of Hubbard's involvement with Parsons and
Crowley's magical rites, he soon turned from these occult explorations

to developing a new "science of the human mind" called Dianetics. As Hubbard himself reflected on the origins of his new science, Dianetics was the result of his exploration and synthesis of a wide array of different philosophical, psychological, and spiritual traditions. As a *bricoleur*, Hubbard claimed to have examined every known approach to the human mind, ranging from hypnosis and narcosynthesis to the occult methods of "automatic writing, speaking and clairvoyance," and even seeking out "the shamans of North Borneo, Sioux medicine men ... a magician whose ancestors served in the court of Kublai Khan and a Hindu who could hypnotize cats. Dabbles had been made in mysticism, data had been studied from mythology to spiritualism. Odds and ends like these, *countless odds and ends.*"[64]

Hubbard's new science initially took the form of an unpublished manuscript in 1948 (later published under the title *Dianetics: The Original Thesis*). Its first published form appeared in an issue of *Astounding Science Fiction*—a popular magazine edited by John Campbell, to which Hubbard had been a regular contributor—in May 1950. The cover of the issue featured a hairy, apelike alien creature with yellow cat's eyes—a figure readers would learn is the evil Duke of Kraakahaym, a special envoy from the Empire of Skontar. But the same cover also announced "Dianetics, the Evolution of a Science," which was not presented as "astounding science fiction" but rather as a revolutionary new science of the human mind. An expanded version of Hubbard's work was then printed in book form later that same year under the title *Dianetics: The Modern Science of Mental Health*. Advertised as nothing less than a radical breakthrough for mankind, Dianetics was said to be comparable to "the discovery of fire and superior to the wheel and arch."[65] As Pendle observes, however, it is not accidental that Hubbard's new science of the mind was published first in a science fiction magazine, since its claims and rhetoric appealed to much the same audience that had devoured his fictional tales for a decade: "*Astounding Science Fiction* didn't class Hubbard's essay as fiction, but its language was clearly tailored to the science fiction fan. Like the Charles Atlas bodybuilding advertisements that also ran in the pulp pages, Dianetics promised to transform the reader's 'normal brain' into an 'optimum brain' and thus help man 'continue his process of evolution toward a higher organism.'"[66] Hubbard

The cover of *Astounding Science Fiction*, May 1950, containing the first published version of "Dianetics"

himself, moreover, claimed that the aim of Dianetics was none other than to create a kind of new man or *Homo novis* with superhuman abilities: "The person ceases to respond like Homo sapiens and has fantastic capability to learn and act."[67] As fellow science fiction writer Jack Williamson put it, Dianetics offered "the promise to liberate the superman trapped inside us."[68]

Indeed, among the first proponents of Dianetics were key figures in the science fiction world—most important among them, John Campbell. As the editor of *Astounding Science Fiction*, Campbell shaped and dominated science fiction during the "golden age," from 1937 on. And he wrote enthusiastically about Hubbard's new science in a letter of 1950: "Fifteen minutes of Dianetics can get more results than five years of psychoanalysis. . . . We've broken homosexuals, alcoholics, asthmatics, arthritics and nymphomanics."[69] Another early convert to Dianetics was A. E. van Vogt, who was ranked with Robert Heinlein and Isaac Asimov at the top of Campbell's science fiction team.

Although Hubbard and the Church of Scientology would later become fierce critics of psychoanalysis, it is difficult not to see the influence of Freud, Jung, Rank, and various other psychotherapists whose work was widely available in the 1940s and 50s. Hubbard himself claimed to have mastered Freud's psychoanalytic theories, having studied under "the tutelage of one of his more brilliant pupils, a Commander Thompson" (referring here to U.S. Navy Commander Joseph "Snake" Thompson). He also acknowledges that he had "used an awful lot of hypnotism in early research. God bless Charcot. . . . And God bless Anton Mesmer."[70] In an article published in 1962, in fact, Hubbard himself noted the many similarities between Dianetics and Freudian psychoanalysis. However, he also insisted that Dianetics had provided more adequate solutions to some of the early life traumas suggested by Freud and by hypnosis:

> In the earliest beginnings of Dianetics it is possible to trace a considerable psychoanalytic influence. . . . [M]any of the things which Freud thought might exist, such as "life in the womb," "birth trauma," we in Dianetics have . . . confirmed and for them provided an adequate alleviation. The discovery of the engram is entirely the property of Dianetics. Methods of

its erasure are also owned entirely by Dianetics, but both of these were pointed to by early Freudian analysis and Hypnotism.[71]

Indeed, mainstream critics of Dianetics quickly dismissed it as a kind of "Poor Man's Psychoanalysis."[72] Others such as fellow writer Jack Williamson were even more skeptical of Hubbard's new science, which seemed to him more like a "wonderfully rewarding scam" and a kind of "lunatic revision of Freudian psychology."[73]

According to Hubbard's new science, the human mind is composed of two fundamental parts: the analytical mind and the reactive mind. While the analytical mind is accurate, rational, and logical—a "flawless computer"—the reactive mind is the repository of a variety of memory traces that Hubbard calls engrams. Consisting primarily of moments of pain, unconsciousness, and loss, these engrams are burned into the reactive mind and cause us a variety of problems in the present, ranging from neurosis to physical illness and insanity. Through the Dianetic process, however, the individual can erase these painful engrams, by returning to the original event, reliving it, and thus clearing it from the reactive mind. This is the process that Hubbard calls—ironically enough—"auditing," or the systemic method by which the patient (called the pre-clear or PC) is questioned by an auditor to identify and remove the troubling engrams.

Although Hubbard had studied hypnosis—and was in fact reputed to be expert in the practice—he explicitly distinguished the Dianetic auditing technique from any form of hypnotism.[74] Dianetic auditing, he claimed, puts the individual into a state of "reverie" in which one has access to all past engrams but without becoming unconscious. However, his description of engrams and the reactive mind bears more than a little resemblance to the work of psychoanalysts such as Otto Rank and his work on the *Trauma of Birth* (1929). Hubbard describes memories that can be traced in the reactive mind all the way back to the womb, where one encounters engrams caused by the pain from a "lover's enthusiasm," the mother's constipation, a douche, morning sickness, an attempted abortion, premature labor pains, and birth.[75]

Ultimately, once all the engrams have been removed, the individual achieves the state called "Clear." As Hubbard claimed, the Clear individual experiences him- or herself and the world in a radically new way, achieving a variety of intellectual and physical benefits, ranging from increased IQ to optimum health and well-being: "His physical vitality and health are markedly improved and all psychosomatic illnesses have vanished. . . . His ability to seek and experience pleasure is great. His personality is heightened and he is creative and constructive. His vigor, persistence, and tenacity are much higher than anyone has thought possible."[76]

Most Scientologists I've interviewed do recount a number of dramatic experiences achieved through auditing. As one individual described his first auditing session at a Detroit, Michigan, center, he was asked a long series of questions about his life and then finally asked to recall a moment of loss. Spontaneously, this question dredged up the memory of his grandfather's death, an event he had not thought about in years. The resurfacing of the memory led to a sudden wave of tears and uncontrollable sobbing; but it was soon followed by a tremendous sense of relief, "like a huge weight had been lifted off my shoulders," he recalled. For an entire week afterward, he felt elated and saw the world with a whole new sense of clarity, freedom, and joy that he had never known before. So began his involvement in Scientology, which lasted for the next twenty-five years.[77]

This individual's experience is not an uncommon one. Indeed, even the most cynical ex-Scientologists I've talked to recount many positive experiences, insights, and realizations achieved through auditing. According to one former member, reaching the state of Clear brought a remarkable feeling of peacefulness and unburdening, giving her, as she put it, a sense of awakening "like the roof came off the top of my head."[78]

Significantly, however, L. Ron Hubbard claimed that auditing would result not merely in a state of optimum *psychological* well-being, but in various forms of *physical* healing as well. In his *Astounding Science Fiction* essay, he had presented Dianetics as the means to cure "colds and arthritis and other psychosomatic ills."[79] Meanwhile, in his book publication, Hubbard asserted that Clear individuals simply "do not get colds" and that Dianetics can treat virtually any psychosomatic illness—that is, any illness created physically within the body by a derangement of the mind. Hubbard's catalog of such illnesses is vast, including arthritis, dermatitis, allergies, asthma, coronary difficulties, eye trouble, bursitis, ulcers, sinusitis, and so on.[80] As we will see in chapter 2, it was precisely these claims to physical healing that would attract the attention of the FDA and other government agencies and eventually lead Hubbard to pursue the "religion angle."

In sum, the goal of "Clear" seemed to represent almost anything the individual hoped and longed for: higher intellectual functioning, brighter personality, more successful career, optimal physical health, and virtually anything else the aspiring Dianeticist dreamed of. Dianetics and Scientology publications from the early 1950s on include a vast array of testimonials from those who had gone Clear, of which the following are but a few examples:

> I'm CLEAR! I'm CLEAR! . . . There are no words to explain or describe the State of Clear. I just AM.[81]
>
> Clear is where it's at. My body feels different! And particularly, I don't have to have noises or voices rambling around in my mind. It's fantastic!
>
> Clear is the culmination of all the yearning and all the striving to be! It has for me . . . an inner calmness.[82]

One of the more unlikely candidates for "Clear" was none other than novelist William S. Burroughs, infamous author of *Naked Lunch* (and later a severe critic of Scientology). Upon becoming Clear number 1163, Burroughs enthusiastically testified that "it feels marvelous! Things you've had all your life, things you think about nothing can be done about—suddenly they're not there any more!"[83]

In many ways, the goal of "Clear" seems to have functioned as a kind of empty signifier, an amorphous but supremely attractive goal that could represent almost anything to anyone: higher IQ for some, better personal relationships for others, career success for some, domestic bliss for others. As sociologist Roy Wallis noted, "[T]he idea of 'clear' like that of 'flying saucer' became a kind of Rorschach blot, a vague and amorphous image upon which any individual could impose his aspirations. Being clear . . . meant being able to do all those things which one could currently not do, and to which one aspired so desperately."[84]

"It Sees All . . . It Is Never Wrong": The Electropsychometer

To aid in the auditing process, Hubbard also began to employ a device known as the E-meter or electropsychometer, a device still central to Scientology auditing to this day. Devices that were alleged to record psychic and/or spiritual states by measuring physical responses had actually been around for some time. Such instruments were first developed in the late nineteenth century and explored by none other than depth psychologist Carl Gustav Jung, who wrote enthusiastically about the uses of "psycho-galvanometers" in the early twentieth century.[85]

The electropsychometer entered into Dianetic and Scientology auditing through Hubbard's early collaborator Volney Mathison, a chiropractor and author of paranormal and science fiction books. Like others in the 1940s, Mathison had been experimenting with early lie-detector devices and developed a meter that was used sporadically in Dianetics auditing in the early 1950s.[86] Consisting of a portable black metal box with knobs to adjust and a big, lighted dial, the Mathison meter was essentially a kind of skin galvanometer designed to measure fluctuations in the passage of a trickle of electricity through the body. The primary component of the meter is an instrument called a Wheatstone Bridge, which measures changes in electrical resistance. As used in Dianetic auditing, the meter is believed to measure physical responses that identify the painful engrams in need of clearing from the reactive mind. While the pre-clear holds two metal cylinders (originally, ordinary tomato cans) attached by wires to the meter, the auditor asks him or her a variety of questions and observes the fluctuations of the meter's needle.[87]

Although little employed in the early days of Dianetics, the E-meter became increasingly central to auditing from 1952 onward. As Hubbard recounted, the Mathison meter was far superior to any lie detector or other instrument available at the time and offered a more precise means to measure the psyche: "Various instruments such as the electroencephalograph and the police lie-detector were used to further this search, but these were inadequate. . . . Finally Volney Mathison applied his electronic genius to the problem and invented the Electropsychometer. This instrument had a range and ability greatly in excess of anything

MATHISON ELECTROPSYCHOMETER
8 patent claims conditionally allowed April 24 1952. 16 claims pending.

Advertisement for the Mathison Electropsychometer. *Aberree* 1, no. 2 (1954): 14. Courtesy of Kristi Wachter

before known."[88] Hubbard's faith in the E-meter was enthusiastic, bordering on fanatical. As he wrote in June 1952,

> The nimble needle of the electropsychometer can detect with accuracy things which would have been otherwise hidden from man forever. . . .
>
> [T]he electropsychometer utterly dwarfs the invention of the microscope. . . . [T]he electropsychometer provides the way for man to find his freedom and to rise . . . to social and constructive levels of which he has never dreamed. . . .
>
> It sees all, knows all. It is never wrong.[89]

Hubbard presented the E-meter as a more scientific, precise, and accurate means to access the unconscious mind that was far superior to Freud's relatively clumsy psychoanalytic techniques. As he wrote in 1952,

the new power of electronics could "give life to Freud's theory" and provide a far more efficient means to access the hidden recesses of the mind:

> [Y]ears after free association as developed by Sigmund Freud had been
> abandoned as a therapy, the development in electronics has revised, at
> least in part, the techniques of the Viennese master. . . .
>
> With the aid of an E-Meter and the technique of associative process-
> ing, it has been estimated that the usual two-year psychoanalysis could be
> cut to three or four months. In the field of Scientology it is said that an
> hour of associative processing is worthy more than fifteen or twenty
> hours of straight memory questioning.[90]

In 1954, Mathison and Hubbard had a falling-out, and use of the
Mathison meter was discontinued. However, Hubbard soon introduced
a new device, with minor modifications, now marketed as the "Hubbard
E-meter." As we see in figure 1, Hubbard believed that his E-meter was
so sensitive that it could even register the pain of a tomato plant, leading

Mark VI model E-meter. Photo by author

him to the conclusion that "tomatoes scream when sliced."[91] The Hubbard E-meter has in turn gone through various incarnations and is still a central part of Scientology auditing to this day.

The "Dianetics Craze": The Success of Hubbard's New Science and the Growth of the Early Movement

Hubbard's *Dianetics* appears to have been wildly more successful than anyone, including its author, could have imagined. Arguably the first major book of do-it-yourself psychotherapy, *Dianetics* became something of a runaway best seller, entering the *New York Times* best-seller list on June 18, 1950, and remaining there until December 24—a full twenty-eight weeks. And it quickly gave birth to a whole new kind of movement—what the *New Republic* called "the Dianetics Craze"—as the book was handed around and thousands of Americans began to sit down and audit one another, either individually or in small, loosely knit clubs.[92] As the *Los Angeles Daily News* reported in September 1950, "Hubbard has become, in a few swift months, a personality of national celebrity and the proprietor of the fastest growing movement in the US."[93] Even those within the movement were astonished by its rapid success. Helen O'Brien, an early executive in the movement and the head of its highly successful Philadelphia center, recalled the early days of Dianetics as follows: "The book met with an overwhelming public response. Sales were high, and the copies were passed from reader to reader. . . . Thousands of dianetic clubs were formed in towns and cities. . . . The boom was remarkable for a while. People everywhere embraced it as though they had found something which they had hungered for all their lives."[94]

Among the thousands who began to dabble in Dianetics was none other than Aldous Huxley, a fellow writer also known for his interest in altered states of consciousness, drugs, and mystical experience. Hubbard actually visited Huxley's home on North Kings Road in Los Angeles to audit Aldous and his wife, Maria, personally. Unfortunately, after three or four sessions, Huxley reported finding no engrams, although Maria apparently "had some success in contacting and working off engrams and has been back repeatedly into . . . the pre-natal state."[95]

To try to manage the rapidly growing movement, Hubbard set up the Hubbard Dianetic Research Foundation (HDRF) in Elizabeth, New Jersey, in April 1950, which was shortly followed by a second foundation in Los Angeles under the direction of fellow science fiction writer A. E. van Vogt.[96] Auditing in the early days went for $25 an hour, while one could enroll in the HDRF auditor's course for $500. As *Look* magazine reported in 1950, much of the attraction of Dianetics was precisely that it offered a form of simplified psychoanalysis that was open to more or less anybody and was an entertaining therapy that could be performed anywhere from a living room to a dinner party: "Hubbard's greatest attraction to the troubled is that his ersatz psychiatry is available to all. It's cheap. It's accessible. It's a public festival to be played at clubs and parties."[97]

As such, Dianetics in its early phase was a kind of wildly proliferating and spontaneous grassroots movement that gave rise to small groups of individuals and clubs all over the United States and the United Kingdom,

L. Ron Hubbard in 1982. Getty Images

who practiced the technique on their own. Thus there was the "Bristol Dianetics Group," the "Connecticut Valley Dianetic Association," and so on, often operating independently of Hubbard and creating no end of organizational headaches for the early movement. As we will see in chapter 2, this grassroots spontaneity was, ironically, both a key to Dianetics's early success and a primarily reason for its rapid disintegration and Hubbard's creation of a more structured, hierarchical movement called the Church of Scientology.

Conclusions: Founder of a Revolutionary New Science or "the Greatest Con Man of the Century"?

Evaluating and making sense of L. Ron Hubbard is no easy task. Whenever I teach Scientology in my religious studies classes, students inevitably ask: "Did he really believe this stuff? Or was he just a con artist? Or was he completely insane?" From the first publication of *Dianetics* in 1950, the media and various government agencies were asking this same question. Some authors of the day described Hubbard as not just *a* con man but indeed as "the greatest con man of the century."[98] As former Scientologist and erstwhile biographer Gerry Armstrong put it, "He was a mixture of Adolf Hitler, Charlie Chaplin and Baron Munchhausen."[99] For the thousands of Scientologists worldwide who still follow his teachings today, however, Hubbard was nothing less than a heroic explorer who uncovered the most arcane mysteries not just from all corners of the earth but from every nook and cranny of the human mind. Yet even the fiercest critics of Hubbard, such as ex-Scientologist Jon Atack, have acknowledged that the man had an astonishing and almost inexplicable charismatic power: it was almost impossible, Atack recounts, to write a convincing picture of Hubbard's charisma or explain "the remarkable devotion that his followers felt for him."[100]

One possible clue to Hubbard's complex persona is provided in a late interview he did with the *Rocky Mountain Times* in 1983, three years before his death. In it, Hubbard comments that his favorite work of nonfiction was William Bolitho's *Twelve Against the Gods* (1929), noting that "the introduction is particularly good."[101] Bolitho's work examines twelve "adventurers," that is, twelve determined, often controversial, and at times even hated individualists whose spirit of independence, defiance, and willfulness changed history. These include Alexander, Casanova, Columbus, Mahomet, Lola Montez, Cagliostro, Charles XII of Sweden, Napoleon, Catiline, Napoleon III, Isadora Duncan, and Woodrow Wilson. As Bolitho describes "the adventurer," he is "an individualist and an egotist, a truant from obligations. His road is solitary, there is no room for company on it. What he does, he does for himself. His motive may be simple greed. It most often is, or that form of greed we call vanity."[102] In his relentless pursuit of "the Atlantic flights, the polar journeys, the Everest climb, the flowering of heroism and endurance above anything in humanity's past," the adventurer is driven by a motive that is both "swinish and godlike. . . . For this greed they have in all their five senses, for gold, for power for vainglory."[103] As Atack suggests, Hubbard's reference to his favorite book may well give us some insight into his own character—the self-proclaimed adventurer and radical individualist who is also motivated by a touch of vanity and greed.[104]

Yet whether we regard him as a heroic adventurer or a greed-driven con man, we do have to appreciate one basic fact about L. Ron Hubbard: in the space of a year, he had risen from a penny-a-word science fiction writer to the leader of the largest and most lucrative self-help group in the United States. As we will see in the next chapter, he would soon become the leader of the fastest-growing and most controversial new religion in the world. In this sense, Hubbard is perhaps best understood neither as a romantic philosopher-hero nor as a cynical con man; rather, he was an extremely savvy entrepreneur and *bricoleur* with an unusually keen sense of the spiritual marketplace of 1950s America. And Hubbard, if we read his myriad bulletins, policy letters, and books, more or less described himself as such. In his own words, he had explored and used "anything that worked," from hypnotism to psychoanalysis to explorations of Eastern religions to build his new science of the mind: "Everybody and everything seemed to have a scrap of the answer. The cults of all the ages, all the world seem, each one, to contain a fragment of the truth. How do we gather and assemble the fragments?"[105] At the same time, however, Hubbard also pushed his followers to likewise employ any and all methods necessary—"anything that worked"—in order to sell his books and to get *Dianetics* into the hands of readers: "Any 'sales tricks' you employ after you have succeeded by use of help, control, communication and interest, in arousing that interest to get them now to inform themselves of the moment of break-through, will be well expended by you. . . . Let's push this book. Let's crowd it into people's hands and demand that they buy it. . . . Push it. Get your people to read it."[106]

In this sense, Hubbard was hardly a strange aberration amidst the rapidly growing spiritual marketplace of the 1940s and 50s. Rather, he was perhaps its very epitome: an enthusiastic, resourceful, and ever-optimistic American entrepreneur. In his quest to explore the terra incognita of the human mind, he was determined to use quite simply "anything that worked." As we will see in chapter 2, the same spirit of tireless experimentation, synthesis, and entrepreneurship would soon lead him to found his own new church.

- TWO -

SCIENTOLOGY, INC.
Becoming a "Religion" in the 1950s

As far as Scientology being a religion is concerned, it has more right to be
a religion than the Catholic Church has and could stand up and be
proven in court to that effect.
—L. Ron Hubbard, *Phoenix Lectures* (1954)[1]

It appeals a great deal to Americans, I think, because they tend to believe
in instant everything, from instant coffee to instant nirvana. By just . . .
doing a few assignments, one can become a god.
—L. Ron Hubbard Jr., interview (1983)[2]

Dianetics was a surprisingly successful and widely popular form of personal therapy—indeed, arguably the first of the many popular self-help
manuals that followed in the next five decades. Although it offered many
remarkable benefits and made many astonishing claims, one thing Dianetics did *not* claim was any sort of religious status. As Hubbard put it,
"Dianetics is a science; as such, it has no opinion about religion, for sciences are based on natural laws, not on opinions."[3] In fact, in many of his
lectures from the early 1950s, Hubbard was quite critical of organized
religion and particularly of Christianity. As he explained in a lecture in
1952, organized religion is primarily about lying and control, that is,
about deceiving and manipulating people through notions of sin and
guilt, rather than freeing them through knowledge: "[R]eligion is always
different than truth. It has to be. Because the only way you can control a
people is to lie to them"; indeed, organized religion is primarily about
instilling guilt and fear in order to dominate individuals: "The church,
actually, will educate people into being sinners and tell them to repent. . . .
'Regret, regret, regret, repent, repent, repent.' You're a sinner, you're a

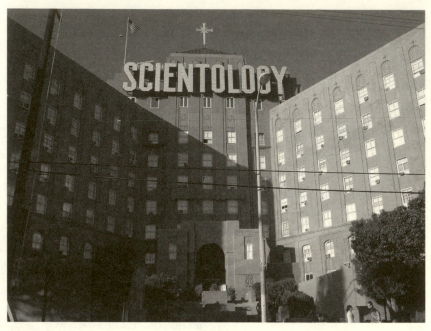

Church of Scientology, Los Angeles, CA. Photo by author

sinner. You shouldn't do this . . . you shouldn't do that, after all. And the reasons you shouldn't is because there's a mysterious and awesome being."[4] Hubbard was especially critical of Christianity, which he described as simply a movement "based on the victim": "Christianity succeeded by making people into victims."[5]

This negative attitude toward religion, however, changed rapidly in the 1950s, as Hubbard began to see the advantage (and perhaps the necessity) of achieving official recognition as a "religion" in order to keep his young movement alive. The reasons for this shift are many and complex. Various individuals—including several fellow science fiction writers and Hubbard's own son—have recalled hearing Hubbard state that the way to make money was to start a religion. As writer and publisher Lloyd Eshbach recalled, Hubbard made the statement over lunch in New York City in 1949, just months before the publication of *Dianetics*: "I'd like to start a religion. That's where the money is!" Plans for this new religion, Eshbach claims, were soon after drawn up in John W. Campbell's kitchen in New Jersey.[6] This rumor about the cynically "religious" origins of Scientology has been repeated by various other writers who knew Hubbard in the 1940s.[7]

However, the transition from Dianetics to Scientology and the birth of a new religion is far too complex to be reduced to a simple money-making or tax-evasion scheme, of which Scientology is so often accused. Hubbard's efforts to redefine Scientology as a "religion," in fact, began gradually, in fits and starts, and largely in response to internal and external events that made such a redefinition of the movement both expedient and necessary. In part, this shift had to do with internal tensions within the early Dianetics movement and challenges to Hubbard's authority; in part, it had to do with mounting attacks from external agencies such as the FDA and the American Medical Association, who were increasingly skeptical of Hubbard's claims to physical healing through auditing; and no doubt it also had in part to do with Hubbard's own fertile imagination as a spiritual entrepreneur who now began to explore the terrain of reincarnation, Eastern religions, out-of-body experience, and supernatural powers.

Not all of Hubbard's early followers were happy with this religious turn, moreover. In the words of Helen O'Brien, the head of the highly successful Philadelphia office of Dianetics, the shift to Scientology seemed to many members like a descent into mystical mumbo jumbo: "Beginning in 1953, the joy and frankness shifted to pontification. The fact-filled 'engineering approach to the human mind' faded out of sight, to be replaced by a 'Church of Scientology' in which Hubbard ordained ministers . . . [I]t resembles nothing so much as a temperate zone voodoo, in its elasticity, unexplainable procedures and mindless group euphoria."[8]

If Hubbard is best understood as an ingenious spiritual entrepreneur and *bricoleur*, then his eclectic entrepreneurial spirit only grew more ambitious in the 1950s as he developed his new church. As Wade Clark Roof suggests, "[S]uccessful religious groups adapt to their environments . . . providing a compelling 'religious product' in exchange for resources," and Scientology appears to have adapted itself remarkably well to the rapidly expanding marketplace of 1950s America.[9] Hubbard's already highly syncretic science of Dianetics quickly morphed into an even more complex *bricolage* of philosophical, spiritual, and science fiction elements drawn from sources as varied as Eastern religions, past-life memories, UFO beliefs, and his own creative imagination.

As historian Patrick Allitt suggests, the American religious landscape in the years after World War II was characterized by a series of apparent paradoxes. America in the 1950s was "simultaneously a highly religious and a highly secular place";[10] it witnessed a tremendous "flourishing of secular science and technology alongside flourishing of religion"; it was a nation that was at once "very wealthy and very religious"; and it was a culture that was "both traditional and technologically sophisticated," with an ability to adapt eagerly to each new technology. In sum, "America in the latter half of the twentieth century was the world's richest nation, with a population much better provided for materially than at any other time in its history. . . . The workings of the massive market economy and its success as a wealth generator profoundly affected religion, enabling Americans to build imposing churches and to fund them to the tune of billions of dollars."[11]

Scientology, I would argue, is a striking embodiment and arguably the epitome of each of these paradoxes within American religion in the years after World War II. Perhaps more so than any other modern movement, Scientology combines religion and secular culture, faith in science and technology with faith in spiritual development, and tremendous material wealth with claims to religious status. Indeed, if we follow Allitt's description of the religious landscape of the postwar era, Scientology would seem to lie close to its ground zero. Yet ironically, Scientology's journey to becoming a "religion" was a long, complex, often convoluted one, responding to various forces both within the movement and without, from both disgruntled members of the early Dianetics community and critical elements within the U.S. government. Hubbard's unique genius as spiritual entrepreneur seems to have been his remarkable ability to adapt, rework, and repackage his new movement to the changing marketplace of America in the 1950s and 60s.

Challenges from Within and Outside the Early Dianetics Movement

Not long after its birth, Hubbard's Dianetics movement faced a series of crises from both within and outside the organization. First, Hubbard's ambitious claims about the efficacy of Dianetics and the abilities of a

"Clear" met with serious challenges and very bad PR. His own wife, Sarah, whom he had at one point pronounced "Clear"—that is, a perfectly healthy, rational individual possessing optimum psychological and physical well-being—had him pronounced "hopelessly insane" by doctors she had consulted and sued for divorce.[12] Still worse, in August 1950, Hubbard presented his first Clear individual to a lecture hall of six thousand in Los Angeles. To his embarrassment, his Clear (who was supposed to have total memory recall) was unable to remember what she had for breakfast that morning or even what color Hubbard's tie was that evening.[13]

Second, in the wake of this negative PR, the Dianetics movement centered in Elizabeth, New Jersey, began to fall into both serious financial trouble and a growing crisis of authority. Already by April 1951, less than a year after the publication of his best seller, Hubbard's movement was facing financial ruin. The foundation temporarily received assistance from Don Purcell, a Wichita businessman and self-made millionaire, who offered funds along with a building centered in Kansas and thus became the foundation's president. Yet very quickly, Purcell and other early supporters such as John Campbell and Joseph Winter reported being frustrated by the increasing dogmatism and authoritarianism of Hubbard, who resisted any attempts to restrain his complete control over Dianetics. Winter resigned from the board of directors in October 1950, followed by Campbell in March 1951. Purcell recounted similar frustrations with Hubbard's poor business sense and finally entered the foundation into voluntary bankruptcy in 1952.[14]

A third tension arose, however, when Hubbard began to introduce the idea of past lives into the movement. As we will see in more detail below, Hubbard believed his research had uncovered experiences in his patients that could only be explained as a result of memories from previous lives. This was an idea that did not sit well with other leaders of the movement who hoped to preserve a more credible "scientific" reputation for Dianetics. Early supporters of Dianetics in the medical community such as Winter became increasingly distressed at what they considered the unscientific orientation that was beginning to prevail in Dianetics. Hubbard himself reflected on this in his *Science of Survival* in 1951: "The subject of past deaths and past lives is so full of tension that as early as last July (1950) the board of trustees of the Foundation sought to pass a resolution banning the entire subject."[15]

Finally, perhaps the most serious problem for Dianetics came from outside the movement. Not long after its inception, the practice of Dianetics generated extreme skepticism and at times fierce criticism from the medical community and the FDA. Dianetics, after all, had made fairly grandiose claims to heal a wide range of physical as well as psychological ills, including arthritis, myopia, heart illness, and asthma, promising that "the whole catalogue of ills goes away and stays away."[16] Not surprisingly such claims drew the attention of the FDA and various state medical boards, and throughout the early 1950s, Hubbard's followers across the United States were arrested for practicing medicine without licenses. Thus in January 1951, the New Jersey State Board of Medical Examiners accused the Hubbard Dianetic Research Foundation Inc. of operating a school for treatment of disease without a license; in March 1953 two Dianetics and Scientology practitioners were arrested as part of an investigation into running an unlicensed school and practicing medicine without a license; and in late 1953, a Scientologist in Glendale, California, spent ten days in jail for practicing medicine without a license.[17] In 1958, the FDA seized and destroyed a consignment of twenty-one thousand tablets of Hubbard's anti–radiation sickness drug, Dianezene, claiming they were falsely labeled for treatment of real illness.[18]

Beyond the Dianezene, however, the FDA also began to take a critical interest in Hubbard's E-meter and his ambitious claims about the meter's healing potential. In response, Hubbard began to explicitly emphasize the distinctly *spiritual* and *religious* nature of the E-meter. Perhaps the clearest example of this religious turn is a policy letter of October 20, 1962, entitled simply "Religion," which includes a special note to "furnish a copy of this to all attorneys dealing with our interests for us." Here Hubbard makes it clear that the E-meter should be presented to the FDA as an inherently *religious* device and explicitly *not* a medical or diagnostic one:

> It is of interest to all organizations that *all* Scientology incorporations are religious in nature. . . .
>
> The use of the E-Meter in Scientology . . . is describable as follows:

"All religions seek truth.

"Freedom of spirit is only to be found on the road to Truth. . . .

"Religions in the 1960's use modern aids. The Electropsychometer is a valid religious instrument, used in Confessionals, and is in no way diagnostic and does not treat". . . .

In view of the "interest" the Food and Drug Administration has in the E-Meter the above data is vital and must be impressed upon investigating agents. . . . They thought that outside the U.S. Scientology was not religious, which is false. The impression must be strongly corrected in the FDA at once.[19]

Apparently, however, Hubbard's directive to emphasize the "religious" nature of auditing and the E-meter did not immediately satisfy the FDA. On January 4, 1963, U.S. Marshals acting on an FDA warrant launched a surprise raid on the Founding Church of Scientology in Washington, DC, confiscating over a hundred E-meters and more than three tons of literature and equipment.[20] After a decade of court battles, the church finally settled with the FDA. The court ruled that the church must include clear disclaimers on its E-meters, warning that they are not for use in any kind of medical treatment but are permitted only as part of a *religious activity*:

The device should bear a prominent, clearly visible notice warning that any person using it for auditing or counseling of any kind is forbidden by law to represent that there is any medical or scientific basis for believing or asserting that the device is useful in the diagnosis, treatment, or prevention of any disease. It should be noted . . . that use is permitted only as part of religious activity, and that the E-meter is not medically or scientifically capable of improving the health or bodily functions of anyone.[21]

Looking back on this period from the vantage point of 1969, Hubbard himself later explained "why Dianetics fell out of use" and why Scientology finally took its place. As Hubbard put it, "[I]n some areas, mainly the US, it was illegal to heal or cure anything"; as a result, Dianetics as a *healing* practice was gradually replaced by Scientology as a *spiritual* practice, which would be outside the scrutiny of government agencies such as the FDA and able to operate freely without interference by the medical establishment: "[T]he ability of Scientology to bring about spiritual freedom therefore received the concentration of efforts by organizations."[22]

Scientology, Inc.: The Decline of Dianetics and the Birth of Scientology

Hubbard's response to the crises from within and outside the movement was essentially to abandon Dianetics and to begin promoting a new, separate system of belief and practice. He called his new science "Scientology"—a term that he claimed to have coined himself, but one that had been used at least twice earlier in English and German texts. (Ironically, we might note, the first usage of the term was far from positive. As early as 1910, it was used by the satirist Allen Upward to describe any pseudoscientific babble that masquerades as fact: "And unhappily scientology is as often mistaken for science as theology is for worship."[23])

Hubbard's turn to Scientology began as early as 1952, when he broke with the Dianetics group in Wichita and established the Hubbard Association of Scientologists (HAS) in Phoenix. In March of that year, he also married his third wife, Mary Sue Whipp, who reportedly helped him come up with the name for his new movement and later became one of its most important and successful organizers. Scientology then operated as a separate practice until 1954, when Hubbard regained control of HDRF and incorporated Dianetics as a sort of minor, introductory technique into the larger structure of Scientology. If Dianetics promised to achieve optimum physical and psychological well-being in this lifetime, Scientology had far more ambitious aims beyond the physical realm. In the earliest texts from 1952, however, Hubbard still does not define Scientology as a religion, but identifies it primarily with *science*: "'Scientology' is a new word which names a new science. It is formed from the Latin word *scio* which means *know*. . . . It is formed from the Greek word *logos,* which means *the word, or outward form by which the inward thought is expressed and made known.* Thus, *Scientology* means *knowing about knowing* or *science of knowledge.*"[24]

Scientology's shift toward an explicitly "religious" identity was not immediate but in fact rather gradual and seems to have been in response to various legal and political challenges in the early 1950s. As we see in a newsletter of April 1953, Hubbard seems to almost toy with the idea of "religion" without really committing himself one way or the other: Scientology auditing, he suggests, is "perhaps allied with religion, perhaps a mystic practice, and possibly just another form of Christian Science or plain Hubbardian nonsense."[25]

The most important document concerning the birth of Scientology as a "religion" is a letter dated April 10, 1953, which was sent by Hubbard to Helen O'Brien, at that time the head of the HAS in the United States. This letter was produced as evidence in the *Church of Scientology v. Gerald Armstrong* case in 1984, and its authenticity has never been contested by the church. In it, Hubbard states quite frankly that he hopes to pursue the "religion angle" in order to both combat psychoanalysis and make money: "We don't want a clinic. We want one in operation, but not in name. Perhaps we could call it a Spiritual Guidance Center. Think up its name, will you? . . . It is a problem in practical business." However, Hubbard also seems to indicate that he has not entirely thought through this religion idea and is asking O'Brien's advice on how to best package and market the rebranded movement: "I await your reaction on the religion angle. In my opinion, we couldn't get worse public opinion than we have had or have less customers with what we've got to sell. A religious charter would be necessary in Pennsylvania or N.J. to make it stick. . . . We're treating the present-time beingness, psychotherapy treats the past and the brain. And, brother, that's religion, not mental science."[26]

Finally, in late 1953, Hubbard appears to have taken the plunge and embraced the "religion angle" as the most advantageous way to rebrand his young movement. In December 1953, Hubbard incorporated three new organizations in Camden, New Jersey: the Church of American Science, the Church of Scientology, and the Church of Spiritual Engineering. This was followed by the opening of a church in California in 1954 and the incorporation of the Founding Church of Scientology in Washington, DC, in 1955. According to the founding church's certificate of incorporation, this is now a *religious* organization, created "to act as a parent church for the propagation of the religious faith known as 'Scientology,' and to act as a Church for the religious worship of that Faith."[27] Among other things, Hubbard clearly hoped that this religious angle would protect the movement from the attacks of the government and medical community. As we see in a publication by an independent Scientologist in 1954, "[T]his stroke will remove Scientology from the target area of overt and covert attacks by the medical profession, who see their pills, scalpels, and appendix-studded incomes threatened. Several auditors . . . in the past have found themselves facing prejudiced courts or behind bars."[28]

In June 1954, a second organizational shift occurred: the HAS was dissolved and replaced by the HASI (Hubbard Association of Scientologists International), which ran the "churches" now incorporated under it. More important, the re-formed HASI was now explicitly defined as a "religious fellowship" and thus—theoretically, at least—protected from state interference. Hubbard emphasized, however, that this organizational change would not affect ordinary Scientologists "except to give auditors and schools complete security from legal interference. The new organization, HASI, is a non-profit religious fellowship, and as such, Ron said, is entitled to the constitutional guarantees of a Supreme Court ruling that no state shall take action to prevent operation of any organization concerned with the study of the human soul."[29]

Thus, by the end of 1954, Hubbard was explicitly defining Scientology as a "religion," focused on the *spirit*, and contrasting it with Dianetics as a "science," focused on the physical being: "Dianetics is a science which applies to man, a living organism; and Scientology is a religion."[30] He also began to introduce a variety of explicitly religious terms and practices, including the titles of "Minister" and "Doctor of Divinity" for practitioners (1954–1955),[31] the celebration of marriages and a formal Scientology wedding ceremony (1955–1956), the wearing of clerical collars (1959), and various other religious ceremonies such as church services, christenings, and funerals (1959).[32] Hubbard made it clear that the Scientologist should attempt to conform to the standard image of a religious minister: "[H]e should dress in a way that does not upset the accepted stable data of what a minister looks like"; thus he should "wear a cutaway and the cross," and he should be prepared and able to explain to Christian ministers that Scientology stands for the same basic principles as did Jesus Christ.[33] Shortly after the formation of the church in 1954, Hubbard also composed the "Creed of the Church of Scientology."

While reminiscent of the Christian Nicene Creed, the Scientology Creed also strongly emphasizes two key points: (1) freedom of religious expression, and (2) the idea that mental healing is properly the domain of *religion* and that *spirit* alone can heal the physical body. Both of these points seem to be in clear response to the FDA's investigations into Dianetics's claims to physical healing:

> We of the Church believe:
>
> That all men of whatever race, color or creed were created with equal rights.
>
> That all men have inalienable rights to their own religious practices and their performance. . . .
>
> That the study of the Mind and the healing of mentally caused ills should not be alienated from religion or condoned in nonreligious fields . . .
>
> That the spirit alone may save or heal the body.[34]

During this same time period in the mid-1950s, Hubbard also introduced the "Scientology cross" as a key symbol for the church. As I and many other observers have pointed out, Hubbard's eight-pointed cross bears a striking resemblance to the eight-pointed cross used by the occult-magical group called the Hermetic Order of the Golden Dawn—of which Aleister Crowley had been a member, and which also adorns the back of Crowley's influential and widely used tarot deck, the Thoth deck.[35] According to Hubbard, however, the eight points of the cross symbolize the "eight dynamics" or the eight urges to survival that we all have, ranging from the urge to survive as an individual physical being up through the urge to survive as a spiritual being and the urge to survive as "Infinity" or "the Supreme Being," also called the "God dynamic." It is worth noting, however, that Hubbard was generally very reluctant to say much about this eighth dynamic or the Supreme Being, even making a point to state, "It is carefully observed that the science of Scn does not intrude into the dynamic of the Supreme Being."[36]

However, Hubbard was also aware that many of his followers would not be happy with this new "religious" turn. As we noted above, key leaders in the movement such as Helen O'Brien were clearly not happy with the shift toward "pontification." In fact, Hubbard wrote several pieces explicitly to address concerns among Scientologists who were uneasy about the language of religion, ministers, and churches. Thus in August 1954, he addressed the question, "Why Doctor of Divinity?" "There has been some stir amongst auditors concerning the fact that Scientology has allied itself with the Church of American Science, why a Church of Scientology has come into existence and why auditors . . . have received ordination as ministers in these churches."[37] He acknowledged that Scientologists should be wary of the invocation of religion, given its historical links to Christianity; however, they should also not fear embracing it as an alternative to modern medicine and psychoanalysis. Indeed, they can use this as an opportunity to *improve religion* itself: "[B]efore you say, 'Religion, grrrr,' think of that—it is a practical religion and religion is the oldest heritage that Man has. . . . The fact is that we do not . . . have any real contact with medicine, certainly not with psychiatry. . . . We can only exist in the field of religion. Of course, it would be up to us to make religion a much better thing than it has been."[38]

However, Hubbard was also fairly blunt about the fact that the turn to the "religion angle" was more *pragmatic* than anything else—that is, it was more a practical, legal, and bureaucratic question than a spiritual or philosophical one. Perhaps the clearest example of this pragmatic approach to religious status is a policy letter of October 1962, in which Hubbard describes his plans for "Scientology 1970," the movement imagined eight years in the future. Henceforth, Scientology is to be planned on an explicitly "religious" foundation. Hubbard makes it clear, however, that its "religious" label will in no way affect the actual operation of Scientology, which would continue as it had all along. The religious designation is simply a bureaucratic detail: "Scientology 1970 is now being planned on a religious organization basis throughout the world. This will not upset the usual activities of any organization. It is entirely a matter for accountants and solicitors."[39]

The Thetan: The True Spiritual Nature of Man

In his efforts to redefine Scientology as a religious rather than simply psychotherapeutic technique, Hubbard began to rework his very understanding of the human person as a *spiritual* rather than simply physical and psychological being. Hubbard's early Dianetics practice had treated the mind and body of the human being, hoping to achieve a state of optimal mental and physical well-being. In the early 1950s, however, Hubbard introduced a new concept called the thetan, which is described as our true identity, our immortal, spiritual selfhood that has potentially unlimited capabilities. Hubbard claimed to have scientifically discovered and "isolated" the thetan or human spirit in 1951–1952, which he then described in his works *Science of Survival* and *What to Audit* (later retitled *The History of Man*):

> Probably the greatest discovery of Scientology and its most forceful contribution to the knowledge of mankind has been the isolation, description and handling of the human spirit. Accomplished in 1951 in the month of July, in Phoenix, Arizona, it was established along scientific rather than religious or humanitarian lines that the thing which is the person, the personality, is separable from the body and the mind at will.[40]

Thus, the difference between Dianetics and Scientology is, in part, the difference between a science that treats the physical organism and one that treats the spiritual self: "Dianetics addresses the body. Scientology addresses the thetan."[41]

As Hubbard defines it, the thetan in its original state is pure consciousness without any connection to the physical universe. The thetan is "the awareness of awareness unit which has all potentialities but no mass, no wave-length and no location"; it is "the being who is the individual and who handles and lives in the body"; and it is "immortal and possessed of capabilities well in excess of those hitherto predicted for man."[42] Thetans in their original state do not require any physical organs or senses to communicate and maneuver; rather, they "communicate by telepathy. They can move material objects by throwing an energy flow at them. They can travel at very high speeds."[43] In Hubbard's early Scientology cosmology, the thetan is ultimately a "godlike" entity that does not now recognize its own powers but can be freed to realize its infinite possibilities. As David Bromley explains Hubbard's cosmology: "In the beginning theta was separate from the physical universe. Theta had no energy or mass, time or location; it was simply energy. . . . At one time thetans were godlike, celestial entities, possessed their own distinctive individuality and created and controlled their own 'Home Universes.'"[44]

Conversely, the present universe in which we seem to exist—the MEST universe of matter, energy, space, and time—is at once an illusion and a trap. The MEST universe is in fact only a kind of collective fiction created by our own continual agreement that it appears to be real. Interestingly enough, fellow science fiction writer Robert Heinlein would use this same idea of reality as mutual agreement in his classic novel *Stranger in a Strange Land*.[45] In fact, the thetan has been "booby-trapped" into identifying with the physical world, and the entire MEST universe is itself nothing more than a "a trap of idiotic simplicity," and "a horrible rat race from which man has been trying to escape, endlessly trying to escape."[46] Meanwhile, the physical or MEST body in which the thetan is trapped is merely "a sort of vegetable."[47]

Hubbard appears to have had no substantive knowledge of the complex body of religious movements known as Gnosticism, which spread throughout the early Christian world during the first several centuries after Jesus's death (and were eventually considered heretical by the dominant Christian churches). However, various observers have noticed that Hubbard's view of the immortal, divine thetan trapped in the material world bears more than a passing resemblance to early Gnostic ideas of the divine spark of the soul trapped in the physical cosmos. Hubbard does, moreover, make passing reference to Scientology as a "Gnostic religion," in so far as it "knows that it knows."[48] And like the early Gnostic heresies, he also saw his own new movement as a persecuted minority unfairly targeted by the dominant orthodoxies of the day.

"Have You Lived Before This Life?" The Thetan's Past Lives

In his early 1950s lectures, Hubbard introduced the idea that the thetan was not simply an immortal spiritual being with unlimited potential, but also that it had been reincarnated in countless forms over many lifetimes. As we will see below, it is likely that Hubbard drew much of his inspiration from ideas of reincarnation in Hindu and Buddhist traditions; but he also added his own elements drawn from science fiction and space travel. Indeed, the thetan's past lives extend throughout the entire history of life on this planet and, ultimately, throughout the history of the entire universe. Very shortly after the birth of Dianetics, as early as mid-1950, practitioners began to report past-life experiences during auditing sessions. Helen O'Brien, for example, experienced a memory of past life in Ireland in 1813, where she had been a woman whose husband was off fighting the British. And Hubbard soon began to incorporate past lives into his lectures and to use the E-meter to audit past-life memories—much to the annoyance of HDRF executives, who feared that talk of reincarnation would be finally disastrous to the movement.[49] As former Scientologist Jim Dincalci told me, moreover, the concept of past lives was one of the elements that first attracted him and others to Scientology in the 1950s and 60s. Interested in reincarnation for some time, he found the first serious discussion of the idea in Hubbard's work and was naturally drawn to it.[50]

One of the most remarkable of Hubbard's early works and the first to deal extensively with past lives is *A History of Man* (1952). On its very first page, the text claims to present "a cold-blooded and factual account of your last sixty trillion years."[51] The cover of the book features a hairy caveman eating a bloody of piece of raw meat—presumably one of our previous incarnations—and its pages trace the history of the thetan on earth from the atom on upward, through volcanoes, birds, sloths, apes, and cavemen to modern humans. Interestingly, Hubbard spends a great deal of time on specific life forms from our prehistory on earth. He devotes a lengthy discussion, for example, to the life of the clam, whose experiences in the ocean can still be "restimulated" and affect us today, even in the most mundane discomforts such as sunburns:

> The clam had an astonishing number of adventures for so minor a creature. It would get things into it shell and be unable to get them out. It would get its shell stuck open and be unable to shut it. . . . And it would become deserted by the tide and left to bake under a frying sun, a quite uncomfortable situation which restimulates sometimes in a sunburn.[52]

Perhaps an even more remarkable work, however, is Hubbard's 1958 text, *Have You Lived Before This Life*, which delves into past lives going far back beyond this earth. The book describes a vast array of past-life experiences uncovered through auditing sessions, recounted in vivid detail. "Man," Hubbard recounts, "has been 'on the way' a very long time, has lived on other planets and in other places. He has engaged, evidently, in space travel, barbarous jungle warfare, has lived as kings and commoners, citizens and commissars, for a very, very long time."[53] Some of these past lives occurred on this earth during recorded history, for example: fighting in the trenches during World War I, being a gondolier in seventeenth-century Venice, or serving as the leader of the Roman Army in North Africa 3,225 years ago.[54] But others occurred tens of thousands or even trillions of years ago on other planets, such as one individual who claimed to have been "a member of a foreign ruling group in a civilization advanced in electronics, space travel and mind control."[55] Many of these past lives do read very much like Hubbard's own science fiction tales, complete with underwater battles with fantastic monsters on other worlds:

> Incident 55,000,000,000,000,000,000 years ago. . . . I was in the sea and had thoughts only for Manta rays, and for a long time in running this I felt I was probably a Manta ray. We went earlier and I was in a flying saucer over the ocean. . . . Later it seemed I was on land in an Atomic War and could smell what seemed like the smell of death or burning bodies.[56]

> The incident began 17,543 years ago on a "Space Command" post on Earth. I had the idea that I could go to Mars incognito to learn how they handled disorder. . . . On landing I was immediately surrounded and interrogated by Martian automatons who recognized me instantly because I did not broadcast the same vibrations.[57]

In one telling incident, the individual being audited recounts a fantastic series of past-life memories ranging from bizarre experiences in outer space to encounters with Christ to the death of a pope; but he then admits that these memories might also have something to do with his previous experimentation with drugs: "Chinese tortures, meeting Christ, a crucifixion, a heart operation, a hanging, rape and attempted murder. All of these, and especially an arrow in the eye and the death of a Pope . . . were extremely real, but I was not sure they had happened to me, because incidents run from this present body's lifetime appear, to my astonishment, less real than any of the above mentioned. This may be because of the drugs I have previously taken."[58]

As unbelievable as these past-life experiences may sound to contemporary readers, they appear to have been extremely persuasive to many Scientologists of the 1950s and 60s. As Hubbard's former physician Jim Dincalci told me, the past-life "memories" he encountered during auditing seemed extremely intense at the time; but that is perhaps not surprising, since Scientologists were thoroughly trained to expect such experiences: "Jungians have Jungian dreams, Freudians have Freudian dreams; Scientologists have past life dreams."[59]

Space Opera and the Origins of the Thetan in This Universe

In addition to this complex history of our previous incarnations on this world and others, Hubbard also began to develop an increasingly elaborate narrative or "space opera" about the history of the universe and the role of the thetan.[60] Like many other writers and new religious leaders of the 1950s, Hubbard played upon the widespread interest in space travel, other planets, and alien invaders that pervaded the cold war era. As Allitt notes in his history of postwar religion, "Throughout the Cold War . . . years when many suspicious objects were flying through the air, a stream of witnesses came forward with the claim that they had been visited by aliens from spaceships and received some form of higher wisdom from them."[61] Not surprisingly, as Wallis found in his early sociological study of the church, the early members of Scientology were "predominantly consumers of science fiction literature."[62] And more than one observer has noted the parallels between Hubbard's science fiction tales and early Scientology. Hubbard's ideal of the all-powerful liberated thetan has more than a little in common with his "Soldiers of Light" roaming the galaxy: "The history of 'scientology' reads like his own fantastic stories about a super-competent future medic, 'Ole Doc Methuselah.'"[63] Hubbard himself admits that this space opera material "sounds awfully wild" because he is describing the past lives of thetans on other planets on spaceships and engaged in all manner of adventures thousands or millions of years ago: "As *wild* as it sounds . . . there are probably two or three people in this room, twelve million years ago or ten million years ago or eight million years ago, were sailing around. And there's certainly at least one person in this room that's blown up a planet and killed everybody on it."[64] But really, the "wildness" of these claims seems to have been one of Scientology's major selling points in the thriving spiritual marketplace of the 1950s.

The most infamous and controversial portion of Hubbard's space opera narrative is contained in the confidential upper levels of Scientology training that describe the mysterious figure of Xenu or Xemu, the ruler of the Galactic Confederacy who lived seventy-five million years ago. This is the narrative that was so viciously satirized in an episode of *South Park* in 2005,[65] and it will be discussed in more detail in chapter 3. However, the Xenu story was itself a relatively late innovation as Hubbard began to develop the advanced levels of Operating Thetan (OT) in the late 1960s. In fact, the Xenu story is really just one part of a far more elaborate, often bewildering set of space opera narratives that began in the earliest Scientology lectures of the 1950s.

Space opera elements are sprinkled throughout Hubbard's Scientology lectures from roughly 1952 onward. Reconstructing a coherent cosmology from Hubbard's various statements about the universe over these decades is difficult, since his comments are fragmentary, scattered, and at times contradictory. Based on his extensive auditing and use of the E-meter, Hubbard believed he had uncovered the "Whole Track" or the entire time line of the universe going back roughly sixty trillion years. As Hubbard told his audience in a lecture from 1952, their past lives had involved a whole series of adventures on other planets, at every level from peasants to kings, from space officers to planetary rulers with the ability to destroy entire worlds:

> So you've been in and out of bodies, you've been thought people, you've been this, you've been that. You've been sheep, goats, spacemen, space officers. You've been governors, kings, princes, ditch-diggers, slaves, glaziers, carpenters, bricklayers, amusement-park barkers, operators. You have turned planets into parks and parks into cinders. You, at one time or another on the track, have had weapons in your hands of sufficient magnitude to just say 'Boom'! and the whole, planet goes up. . . . You talk about drama.[66]

You can take somebody and process only space opera, the two or ten million years somebody spent in space: spaceships, invader forces, thought people. Fascinating stuff, just fascinating. Drama—lots of it.[67]

In these early lectures from the 1950s, Hubbard also explains how it is that we thetans—who are immortal and of unlimited ability—came to be enmeshed in this universe of matter, energy, space, and time. As he explains in a lecture from 1952, the thetan originally had its own "home universe," which it had created for itself out of its own infinite power. Unfortunately, for some reason that is not entirely clear, the thetan was unwittingly absorbed into the MEST universe, which gradually expanded and swallowed the thetan into the realm of mundane time and space: "[T]hey invented this universe, and it's a perfectly good universe, and one day all the stars fell down in it. Why? Somebody else got a universe invented and it just got over and kind of ate it all up. And that's what the MEST universe is doing. Evidently it is an expanding universe and it just keeps eating into everybody's time and space."[68] Hubbard goes on to explain that thetans entered the MEST universe beginning roughly sixty trillion years ago and that this sixty-trillion-year period constitutes the entire "Time Track" of our past lives in this universe. Thetans entered MEST in a series of six waves of "Invader Forces," which each in turn tried to conquer the MEST universe and were successively conquered and replaced by the next Invader Force:

> Counting from the first time you hit the track, about sixty trillion years ago in the MEST universe—some of you hit the track sixty trillion years ago MEST universe, some of you didn't get into the MEST universe til about three trillion years ago—that's Invader Force One and Invader Force Two. . . . The reason you say "invader force" at all is because, at some time along the line fairly early in its youth, it took off to conquer the whole MEST universe, gobble glop. And you succeeded, of course, until Invader Force Two came along and you got rickety. . . . And all of a sudden out of nowhere, . . . Invader Force Two suddenly showed up, gunned you down, manhandled you, put you into bodies, made slaves out of you who had been emperors and kings.[69]

This particular planet Earth, Hubbard explains, is more or less the last and lowest rung on the cosmic hierarchy, a physical prison where we have almost completely forgotten our true spiritual nature and have been deluded into identifying with our MEST bodies: "This is the final dumping ground. Earth is a sort of prison."[70]

Throughout his lectures from the 1950s and 60s, Hubbard mentions various other events in the past history of the universe. There is, for example, the Marcab Confederacy, which is a group of planets united into a vast civilization that emerged about two hundred thousand years ago and looks very much like our own, complete with "automobiles, business suits, fedora hats, telephones."[71] Another significant event occurred one trillion years ago, when we were captured by the "Arsclycans" (beings from Arsclycus, a "City in Space"). Apparently, the Egyptian period here on Earth was also very "space opera," witnessing a complex battle between the fourth invader force from Space Command and the fifth invader force from Martian Command from about 1135 to1230 BC.[72] And then there was the "totally electronic society of Atlantis," which was also a "kind of space opera society," complete with all sorts of drama such as "people blasting walls down with disintegrators" and the like. If one explores the time track further, one encounters even more complicated sorts of space opera elements, such as "fish people" who lived sixty-five thousand years ago, sea monsters, and so on.[73]

It is difficult not to see a direct continuity between Hubbard's imaginative science fiction tales of the 1930 and 40s and his equally elaborate space opera accounts of the 1950s and 60s. In many ways, the more mundane, earthbound science of the mind described in *Dianetics* seems to be a brief departure from the trajectory of Hubbard's writings from the 1930s onward, both fictional and religious, which were more concerned with other worlds, space flight, and paranormal phenomena. Hubbard himself was fairly explicit about the links between science fiction and his own description of the universe. The author of science fiction, he suggests, is in fact partially remembering the *past* history of the universe, but mistakenly projecting it *forward* in time: "[T]he science fiction writer's memory is faulty and he gets himself all restimulated and so forth, and he doesn't remember straight. Some of them remember quite well, but then they reverse their time . . . and put it all into the future."[74] Moreover, the true history of space is far more remarkable than any science fiction writer has yet been able to imagine. As Harriet Whitehead notes, it seems likely that Hubbard found in Scientology a practical means to embody the space opera narratives elaborated in his novels, now offering his followers the same adventures once described in his tales for *Astounding Science Fiction*: "Hubbard had finally found a place for the high adventure of which he was so fond. . . . [T]he spirit's previous existences comfortably encompass not only what we know of conventional history . . . but also much of what is customarily assigned to the realm of myth and science fiction."[75]

"Be Three Feet Back of Your Head": Exteriorization of the Thetan and the Grand Tour of the Universe

Not only did Hubbard describe in elaborate detail how it was that thetans became enmeshed within this illusory MEST universe, but he also developed specific techniques to help thetans get *out* of the MEST universe. Many of Hubbard's lectures of the 1950s contain auditing exercises designed to help the thetan "exteriorize" or move outside of its physical body and so realize its true potential as a spiritual being of unlimited power. Although Hubbard himself eschews the phrases "astral body" and "astral projection,"[76] his description of exteriorizing the thetan is extremely similar if not identical to descriptions of astral projection in occult literature popular in the United States and United Kingdom from the late nineteenth century to the 1960s. The astral body was regularly discussed by occult groups such as the Theosophical Society, which drew upon the concept of the subtle body in Indian yogic traditions[77]; and the idea of "exteriorizing" the astral body was later popularized through works such Sylvan Muldoon's widely read *Phenomena of Astral Projection* (1951). As Muldoon described it, the astral body could be "detached and sent on long journeys, traveling at a rate of speed only less than that of light-waves."[78] Muldoon also describes the astral body as being connected to the physical body by a long thin, elastic cord (virtually identical to the one described in Hubbard's "Excalibur" vision, we might note). Astral projection is also a central theme in Aleister Crowley's classic occult work, *Magick in Theory and Practice*, which Hubbard had quoted directly in his 1952 Philadelphia lectures.[79]

Hubbard's lectures from the 1950s give clear directions about teaching the individual to exteriorize from the MEST body. As Hubbard summarizes the goals of Scientology in 1952, "the entire technique consists of getting the thetan out of the body immediately, unburdening some of the sympathy for the body and . . . bringing him up to complete self-determinism."[80] According to the introduction to his *Philadelphia Doctorate Course*, Hubbard's extensive research had revealed that the thetan could be easily exteriorized from the body using a very simple command: "It could be accomplished, in about 50 percent of the cases, with the precise command to 'be three feet back of your head.' By exteriorizing the thetan from the body, the long-sought goal of religion—spiritual existence independent of the body—had been accomplished."[81]

Once the thetan has successfully been taken three feet in back of the head, it could then be directed to go much farther, practicing more adventurous journeys outside the body. Indeed, in early lectures such as *The Creation of Human Ability* (1954), Hubbard directs the auditor to take the thetan from Earth to the moon and then venture to other planets: "Be near earth, be near the Moon, be near the Sun. . . . Now find a rock. Be inside of it, be outside of it. . . . Be in the center of the Earth, be outside the earth . . . be near Mars. Be at the center of Mars."[82] (Thus an illustration to the *Creation* lectures shows the symbol Θ for the thetan flying through the solar system.)[83] Then the thetan should be instructed to embark on a "Grand Tour of the Universe," exploring the surface of other planets, sliding down plumes on the sun, even going inside black stars:

> One of the common practices in the Grand Tour is asking him to be inside a black star, outside it, inside it. . . . And oh, boy does that rip him to pieces, because there are black stars up there which are so heavy and dense that electrons can't escape from them.[84]

> So you say, "Find a plume and slide down on it to the face of the Sun". . . . You could have him find Mars. "Be outside Mars and move down on the surface." But he's immediately going to discover the force field of Mars. . . . It's not science fiction.[85]

However, Hubbard emphasizes that this process of exteriorizing the thetan and touring the universe is *not* an imaginary exercise. The individual *really is* engaged in an out-of-body planetary tour and should recognize it as such: "It should be clearly understood . . . that the preclear does not simply think about these things or mock them up and view them. The auditor wants the preclear, exteriorized, to go around various places in the actual physical universe and *look* at things."[86]

"Create Your Own Universe": Becoming Superman with Super Powers

Ultimately, in Hubbard's early lectures, the goal of Scientology is to realize and unleash the unlimited power of the thetan. The thetan, after all, is a spiritual being of infinite potential, capable of creating its own universe, and therefore the goal of auditing is to release the thetan from its entrapment in MEST and so reawaken its tremendous power. As another science fiction writer, Jack Williamson, points out, Scientology has more than a few things in common with Hubbard's own science fiction tales from the 1940s, including his Ole Doc character and the Brotherhood of Light. Like the appeal of so many science fiction stories of the era, Scientology also offered "the promise to liberate the superman trapped inside us."[87] As Hubbard described it, the truly Clear individual is none other than a *Homo novis*, a "godlike" being; meanwhile, a liberated thetan or Theta Clear is even infinitely far beyond that: "Compared to a Homo sapiens, Homo novis is very high and godlike. Compared to a truly self-determined being, Homo novis is an ant ready to die under anybody's misstep."[88]

Indeed, both Hubbard's early lectures and various testimonies from Scientologists claim an array of remarkable powers for the liberated thetan. These include not just optimal psychological and physical health, but more "paranormal" abilities such as the power to see through walls, telepathy, "remote viewing" or seeing events from distances outside the body, and even the ability to rearrange molecules in order to fix broken appliances such as coffeemakers and air conditioners. Scientology publications such as *Advance!* and *Source* include numerous success stories from individuals who acquire powers both miraculous and mundane: some recount being able to prevent rain from falling, while others claim to be able to remotely shut off a neighbor's annoying, noisy sprinkler system.[89] Others report the power to heal sick goldfish and a cat with a bad eye.[90] "I love it," wrote one enthusiastic member, "like Superman!"[91]

Super Power Building, Clearwater, FL. Photo by author

Eventually, Hubbard would also offer a special series of training sessions known as the "Super Power Rundown." According to the *Dianetics and Scientology Technical Dictionary*, this series is nothing less than "a super fantastic, but confidential series of rundowns . . . that puts the person into fantastic shape unleashing the Super Power of a thetan. This means that it puts Scientologists into a new realm of ability enabling them to create a new world."[92] At the time of the writing of this book, the church was still at work on a huge (and hugely expensive) "Super Power" building in Clearwater, Florida. As advertised in Scientology's *Source* magazine, the Super Power building is "an entirely New Universe" and "ideal in every detail": "Expanding on technology developed by NASA astronauts, it's now combined with everything else they never conceived of in terms of space."[93] Photos of the interior of the building feature space-age-looking rooms with large shiny orbs and a GyroSpin device. Begun in 1998, the Super Power building was still incomplete as of 2010, while the projected cost has doubled to over $50 million.[94]

Ultimately, at its highest levels of operation, the power of the thetan is infinite and unlimited. Indeed, one of the basic definitions of the thetan or spirit is that it can conquer, manipulate, and organize the physical universe. For example, an exteriorized thetan can heal the physical body, fix broken objects, and manipulate others' bodies from a distance. In fact, it can cause the MEST universe itself to manifest or dissolve: "What we're doing is simply taking the MEST universe, and we can make it appear or disappear at will."[95]

Not only can a thetan alter the MEST universe, but ultimately, the thetan has the ability to "create its own universe."[96] As he developed Scientology in the 1950s, Hubbard described different states of the thetan, such as "Cleared Theta Clear" and finally "Operating Thetan" (OT). Thus, someone who has achieved Cleared Theta Clear is "a person who is able to create his own universe or, living in the MEST universe, is able to create illusions perceivable by others at will, to handle MEST universe objects without mechanical means and to have and feel no need of bodies or even the MEST universe."[97] Any universe the Cleared Thetan chooses to create will be far better and in fact more "real," that is, "sharper and brighter," than the MEST universe itself.[98]

One who has achieved the state of "Operating Thetan," meanwhile, can essentially do *anything* it pleases. As Hubbard describes it, the state of OT is one in which the thetan is not just liberated but enabled to do anything it chooses: the OT is completely free to create anything, to be anything, to go anywhere its will desires: "[H]e would be able to be anywhere as a finite point or be everywhere as a generalized area. . . . [H]e could be *anything* at will."[99] The liberated thetan could even freely create a personal paradise, populating it with heavenly beings and infinite pleasures at will:

> "You make forty mock-ups and they dance back and forth; put blue veils on them and put them in a sky with clouds and you have a Mohammedan heaven. You mean, I can do all this?" Well he can not only do all that, but he can fix them up three-dimensionally and he can give them actual separate beingnesses and personalities.[100]

As such, the thetan who truly realized his power to create and destroy universes would in effect be "beyond God"—that is, he would be beyond whichever so-called god happened to create this particular MEST universe. In fact, the thetan has been deceived into worshiping such a God by mainstream religion and so forgotten its own godlike power to create and destroy universes: "[W]hat passed for God for the MEST universe is not the goddest God there is by an awful long ways. . . . [W]hoever made that MEST universe . . . was a usurper of one's own universe. And this has been sold to the individual and it has sold the individual out of his ability to make a universe."[101] Such an idea was clearly appealing to many aspiring Scientologists. As Cyril Vosper, a former member of Hubbard's staff, recalls, "I thought it would give me total control over my own life. . . . He was saying that you and everyone else, with the use of Scientology . . . could become a god. And we were all, if you like, fallen gods."[102]

Quite strikingly, in a 1952 lecture, Hubbard also explicitly compares the thetan's divine ability to create new universes to the ability of a writer, who similarly creates new universes with his imagination: "Highest potentiality of theta is evidently the creation and management of universes. . . . Now, let's take a writer sitting at his desk, he's pounding a typewriter and so what's he doing? Inventing time and space and energy and matter." The only difference, Hubbard notes, is that the rest of society sees the writer's invented universe as fiction and the physical world as "real." But in fact, they are *both* fictional illusions, and it is precisely by creating *new* universes through our divine ability that we can free ourselves from the MEST universe.[103]

"Am I Metteyya?" The Turn to Eastern Religions

Interestingly enough, when Hubbard first began to make claims to a "religious" status for Scientology, he did not initially turn to Christianity as its closest spiritual kin. This may have been due to Hubbard's apparent disdain for mainstream Christianity, which we can see in his early lectures. Instead, from 1954 onward, Hubbard began to argue that Scientology has most in common with Eastern religions, particularly Hinduism, Buddhism, and Taoism: "A Scientologist is a first cousin to the Buddhist, a distant relative of the Taoist, a feudal enemy to the enslaving priest."[104] Again, Hubbard is at least in part responding and adapting to the expanding spiritual marketplace of the United States in the 1950s. While various strands of Hindu philosophy and yoga had been spreading throughout the United States since the late nineteenth century, newly imported forms of Hinduism and Buddhism were just beginning to become popularized through the influence of teachers such as D. T. Suzuki and numerous American enthusiasts such as the Beat poets and writers, Gary Snyder, Jack Kerouac, and Allen Ginsberg.[105]

Thus, in his 1954 *Phoenix Lectures*, Hubbard presents the "religious and knowledge background of Scientology," suggesting that its earliest ancestor was the Veda, or the most ancient and revered sacred scripture of Hinduism. Significantly, he also strongly emphasizes the fact that the Veda *is a religion*, and one with the same goal of "knowingness" as his own system of Scientology: "[W]e find Scientology's earliest, *certainly known* ancestor in the Veda. The Veda is a very, very interesting work. . . . It is a religion. It should not be confused as anything else but a religion. And the very word *Veda* simply means 'lookingness' or 'knowingness'"[106]—which is of course exactly how Hubbard defines Scientology.

Elsewhere, however, Hubbard argued that Scientology has perhaps most in common with Buddhism. The Buddha, after all, never claimed to be a God but was simply a man—like Hubbard himself—who had by his own exploration figured out how the universe works and how we might reach ultimate liberation. As Hubbard put it in a bulletin from 1960, "Scientology's closest spiritual ties with any other religion are with Orthodox (Hinayana) Buddhism, with which it shares an historical lineage."[107] Again, Hubbard distinguishes the more enlightened "religion" of Buddhism from the more "barbaric" priesthood of Christianity, identifying Scientology's lineage with the former: "[T]hose men (the Buddhas) responsible for what Western culture calls their religion, called themselves priests. . . . Only a barbaric minister is a 'Man' of God. In all enlightened religions such men are called 'Men of Wisdom.'"[108]

Thus Hubbard suggests that the key Buddhist concept of *dhyana* (meditation or concentration) is no different from Scientology, which is also defined as the control of knowledge and thought: "Dhyana could literally be translated as Indian for Scientology"; and he quotes the Buddha's words in the *Dhammapada* (apparently from Paul Carus's popular 1898 translation, *The Gospel of Buddha*) that "[a]ll that we are is the result of what we have thought: it is founded upon our thoughts, it is made up of our thought."[109] The Buddhist goal of enlightenment, moreover, is no different from the goal of Clear offered by Dianetics and

Scientology—the only difference being that this once elite goal of monks is now available for everyone: "The dream of Buddha, attained by the few, was a reality. Man could be a Clear."[110] Moreover, the remarkable claims that Hubbard made about the states of Clear and Operating Thetan included almost all of the supernatural abilities (*siddhis*) claimed by enlightened Buddhas and by Hindu yogis. These include knowledge of previous lives; the power of great sight; the ability to change size; the power of great hearing; the power to cause events; the power to be anywhere; the power to be invisible; and the power to walk on air, among others. Hubbard himself also claimed that the ability to "exteriorize" the thetan from the body was also one of the supernatural powers claimed by the lamas of the Tibetan Buddhist tradition.[111]

But perhaps the most audacious claim for his ties to Eastern religions appeared in a poem of Hubbard's entitled "Hymn of Asia," said to have been composed on the occasion of the Buddhist convention of 1955–1956 celebrating the 2,500th year of the Buddhist era. The poem centers on the Buddhist prophecy of the future Buddha, Metteyya or Maitreya, who will come to restore the Buddhist teaching at the end of the age. The introduction to the poem begins with an alleged Tibetan prophecy about the coming of Metteyya/ Maitreya (the origins or authenticity of which I have been unable to establish) that proclaims: "When he shall be seen in the West, seated in the Western fashion, his hair like flames about his noble head, discoursing, then shall the inhabitants of the Three Worlds rejoice." The "hair like flames" is clearly meant to be a reference to Hubbard's own famous red hair. The poem then begins with the question "Am I Metteyya?" and then proceeds to answer in the affirmative:

> I come to bring you all that Lord Buddha would have you know
>   life, Earth and Man.
> I come to you with Freedom
> I come to you with science.
> I come to teach you
> I come to help you.[112]

Yet significantly, despite his many claims about the links between his philosophy and that of the Buddha, Hubbard also clearly distinguishes the final goal of Scientology from that of Buddhism. Whereas Buddhism—as he understood it at least—aimed to extinguish the individual in the nothingness of nirvana, Scientology has the technology that can liberate the thetan into a state of individual freedom, autonomy, and unlimited power to do anything it chooses: "We are Scientologists. We won't fall into the abyss. And we won't join Nirvana. We have meters and a map. . . . Nirvana is choked with the overwhelmed. . . . We are Scientologists. We have won."[113] In contrast to Hindu and Buddhist holy men, Hubbard wrote in 1952, the Scientologist does not seek to become "one with the universe but maintains his own individuality" and ultimately becomes capable of doing anything he desires:

> Thetans are individuals. They do not . . . merge with other individualities. They still have the power of becoming anything they wish while still retaining their individuality. . . . There is evidently no Nirvana. . . . When he goes upscale, he becomes more and more an individual capable of creating and maintaining his own universe.[114]

Hubbard's turn to Eastern religions to support Scientology does not appear to have been accidental. As Stephen Kent has argued, Hubbard began to make links between Eastern religions and Scientology at crucial moments when his fledgling movement was most threatened by attacks from government agencies and medical authorities. The key moments when Hubbard began to turn to the East—most notably, in 1954–1955, 1960, and 1962—coincided almost exactly with those times when Scientologists were being investigated—and at times arrested—for practicing medicine without a license. In short, "at crucial moments in Scientology's history, he attempted to shield his organisation's self-asserted healing efforts behind religious claims. . . . Hubbard used religious claims to protect his organization from governmental and medical scrutiny over practising medicine without a license and related fraudulent healing claims."[115]

Because of his disdain for Christianity, and perhaps because of the newly imported forms of Hinduism and Buddhism then entering the United States, Eastern religions were a more likely candidate for the "religion angle" than the Gospels. Yet ironically, in Hubbard's increasingly complex religious *bricolage*, Eastern ideas of past lives and Buddha-like supernatural abilities were melded together with a cross, ministerial collars, and the overall appearance of a "church." Such a unique fusion of East and West, however, was clearly appealing to many Americans during these decades. One woman who had been on staff in the Berkeley Scientology mission explained its appeal to many young people in particular. Combining Eastern religions with Western science, Hubbard's church seemed to offer a far more practical, less otherworldly road to enlightenment and a more direct engagement with the external social world: "Now Scientology had an Eastern flavor with a Western technology. . . . It suddenly combines two important things for young people at that time. They didn't have to go to India and sit in a cave and meditate for twenty years to get enlightened. . . . They could bring about social change and reform with a technology that they could learn."[116]

Conclusions: Combining the "Precision of the Gautama Buddha with the Urgent Productive Practicality of Henry Ford"

In sum, if Hubbard's early science of Dianetics is best understood as a complex *bricolage* that brought together his various explorations in psychology, hypnosis, and science fiction, then Scientology is an even more ambitious sort of *religious bricolage* adapted to the exploding new religious marketplace of 1950s America. While Dianetics had been a relatively brief cultural fad, his new model of Scientology was far more eclectic, wide-ranging, and much bolder in its claims to spiritual authority, combining notions of an immortal thetan with past-life memories, exteriorization from the body, superhuman abilities, space opera histories of the universe, and various elements of Eastern philosophy. In effect, "Scientology emerged as a religious commodity eminently suited to the contemporary market" of postwar America.[117] As Hubbard's own son, L. Ron Jr., recounted in an interview, his father's spiritual *bricolage* seemed to be uniquely suited to the individualism and quick-fix mentality of 1950s America: by just doing a few assignments, "one can become a god."[118]

In the introduction to Hubbard's 1973 work, *Mission into Time*, the editors suggest that Hubbard's research had been from its very origins "religious" in nature; hence the founding of a "church" was in perfect keeping "with the religious nature of the tenets dating from the earliest days of research. It was obvious that he had been exploring religious territory all along."[119] If we look closely at the history of Dianetics and the birth of Scientology, however, it seems far less obvious that Hubbard had been planning a religious movement all along. On the contrary, it appears that his exploration of the "religion angle" began somewhat slowly and tentatively, in fits and starts, and initially in response to external pressures such as investigations by the FDA (and later, as we will see in chapter 5, by the IRS).

In the previous chapter, we asked the basic questions (which many readers are no doubt still asking): Did Hubbard himself really believe any of this stuff? Did he really believe the material we have encountered in this chapter, such as past lives, space opera on other planets, and super powers? Or was he just simply fabricating all of this in the same way he had fabricated his science fiction novels, only now with the hope of creating a kind of "simulacrum" of a religion that would be protected from government intervention? I think the answer to this question is actually far more complex than simply answering, "Did he make it up, or did he really believe it?" If we look back at Hubbard's science fiction writings and his early Scientology lectures, we see that he regarded the physical universe itself as an illusion and a fiction; moreover, he also suggested that the imaginative universes created by the thetan—like the new universes created by the science fiction writer—are actually *more real* than the MEST universe itself. And it is precisely by creating new, alternative universes that we can *free* ourselves from the illusory trap of the physical realm. As Hubbard acknowledged in one very telling lecture during his *Philadelphia Doctorate Course*,

> Now, all this of course is—I'm just kidding you mostly. I don't believe that you've been in the universe seventy-six trillion years. . . . I don't believe any of these things and I don't want to be agreed with about them. . . . All I'm asking is that we take a look at this information, and then go through a series of class-assigned exercises. . . . [L]et's see if we can't disagree with this universe, just a little bit.[120]

In this sense, Hubbard's new religion of Scientology with its elaborate cosmology might best be understood as his own imaginative attempt to "disagree with this universe"—that is, to create an alternative universe in which the unlimited potential of the thetan might be liberated.

Whatever its precise origins, however, Hubbard's new church soon began to enjoy far more lasting success than had his loose and chaotic Dianetics movement. Now "incorporated," the church actually began to function with the efficiency and productivity of a well-run corporation. Indeed, as Hubbard himself acknowledged in an interview with the *Saturday Evening Post*, "I control the operation as a general manager would control any operation of a company."[121] And more than one observer has noted that Scientology's early organizational structure resembles less a traditional church than it does "multi-national enterprises such as the Ford Motor Corporation, Coca Cola or International Telephone and Telegraph."[122] In the words of the respected sociologist of religion Bryan R. Wilson, Scientology combines the "precision of the Gautama Buddha with the urgent productive practicality of Henry Ford."[123] Soon after the birth of HASI and the Church of Scientology, Hubbard began "franchising" (a term he used frequently) new churches throughout the United States and the United Kingdom. As one former member put it, Scientology had become the "McDonald's hamburger chain of religion," increasingly adopting the mass-production and marketing aspects of American commerce.[124]

By the end of the 1950s, Hubbard's church was profitable enough to purchase Saint Hill Manor, an impressive eighteenth-century building near the hamlet of East Grinstead in Sussex County, England. Previously owned by the Maharaja of Jaipur, Saint Hill Manor became the headquarters of the expanding Scientology empire from 1959 until Hubbard's departure in 1967. The complex corporate structure of Scientology helped make it perhaps the most lucrative and powerful new religion in the United States from the 1970s onward. Yet as we will now see in chapter 3, Scientology's corporate structure was also closely tied to the obsessions with secrecy, surveillance, and information control that characterized the cold war period as a whole.

- THREE -

A COLD WAR RELIGION
Scientology, Secrecy, and Security in the 1950s and 60s

Up there are the stars. Down in the arsenal is an atom bomb. Which one
is it going to be?
—L. Ron Hubbard, "Dianetics: The Evolution of a Science" (1950)[1]

In my opinion the church has one of the most effective intelligence
operations in the U.S. rivaling even that of the FBI.
—Ted Gunderson, former head of the FBI's Los Angeles office,
quoted in Behar, "The Thriving Cult"[2]

The Church of Scientology was born in, flourished amidst, and gained
its greatest popularity in the decades from the early 1950s to the late
1980s—in other words, a period that almost exactly coincided with the
decades of the cold war. Indeed, the years from the birth of Dianetics in
the late 1940s to the death of Hubbard in 1986 closely parallel the years
from the dawn of the Red Scare after World War II to the collapse of the
Soviet Union in the late 1980s and early 90s. This historical overlap with
the cold war is hardly accidental. In its beliefs, practices, organizational
structure, and above all its obsession with secrecy, Scientology could be
described as not just a reflection, but perhaps the very epitome of American religion during the cold war.

As Patrick Allitt suggests, the United States in the 1950s was experi-
encing a kind of "Cold War of the Spirit," as the hot war against Hitler's
Germany was being replaced by anxieties about the Soviets' newly acquired nuclear weapons. Amidst mounting fears of Communist threats
not just from abroad but from within America itself, this Cold War
of the Spirit gave birth to intense new concerns with information control, secrecy, and espionage: "Inside America, first the government then

numerous private agencies began searching for evidence of internal espionage and Communist subversion. . . . The Korean War heightened
anti-Communist fears and gave Senator Joseph McCarthy . . . his chance
to exploit them with claims of an immense conspiracy to subvert America."³ Meanwhile, on the level of the popular imagination, these Cold War
anxieties were also reflected in the widespread fascination with UFOs
and other unidentified phenomena filling the skies of 1950s America:
"UFOism combined signs and wonders in a contemporary idiom with
moral teaching attuned to the deep anxieties and dreams of the day. In a
world beset by McCarthyism and Cold War, with nuclear disaster only a
button away, it is not surprising that some . . . looked for better signs in
the skies than in Bombers and missiles."⁴

Scientology, I would suggest, was in many ways the very embodiment
of this Cold War of the Spirit. Not only did Hubbard's elaborate "space
opera" narratives reflect the larger preoccupation with UFOs and alien
beings; but from the outset, Hubbard presented Scientology as the ultimate solution to the frightening new challenges of the nuclear era, the
one means of "controlling man" that could save Earth from nuclear annihilation. Hubbard was, moreover, quite obsessed with Communism,
writing numerous letters to the FBI to identify potential subversives
both within and outside his own movement and offering Dianetics as
the surest means to combat Communist infiltration. As Russell Miller
notes, Hubbard's new science was thus perfectly attuned to the anxieties
of the cold war: "The atomic bomb had been dropped . . . McCarthyism
was rife. . . . Then along comes Hubbard with the idea that if we would
increase the overall sanity of man . . . it would be a solution to the threat
of nuclear war."⁵

Particularly in the 1960s, Hubbard's church also created its own elaborate network of secrecy and information control. Beginning in 1966,
Hubbard introduced a series of increasingly esoteric levels of training
known as the "advanced tech" or Operating Thetan (OT) levels, which
reveal the true history of the universe and are surrounded with an aura
of intense secrecy. At the same time, Hubbard also introduced an elaborate system of surveillance to identify "suppressive" elements within the
church and defend it from external threats. These included a series of
auditing sessions known as "Security Checks" and a policy called "fair

game," designed to respond very aggressively to any perceived enemies of the church. In the late 1960s, the church even established its own intelligence agency, the Guardian's Office, which undertook programs of espionage, infiltration, and surveillance that read like a cold war spy novel.

As such, more than one observer has compared Scientology's preoccupation with secrecy, surveillance, and information control with that of the FBI and CIA.[6] And conversely, throughout these decades, Scientology and its founder also became an object of growing interest to the FBI. As one critic put it, "[T]he FBI was quite as paranoid about Hubbard as Hubbard was about the FBI."[7] Thus Scientology and the FBI might be regarded as almost two sides of same coin in cold war America, both expressing a larger concern with secrecy, espionage, and information control that at times bordered on fanatical. Indeed, the church believed—in some cases with good reason and in other cases fancifully—that from the early 1950s onward it was being investigated by a wide range of government agencies, including the U.S. Air Force and Army, the Secret Service, the CIA, the FDA, the IRS, the BATF, the Selective Service, the State Department, the Department of Labor, and even the Coast Guard.[8]

In sum, the religion of Scientology as it took shape in the 1950s and 60s needs to be understood as a product of the cold war—that is, as a reflection of the larger concerns with secrecy, surveillance, UFOs, Communist infiltration, and nuclear war that pervaded these decades. Again, Scientology is not so much a strange aberration from mainstream American culture but in many ways an extreme example or even a microcosm of the broader anxieties of the Cold War of the Spirit, and above all, its preoccupation with secrecy.

To conclude, I will suggest that Scientology is an ideal example of what I call the dual and ambivalent nature of religious secrecy. On the one hand, as sociologists such as Georg Simmel have shown, secrecy very often serves as a kind of "adorning possession," that is, a source of status and symbolic power for the one who claims possession of rare, mysterious, esoteric knowledge. Yet on the other hand, secrecy can also become a serious liability for its owner, a source of suspicion and accusations of subversive or illegal behavior.[9] Scientology, we will see, was among the most extreme examples of both these aspects of secrecy, both the allure of the secret and its potential liability. As Hubbard himself put it in 1954, "Secrets, secrets SECRETS! Ah, the endless quest, the far, far search, the codes, the vias, the symbols, the complications, the compilations, the mathematicity and abstracticity of secrets, secrets, SECRETS!"[10] The highly esoteric levels of Scientology's advanced tech represented a mysterious (and expensive) commodity amidst the spiritual marketplace of American religions. But the church and its highly secretive Guardian's Office also became the target of one of the largest FBI investigations in U.S. history. As such, the case of Scientology also has much to teach us about our own historical moment in post-9/11 America, where the issues of religious secrecy and government surveillance have reemerged in perhaps an even more intense form.

A Culture of Secrecy: Concealment, Security, and Religion in Cold War America

If the Church of Scientology seemed preoccupied with secrecy, surveillance, and information control during the late 1950s and 60s, it was largely a reflection of the historical moment in which it emerged. Particularly after 1949, when the Soviet Union detonated its own atomic bomb, the threat of Communism suddenly seemed not far off in some distant land but an insidious presence that could strike on American soil itself. As Stephen Whitfield observes in his study, *The Culture of the Cold War*, "[T]he specter that, a century earlier Marx and Engels had described as stalking the continent of Europe, was extending itself to the United States."[11]

Of course, the Soviet Union was every bit as worried about the United States' own military power, and the result of their mutual paranoia was the growth of the most elaborate networks of secrecy, espionage, and counterespionage the world had ever seen. As Angus MacKenzie notes in his study of secrecy and the CIA during the Cold War,

> The U.S. government has always danced with the devil of secrecy during wartime. By attaching the word "war" to the economic ideological race for world supremacy between the Soviet Union and the United States, a string of administrations continued this dance uninterrupted for the last fifty years. The cold war provided the foreign threat to justify the pervasive

Washington belief that secrecy should have the greatest possible latitude and openness should be restricted as much as possible—constitutional liberties be damned.[12]

In the United States, the fear of Communist infiltration was soon extended not just to undercover agents but to ordinary citizens. Thus the FBI began to compile dossiers on novelists who seemed unduly critical of their native land and even filmed patrons of left-wing bookstores. Under both the Truman and Eisenhower administrations, extensive security programs were put into place throughout the civil service. Political testing was not uncommon, as both government agencies and private employers sought to distinguish between those who were truly patriotic and those who might harbor un-American tendencies. Even ordinary citizens were enlisted in the cold war, called upon to identify those who displayed a lack of patriotic spirit or suspicious degrees of "neutrality."[13]

Religion, too, played a crucial role in cold war American culture and in the struggle over the boundaries between the public and the private. Indeed, more than any other Western country, the United States saw a remarkable increase in religious affiliation after World War II. Church membership rose from roughly 43 percent in 1920 to 82 percent by 1950 and 69 percent by the end of the 1950s, the highest it would ever be in the twentieth century.[14] One of the most threatening features of the rise of Communism, for many clergymen and politicians alike, was its "godless and atheistic" nature. This made commitment to Christian faith even more needed for true patriotism and the struggle against the Soviet menace: "Even as some clergymen were advocating ferocious military measures to defeat an enemy that was constantly described as 'atheistic,' government officials were asserting that the fundamental problem presented by Communism was not political but spiritual."[15] Few preachers of the 1950s were more outspoken in their patriotism and anti-Communism than Reverend Billy Graham. "If you would be a true patriot, then become a Christian," Graham exhorted his audience; and so, "if you would become a loyal American, then become a loyal Christian." In short, in the mid-1950s, an old-fashioned Americanism was equated with "the way to the Cross" as the most effective shield against "Satan's version of religion," which was Communism.[16] Not surprisingly, many churches during this period undertook "Red Hunts" of their own, even as some of their more radical members came under suspicion of Communist sympathies.[17]

Scientology, ironically enough, would soon become both one of the most outspoken voices warning about Communist infiltration from the Red Menace and one of the primary targets of investigations by the FBI and other government agencies. According to an article in the *New York Post* describing the "The Secret War at Home" that took place during the 1950s and 60s, "Starting in 1956, the FBI undertook literally thousands of 'counterintelligence' operations against organizations deemed 'radical' or 'immoral' or 'extreme.' The activities—defamation of individuals and groups, infiltration, provocations and disruptions—are all familiar to the CIA and other espionage agencies. . . . The targets included the National Urban League and the Congress of Radical Equality along with the Ku Klux Klan, the John Birch Society and the Founding Church of Scientology."[18]

Cold war anxieties were by no means limited to fears of Communist infiltration and nuclear war, however. Another obsession that spread throughout popular culture during the 1950s and 60s was the belief in UFOs, which began in the United States in June 1947 after the first widely reported UFO sighting by a pilot near Mount Rainier, Washington. The obsession was quickly fueled by the crash of a mysterious object near Roswell, New Mexico, which UFO enthusiasts took to be evidence of an alien spacecraft and conspiracy theorists assumed to be a vast government cover-up. By the early 1950s, popular films began to appear—often laden with religious themes—such as *The Day the Earth Stood Still* (1951), as well as entire new religious movements based on contact with alien races such as the Aetherius Society (1954).[19] In this sense, L. Ron Hubbard's elaborate speculations about alien races, space opera, invader forces and the imminent crisis facing planet Earth were by no means outside the mainstream, but very much in keeping with the popular imagination of the cold war. As Mikail Rothstein comments, "[T]he driving force in the creation of the UFO or flying saucer myth that swept through the United States . . . was based on Cold War fears, especially people's concern about atomic bombs . . . Hubbard was in alignment with the minds of his contemporaries."[20]

A Religion for the Nuclear Age: Scientology
and the Climate of Cold War America

From the first publication of *Dianetics* in 1950 and continuing with the
Church of Scientology in the 1960s, Hubbard stated emphatically that
his new science was born as a response to the threat of nuclear war. *Dianetics* emerged in the same crucible as the bomb, and, as a science
of the human mind, it is the only tool available that can help us *save
ourselves* from the imminent risk of nuclear annihilation: "There is no
problem in the control of these weapons. . . . The problem is in the control of man."[21]

> With man now equipped with weapons sufficient to destroy all mankind
> on Earth, the emergence of a new science capable of handling man is vital.
> Scientology is such a science. It was born in the same crucible as the atomic
> bomb. . . . The only race that matters at this moment is the one being run
> between Scientology and the atomic bomb. The history of man . . . may
> well depend on which one wins.[22]

Scientology is thus presented as a potent "weapon" of its own, and in fact
the only one that can counter the horrors of the atomic bomb: "We have
today very easily the most powerful 'weapon' extant. . . . That weapon is
Scientology. We are not using it for evil, we are using it for good. Therefore, we will win with it."[23]

This appeal of *Dianetics* in an age of nuclear fear was also noted by the
first critics and reviewers of the book. As Milton Sapirstein wrote in his
review of *Dianetics* for the *Nation*, one of the primary appeals of Hubbard's therapy was precisely its "continuous repetitive emphasis on SUR-
VIVAL. This word is used constantly in capitals as the . . . goal of all human
behavior. For a world frightened by atomic-bomb destruction . . . no
more hypnotic slogan could have been used to entrance people and to
allay their fears."[24]

Hubbard himself was more than a little concerned about the possible
impact of nuclear war. He was particularly interested in the effects of
radiation following an atomic explosion and how survivors might counter radiation sickness. The early HASI center in Phoenix, he notes, "was
there at a time when a great deal of bomb testing was being done in

Nevada only 150 miles away.... [B]eing in possession of instruments which could measure radiation, we were quite shocked to discover that the atmosphere ... began to count somewhat alarmingly."[25] In April 1957, Hubbard hired the Royal Empire Society Hall in London to preside over a "Congress on Nuclear Radiation and Health" and then published his own manual entitled *All About Radiation*. Advertising its author as "one of the first nuclear physicists in the United States,"[26] the book offers Scientology as the most effective solution to the anxieties of a radioactive age:

> Atomic radiation does constitute a real threat in today's society.... We are talking about an unsolved problem, one which could be solved with some brilliant work. Scientology is already doing its part in solving it.[27]

> The anguish of Earth has been multiplied by bomb terror. You can survive with Scientology.[28]

Finally, Hubbard also began to promote the use of a drug called "Dianezene," which was alleged to provide protection against radiation sickness and to counteract cancer. Unfortunately, as we saw in chapter 2, the FDA was less than persuaded by Hubbard's claims and destroyed twentythousand tablets of the antiradiation compound in 1958.[29]

Hubbard, Communism, and the FBI

The clearest example of Hubbard's Cold War mentality, however, lies in his attitudes toward the Soviet Union and the specter of Communism, which seems to have preoccupied him for much of the 1950s and 60s. As Kevin Victor Anderson noted in his report on the church for the state of Victoria, Australia, "Scientology is almost rabidly opposed to Communism which Hubbard frequently denounces in flamboyant and intemperate terms.... Scientology had its beginnings in the early 1950s in America when McCarthyism was rampant, and Hubbard readily appreciated the value of discrediting any opposition ... by denouncing any attack on scientology as Communist-inspired."[30]

From an early date, Hubbard was in correspondence with the FBI, sending many letters to J. Edgar Hoover regarding the Red Threat and the presence of subversive Communist elements in the United States.

And Hoover himself, in turn, wrote a number of memos and letters regarding Scientology during the 1950s and 1960s, though most of them noting with some annoyance the obsessive correspondence coming from the movement's founder.[31] As Hubbard wrote in a letter to the FBI in 1951, "The Foundation has assumed a highly punitive stand upon Communism. I shall shortly be in Washington to go over this matter with the government."[32] Hubbard identified numerous individuals in the letter—including his own ex-wife and her lover—as Communists and seemed convinced that Communist influences were attempting to infiltrate his new movement. Thus in a long letter to the attorney general in 1951, Hubbard warned that Communists were vying to take control of his movement for their own nefarious purposes:

> [M]embers of the Communist Party have in the past year wiped out a half a million dollar operation for me, have cost me my health and have considerably retarded material of interest to the United States Government. . . .
>
> Dianetics is important politically. It indicates ways of controling [sic] people or de-controling [sic] them and of handling groups which is good technology. It is an American science. . . .
>
> The field of Group Dianetics could become an ideology if anyone let it. Who controls dianetics, its technology and research can be a menace to the security of this country. . . .
>
> Dianetics and the Foundation, potent forces, almost fell into complete Communist control. . . . I cannot fight the battle of Communism vs the world as the only opponent or threat. Certainly some one else must be at least faintly interested. My life has been in danger, my work has suffered, my life is still in danger. My reputation is almost ruined so these vermin Communists . . . can take over a piece of society and a technology.
>
> If Russia possessed the notes I have on psychological warfare, she would be that much more potent.[33]

Hubbard's suspicion of Communist infiltration was by no means limited to his own movement. In an executive directive entitled "The War," Hubbard made much broader accusations, identifying the World Federation of Mental Health and all psychiatrists as "card carrying Communists," comparable to Russian storm troopers who have "infiltrated boards of education armed services, even the churches."[34]

At the same time, Hubbard also claimed that the Communists were trying to lure him to the Soviet Union to acquire the secrets of his "American science," Dianetics. In 1951 an FBI agent interviewed him and reported as follows: "Hubbard stated that he strongly feels that Dianetics can be used to combat Communism. . . . He stated that the Soviets realized the value of Dianetics. . . . [A]n official from Amtorg . . . contacted him to suggest that he go to Russia and develop Dianetics there."[35] In an interview with the *Saturday Evening Post* in March 1964— just a year and a half after the Cuban missile crisis—Hubbard claimed that he had been approached by the governments of both Cuba and the Soviet Union. The Communists, he said, had recognized the awesome strategic potential of Scientology, which the Americans had foolishly ignored. Indeed, as early as 1938 the Russians had been angling for his services: "I was put under considerable argument and stress. . . . They offered me $200,000, all laboratory facilities, everything I needed in Russia." And the abilities offered by his new techniques known as Scientology would be an invaluable weapon in the hands of any government: "We can raise the I.Q. of a scientist one percent per hour of processing, and we can reduce the reaction time of a pilot at will up to 1/60th of a second. If offered to a foreign state, Scientology could cause the U.S. to suffer a reverse in war. This is a hot package, and I don't care to have it in my hip pocket forever."[36]

One of the stranger episodes in this Cold War narrative occurred in 1955, when Hubbard submitted an alleged Soviet brainwashing manual to the FBI. Entitled *Brain-Washing: A Synthesis of the Russian Textbook on Psychopolitics*, the book begins with a speech purportedly given by the chief of the Soviet secret police, Lavrenti Beria, to American students at Lenin University about how to subvert societies through the imposition of "psychopolitics" on populations under the guise of "mental healing."[37] The timing of this text is surely not accidental, since the CIA had also been exploring research into brainwashing since the 1940s, and discussions of Communist brainwashing and U.S. methods of counterbrainwashing were being widely circulated during these decades.[38]

As most observers have noted—starting with Hoover and the FBI— the entire text is clearly fraudulent, and most agree that all indicators point to Hubbard as its probable author.[39] Ironically, however, Hubbard argued that this powerful Communist text on psychopolitics could be turned around and used against the vermin Communists themselves: "It may well be that we will also use this in anti-Communist campaigns. . . . We have been seriously hurt by Communists and Communism and we see nothing wrong in our using their tactics against them."[40]

Initially, at least, the FBI does not appear to have taken Hubbard or his new science very seriously. As M. A. Jones wrote in an FBI memo of 1957, little of Hubbard's correspondence with the bureau seemed worth serious attention, owing to its confused, meandering, and irrelevant nature: "Hubbard has written a number of letters to the Bureau which were not acknowledged because of their rambling, meaningless nature and lack of any pertinence to Bureau interests."[41] A couple of FBI memos note that Hubbard had made some potentially "subversive" antigovernment comments in his lectures and had also referred to J. Edgar Hoover as "an awfully good guy, stupid, but awfully good."[42] But for the most part, throughout the 1950s, the FBI seems to have regarded Hubbard more as an annoying crank than as a serious threat. The CIA, likewise, initially dismissed Scientology as simply a silly but lucrative racket. According to the *Los Angeles Times*, a memo circulated within the agency described Hubbard as "a shrewd businessman who has parlayed his Scientology 'religion' into a multi-million dollar business by taking advantage of that portion of society prone to fall for such gimmicks."[43]

This attitude changed quickly, however, in the 1960s, as Scientology came into increasing conflict with a variety of government agencies, including not just the FDA (as we saw in chapter 2) but also the IRS (as we will see in chapter 5), and an array of other organizations both at home and abroad. As William Willoughby wrote for the *Washington-Star News* in 1974, "Well, no one—except the FBI and the IRS and the FDA—takes the church seriously."[44]

Exactly how much of the government's surveillance of Scientology was real and how much was the product of Hubbard's paranoid imagination is a matter of some debate. In a large collection of documents obtained through the Freedom of Information Act (FOIA), published under the provocative title *The American Inquisition*, the Church of Scientology has alleged that Hubbard and his followers were consistently surveilled by an array of government agencies. These include, in addition to the FBI and FDA, the Labor Department, the CIA, the Coast Guard, and the Secret Service. The documents accuse Scientologists of everything from the use of LSD and electric shock, to "hypnosis, carbon dioxide gas, and barbituates," and even acts of "murder, extortion, dope smuggling, and carrying US money to Communists."[45]

At least some of these fears of government surveillance appear to have been imaginary. Thus the church claimed that then vice president Richard Nixon had sent two U.S. Secret Service agents to the Founding Church of Scientology in Washington, DC, in order to intimidate the staff for a slighting reference to Nixon in a church magazine in 1958. Later, under President Nixon's administration, the church claimed that it was placed on the famous "enemies list." However, the Secret Service says it has no record of such a visit, and there is in fact no mention of Scientology on Nixon's enemies list.[46]

As we will see in more detail in chapter 5, however, the FBI and other government agencies would eventually begin to take the church a bit more seriously. Indeed, Scientology would later become the target of one of the largest raids in the bureau's history.

Secrecy and Hierarchies of Knowledge

Even from his early science fiction tales and his first "Excalibur" vision, Hubbard appears to have been fascinated with secrecy and esoteric knowledge. This interest in secrecy escalated rapidly in the 1960s as Hubbard elaborated the various levels and grades of the Church of Scientology and also struggled with the various government agencies now taking an interest in his movement. Indeed, the increasing secrecy, information control, and esotericism of Scientology during this period is a strange mirror image of the increasing secrecy of the FBI and other agencies during these cold war years.

Throughout his Dianetics and especially his Scientology lectures and writings, Hubbard had used a complex, often confusing terminology, not easily understood by those outside the movement. As one CIA agent assigned to reading all of Hubbard's works concluded in 1957, "Hubbard's works contained many words, the meaning of which are not made clear for lay comprehension and perhaps purposely so."[47] But this sort of esotericism accelerated rapidly in the late 1960s, as Hubbard developed a series of increasingly "confidential" levels of training organized hierarchically in increasingly esoteric (and expensive) grades. Indeed, "The belief system of the movement became increasingly esoteric, and a 'hierarchy of sanctification' emerged. Members could locate themselves on levels of initiation into the movement's mysteries."[48] More than one observer has thus compared Scientology to a form of "mystery religion," not unlike the Greek mysteries or various other secret societies and esoteric orders.[49]

While Hubbard's rather "exoteric" science of Dianetics had sought to achieve the goal of Clear or optimum well-being in this lifetime, the higher levels of Scientology training are known as "Operating Thetan" (OT), in which one realizes the ever-expanding power of the thetan. Beginning in July 1966, Hubbard released the first of these advanced levels, OT I and II, and unveiled five higher levels over the next three years.[50] Although the church lists fifteen of these advanced OT grades on its official "Bridge to Total Freedom," only seven or eight appear to have been completed before Hubbard's death. According to an advertisement from the church's *Advance!* magazine, Hubbard's discovery of the OT levels simply "tore the lid off the secrets of the universe" and revealed our true nature as spiritual beings "superior to matter, energy, space and time."[51] As the individual progresses through the levels, he or she thus achieves ever-greater abilities and spiritual powers:

> The OT levels contain the very advanced materials of L. Ron Hubbard's researches and it is here the person achieves the ultimate realization of his own nature and his relationship to life and all the dynamics. Abilities return as he advances up through the OT levels and he recovers the entirety of his beingness. Some of the miracles of life have been exposed to full view for the first time ever on the OT levels. Not the least of these miracles is knowing immortality and freedom from the cycle of birth and death.[52]

As such, the advanced OT materials must be handled with utmost secrecy and care, so that no trace should be leaked to those who are not prepared for their profound contents. Those moving through the OT levels often carry the materials in locked briefcases and are instructed to keep them in secure locations. They are forbidden to discuss any aspect of the materials with anyone, including family members.[53] According to a policy letter of January 8, 1981, "NO UNAUTHORIZED COPIES OF UPPER LEVEL MATERIALS ARE TO BE MADE. This means NO notes, NO photocopies. . . . Any student possessing 'notes' or 'study aids' on any Advanced Courses issues . . . must immediately destroy them completely."[54] In sum, the OT levels are surrounded by an aura of mystery that surely adds to the awesome yet potentially dangerous power believed to be contained within them.

The Wall of Fire: OT III and the Xenu/Xemu Story

Arguably the most complex, controversial, and litigious aspect of all Scientology's many controversies surrounds the alleged contents of the advanced tech level OT III. The OT III materials have been the subject of massive media spectacle, popular satire, church denial and, perhaps most damaging, a 2005 episode of the satirical animated show *South Park*, which claimed to have revealed the innermost secrets of OT III for the entire world to see (and ridicule).[55] The contents of OT III are surrounded by a profound aura of mystery and power. According to Hubbard's audio journal of 1967, this level is "so occluded that if anyone tried to penetrate it . . . they have died."[56] Yet Hubbard risked his own life and health in order to achieve the dramatic breakthrough to OT III, passing through the "Wall of Fire" to uncover the secret history of our galaxy and the means to recover our ultimate potential as spiritual beings: "A research accomplishment of immense magnitude, OT III has been called 'the Wall of Fire.' Here are contained the secrets of a disaster which resulted in the decay of life as we know it in this sector of the galaxy. The end result of OT III is truly the stuff of which dreams are spun: The return of full self-determinism and complete freedom."[57]

Because this knowledge is so profound and mysterious, access to it is tightly controlled. A Scientologist must be "invited" to do OT III, then pass through intensive auditing and promise never to reveal its inner secrets: "They sign a waiver promising never to reveal the secrets of OT III, nor to hold Scientology responsible for any trauma or damage one might endure at this stage of auditing. Finally, they are given a manila folder, which they must read in a private, locked room."[58] Indeed, OT III is said to be fatal to the uninitiated, causing pneumonia and death to those who are exposed to it without proper preparation.[59]

I am not personally an OT III Scientologist, so I cannot claim to know with any certainty the true contents of this particular level of auditing. Nor do I have any interest in exposing the secrets of Scientology's esoteric grades (something already done at length by former Scientologists and on innumerable websites). Here I will simply recount what has been reported in public records such as court transcripts involving current and former Scientologists. The two most important court cases were Larry Wollersheim's suit against Scientology in 1985 (after which the OT III story was leaked to the *Los Angeles Times*) and the church's suit against Steven Fishman in 1993 (after which the OT III documents were posted online, where, as we will see in chapter 6, they continue to circulate today).[60]

In order to avoid any risk of copyright violation or lawsuits myself, I will not reproduce the texts of the Xenu story here. However, according to the documents produced during the Fishman and Wollersheim cases, the story goes something like this: seventy-five million years ago, there was a Galactic Confederacy consisting of seventy-six planets, ruled by a dictator named Xenu (or Xemu in some versions of the story). In order to solve the problem of overpopulation in his federation, he brought billions of people to Earth (then called "Teegeeack") and placed hydrogen bombs in the earth's volcanoes in order to destroy them. The thetans from these individuals, however, survived and eventually adhered to the bodies of modern human beings. Hence, each one of us today has a mass of "extra-body thetans" stuck onto ourselves, which are in turn causing us pain and unhappiness in this lifetime (even more fundamental than engrams). These extra-body thetans must therefore be "run" and "cleaned off" through advanced auditing in order to liberate the full power and potential of one's own true thetan.[61]

A more elaborate version of the Xenu/Xemu story appears in a lecture attributed to Hubbard from September 1968, also now widely available online. This provides further details of Xemu's evil plot: apparently, the thetans were placed into refrigerated units, put onto DC 8 planes, and then blown up in the volcanoes. After that, the disembodied thetans were collected, packed into boxes, and forced to watch 3-D movies. Meanwhile, a group of loyal officers revolted and captured Xemu, locking him in the center of a mountain with an electric fence.[62]

The *South Park* episode that satirically narrates the Xenu story runs a caption stating "THIS IS WHAT SCIENTOLOGISTS ACTUALLY BELIEVE." However, when asked about the Xenu story today, many Scientologists often refuse to answer the question, profess ignorance, or simply deny its existence outright.[63] Numerous ex-Scientologists who have come forward, on the other hand, have corroborated this story in more or less every detail.[64] Moreover, in at least one major court case, Religious Technology Center (RTC) director Warren McShane frankly acknowledged that "the discussion of the . . . volcanoes, the explosions, the Galactic confederation 75 million years ago, and a gentleman by the name Xemu" are a core part of Scientology's advanced materials; indeed, he did not even defend the story itself as a trade secret, but stated that the only trade secret is the "actual technology itself and how to undo that great catastrophe that occurred"—that is, how to remove the extra-body thetans through auditing.[65] Finally, and perhaps most ironically, the entire Xenu narrative was written and circulated in another—apparently far less esoteric—form as a movie screenplay by Hubbard in 1977 entitled *Revolt in the Stars*. According to Gerry Armstrong, who was assigned to proofread the screenplay, its narrative of the Galactic Confederacy and the oppressive ruler described in the screenplay is essentially identical to the narrative revealed to him when he reached OT III.[66] However, it is unclear why Hubbard would want to produce a movie about a story that was supposed to cause pneumonia and death when exposed to anyone not prepared by advanced Scientology training.

Readers might justifiably wonder: what is the point of all the obsessive secrecy surrounding the OT levels? From Scientology's perspective, these advanced levels are both extremely powerful and potentially dangerous in the hands of those unprepared for them. Just as one would not entrust nuclear technology to just anyone, so too, one cannot distribute the OT materials to anyone who has not undergone the training and met the "ethical standards" to handle them correctly.[67]

Critics of the church and ex-Scientologists, however, typically offer a more cynical explanation for the secrecy. As author William S. Burroughs recounts his experience with Scientology, this is largely a ploy to create an aura of tantalizing mystery and also help justify the exorbitant prices of the OT levels (see chapter 4). "The upper levels of Scientology processing are classified as 'confidential,' which means that only those who have completed the lower grades, passed security check and paid the large fees in advance are allowed to see and run this material. . . . Obviously it is very much to [Hubbard's] financial advantage to keep this material secret."[68]

While I would not discount this more cynical interpretation, I would suggest two reasons for the obsessive secrecy in the OT materials. First, this sort of secrecy is in perfect keeping with the historical moment in which the OT levels emerged, at the height of the cold war, amidst the intense fascination with both "confidential information" and UFOs. If we place the Xenu story in its historical context, amidst cold war obsessions with nuclear war, secrecy, and UFOs, it really does not appear very surprising at all.

Second, the intense secrecy surrounding the OT materials also clearly helped surround these with an aura of mystery and power that made them appear extremely alluring, attractive, and valuable. As Simmel suggests in his famous sociological study of secrecy, the practice of concealment can often serve to transform an ordinary piece of knowledge into a kind of "adorning possession." Like a piece of expensive clothing or jewelry, secret knowledge can become a rare, highly valued, and sought-after good that enhances its owner's status precisely by virtue of what it conceals. Secrecy can thus be a powerful form of what sociologist Pierre Bourdieu calls "symbolic capital," that is, the quality of distinction and status that comes from acquisition of scarce, rare, and highly valued resources. Similar strategies of concealment and symbolic capital can be seen in many secret societies and esoteric orders, ancient and modern, ranging from the Freemasons and the Theosophical Society to the Ordo Templi Orientis (a group with whom Hubbard had some experience).[69] As we will see in chapter 4, Scientologists have been willing to pay tens of thousands of dollars to gain access to these OT materials, which suggests that they serve as a very effective sort of "adorning possession" indeed.

Surveillance, Security, and Suppressive Persons

Not only did Scientology develop an elaborate, increasingly esoteric hierarchy of information, but it also began to develop powerful new forms of internal surveillance throughout the 1960s. Indeed, more than one observer has compared Scientology's methods of security and surveillance to those of the FBI, CIA, and Defense Department. As one former Scientologist put it, "[N]ot even the Pentagon has better security than Scientology."[70] According to sociologist Susan Raine, some former members compare the church's surveillance apparatus to the "Thought Police" in Orwell's *Nineteen Eighty-four*.[71]

Already in 1951, in a long letter to the U.S. attorney general, Hubbard noted that the E-meter had been used as a kind of "lie detector" to weed out subversive and Communist elements from the early church: "turbulence in the new Foundation ceased the moment I began to use only personnel screened by a 'lie detector.' This present organization is secure."[72] But particularly in the late 1950s and early 1960s, as the movement faced mounting governmental and media criticism, Hubbard grew increasingly worried about the possibility of subversion from both within and outside his church: "As the Organization rapidly expands," he warned in 1962, "so will it be a growing temptation for anti-survival elements to gain entry and infiltrate."[73] In turn, Hubbard developed an elaborate code of Scientology "Ethics" designed to protect the church and to weed out individuals dubbed "potential trouble sources" (PTS) and "suppressive persons" (SPs). SPs were identified as any persons who might pose a threat to the functioning of the church. These included those who questioned Hubbard's authority, those who revealed classified information to unqualified recipients, and those who sold Scientology materials at a cut-rate price.[74] Using the E-meter and a series of interrogations, Ethics Officers could identify potential threats to the church. As author and former Scientologist William S. Burroughs reflected on his own experience in the church, "Scientology is a model control system, a state in fact with its own courts, police, rewards and penalties. It is based on a tight in-group like the CIA. . . . Inside are the Rights with the Truth. Outside are the Commies . . . the Suppressives." In Burroughs's opinion, Hubbard's meter is not very different from the

lie detector used by government agencies to identify potential dissi-
dents: "The E-Meter is among other things a reliable lie detector in expert hands. The CIA also uses lie detectors. . . . With this simple device
any organization can become a God from whom no thought or action
can be hidden."[75]

Interestingly enough, however, Hubbard himself explicitly defended
Scientology's Ethics on religious grounds. In case of "any challenge to
the validity and religious nature of our Ethics system," he wrote in 1966,
Scientologists should refer to the example of early Buddhist monastic
rules. Just as Buddhist monks had to follow a set of elaborate moral
codes called the *vinaya*, so too, the religion of Scientology has rigorous
ethical rules that govern members' conduct.[76]

Beginning in the early 1960s, Hubbard introduced a series of intensive audits called "Security Checks" or Sec Checks designed to identify
suppressive elements within the church. As we see in his letters and bulletins from these years, the Sec Checks were designed to critically examine Scientology members and seek out any subversive or disloyal tendencies. According to a bulletin on "Security Checks" written in 1960,
"Remember as a security checker you are not merely an observer, or an
auditor, you are a detective."[77] Most of the questions in the Sec Checks
centered on matters of secrecy, disloyalty to the church, and criticism of
Hubbard. In a series of Sec Checks from 1961, for example, one is asked:
"Are you guilty of anything? Do you have a secret you are afraid I'll find
out? Have you ever assaulted anyone, practiced cannibalism, been in
gaol, . . . Have you ever had any unkind thoughts about L. Ron Hubbard
or Scientology?"[78] In keeping with Hubbard's preoccupation with the
Red Menace, many of the questions also focus on Communism and
potential socialist tendencies in the individual being checked; for example: "What is Communism? Do you feel Communism has some good
points?" Other questions, however, focus on more personal matters such
as sexual aberrations, deviations, and promiscuity, such as: "Have you
ever committed adultery? Have you ever practiced Homosexuality?"[79]

While these Sec Checks probe the present life of the individual being
audited, Hubbard also designed a more elaborate Security Check of "the
Whole Track"—that is, an interrogation of the individual's subversive
activities along the great time track going back through myriad past

lives, as well. In keeping with Hubbard's interest in the "space opera" themes of past lives on other worlds, some of these questions involve activities millions of years ago on other planets, amidst struggles between alien civilizations. A brief sampling of the 400+ questions includes the following: "Have you ever enslaved a population?" "Have you ever poisoned an atmosphere?" "Did you come to Earth for evil purposes?" "Have you ever eaten a human body?" "Have you ever zapped anyone?" and "Have you ever been a religious fanatic?"[80]

The practicing of Sec Checking was officially abolished in 1968. However, various ex-Scientologists have repeatedly testified that the practice has continued to this day and is still used to weed out subversive elements within the organization.[81]

Fair Game

Not only did Hubbard launch an intensive program of surveillance within the church itself, but he mounted an equally intensive counterattack against perceived enemies from outside the church as well. Throughout the 1960s, Hubbard was increasingly concerned about "attacks on Scientology" and outlined various means to counter such attacks, including "suits against sources of libel and slander" and "investigating noisily the attackers." In the case of investigations of attackers, he especially recommended delving into the attacker's secrets, exposing them openly, and thus making the attacker the attacked: "These people who attack have secrets. And hidden crimes. . . . And when *we* investigate all this recoils on the attacker."[82]

The most infamous form of this aggressive policy of counterattack was known as "fair game." First introduced in a 1965 letter entitled "Suppressive Acts, Suppression of Scientology and Scientologists," the policy directed that enemies of Scientology (SPs) could be fought using any and all means at one's disposal. Not subject to any rights, the SP is simply "fair game": "A Suppressive Person or group becomes 'fair game.' By Fair Game is meant, without rights for self, possessions or position, and no Scientologist may be brought before a Committee of Evidence or punished for any action taken against a Suppressive Person or group."[83] An even more explicit description of the fair game policy was issued in a letter in October 1967, entitled "Penalties for Lower Conditions." Here, an enemy of the church is defined simply as: "Fair game. May be deprived of property or injured by any means by any Scientologist without any discipline of the Scientologist. May be tricked, sued or lied to or destroyed."[84]

The use of the specific phrase "fair game" was officially ceased in October 1968. However, in his policy letter declaring the cancellation of fair game, Hubbard makes it clear that it was only the specific *phrase* "fair game" that was canceled—and largely for PR reasons—while the actual *tactic* of targeting enemies of the church was to continue as before: "The practice of declaring people FAIR GAME will cease. FAIR GAME may not appear on any Ethics Order. It causes bad public relations."[85] Most critics of the church, moreover, contend that fair game was discontinued in name only and that Scientology continued to retaliate against its enemies as aggressively as ever. As Vicki Aznaran, former president of the Religious Technology Center, stated in her declaration for the Fishman case in 1994: "In reality, the purported cancellation of fair game is at most a matter of semantics. Enemies of Scientology are treated as fair game."[86]

Interestingly enough, in two separate lawsuits (both long after the policy was officially canceled), the church argued that the policy of fair game is in fact defensible as a *religious practice*. In the appeal following Larry Wollersheim's lawsuit against Scientology, the church asserted that fair game was a "core practice of Scientology" and therefore protected as "religious expression."[87] In a statement on behalf of Scientology in their case against Gerald Armstrong in 1984, religious scholar Frank Flinn made a similar argument. Fair game, he argued, is "a typical religious phenomenon for the purpose of protecting the faith and doctrine and practices of the religious group"; as such, it is comparable to the "exclusion" of members from a religious community found in texts such as the book of Leviticus and St. Paul's epistles.[88]

Scientology's "Private CIA": The Guardian's Office

In addition to the practices of Fair Game and Security Checks, the church also created its own intelligence branch dedicated to the defense of Scientology against its many real and imagined enemies. Formed in March 1966 under the direction of Mary Sue Hubbard, the Guardian's Office was responsible for responding to any attack on Scientology, for public relations, for legal actions, and for gathering of intelligence. In 1969, a particularly devoted Scientologist named Jane Kember assumed the title of Guardian Worldwide, while Mary Sue remained the interface between Hubbard and the GO. In the words of Scientologist Bob Thomas, quoted in 1974, "We had to establish a separate arm of the church called the Guardian's Office . . . which deals primarily with the defense of the church against attacks of its enemies, who use the media, government agencies. We have had to become experts in . . . all those things germane to a war of ideas."[89] Compared by some to a kind of "private CIA within the Church," the Guardian's Office undertook a series of highly sophisticated and often astonishingly bold intelligence operations against perceived enemies in the media and government.[90]

By the late 1970s, the Guardian's Office had managed to infiltrate and place Scientologists into a remarkable array of government and private offices, mounting covert operations that impressed even senior U.S. intelligence officers. According to the sentencing memorandum in the trial of Jane Kember, the GO had infiltrated a stunning array of government and private organizations, ranging from the IRS and the Better Business Bureau to the American Medical Association, in a series of "brazen, systematic and persistent burglaries" of government and other offices.[91] As the Los Angeles Times reported in 1978,

> For more than a decade, the worldwide Church of Scientology . . . has conducted sophisticated intelligence and propaganda operations on an international scale against government agencies, private organizations and individual critics the church perceives as its enemies. . . . [I]n addition to federal agencies such as the International Revenue Service, and the Justice Department, Scientologists obtained jobs in key offices of the American Medical Assn., the Council of Better Business Bureaus and the Los Angeles office of the California attorney general.[92]

In 1983, Time magazine found evidence of even further Scientology espionage—indeed, of a "vast spying operation"—that also involved the infiltration of the offices of the Federal Trade Commission, the Drug

Enforcement Administration, and the Justice, Treasury, and Labor departments. According to *Time*, "One Scientology document identifies 136 governmental agencies at home and abroad. At its height, the espionage system . . . included up to 5,000 covert agents who were placed in government offices, foreign embassies and consulates."[93]

The Guardian's Office undertook a series of major operations during the late 1960s and 1970s. The most infamous of these—its "Operation Snow White" against the IRS—will be discussed in chapter 5 as we look in detail at Scientology's war for tax exemption. However, other infamous GO Operations included "Operation Italian Fog," launched against Gabe Cazares, the mayor of Clearwater, Florida. When the church initially bought up property to establish its new "land base" in Clearwater in 1975, it had done so under the innocuous and generic name of the "United Churches of Florida" (UCF). Cazares campaigned for the disclosure of the true purposes of the UCF and, when its ties to Scientology were uncovered, the mayor became increasingly critical of the church. In response, the GO began "covert operations designed to remove him from office," which included, among other plans, an attempt to spread rumors about a sex scandal and then to accuse him of bigamy.[94]

Another of the more astonishing GO projects was "Operation Freakout," launched against journalist Paulette Cooper. Cooper's 1971 book, *The Scandal of Scientology*, was one of the first and most devastating attacks on the church as a dangerous cult, and it met with an equally devastating response from the GO. According to a document of April 1, 1976, the primary aim of Operation Freakout was "to get P.C. incarcerated in a mental institution or jail, or at least hit her so hard that she drops the attack."[95] A U.S. court sentencing memorandum gave the following, rather chilling account of the operation, which involved a multistaged, well-orchestrated plot to frame Cooper for terrorism against the very highest levels of office—including none other than Henry Kissinger (!):

Operation Freakout had three different plans. The first required a woman to imitate Paulette Cooper's voice and make telephone threats to Arab Consulates in New York. The second scheme involved mailing a threatening letter to an Arab Consulate in such a fashion that it would appear to have been one by Paulette Cooper. Finally, a Scientologist field staff member was to impersonate Paulette Cooper at a laundry and threaten the President and the then Secretary of State, Henry Kissinger.[96]

Following the FBI raids of church offices in 1977, Scientology's role in all of this was uncovered, and Cooper finally reached an out-of-court settlement with the church in 1985. Yet the chilling effect of "Operation Freakout" would continue for the next several decades to discourage journalists and scholars from looking too closely at the church.

As the court concluded in the sentencing of Jane Kember after the FBI raids, the GO had become a bizarre secret espionage program that at times simply defied imagination. Indeed, the GO was in many ways a weird, religious mirror of cold war secrecy and surveillance, the same kind of surreal, spy-novel story that only L. Ron Hubbard could have written: "The crimes committed by these defendants is of a breadth and scope previously unheard. . . . No building, office, desk or file was safe from their despicable scheming and warped minds. The tools of their trade were miniature transmitters, lock picks, secret codes, forged credentials, and any other devices they found necessary to carry out their heinous schemes."[97] The GO was officially disbanded in 1983, and much of its operations were transferred over to a new intelligence organization called the Office of Special Affairs—but not before, as we will see in chapter 5, the GO had undertaken its greatest covert operation against the IRS.

Remote Viewers: Scientologists and Secret CIA Psychic Research

Most of this chapter thus far has focused on Scientology's war with government agencies such as the IRS, FBI, FDA, and numerous others. But surely one of the most surreal chapters in the history of Scientology in cold war America was its more positive connection with the CIA and the agency's secret research into psychic abilities. The astonishing story of the CIA's secret psychic research since has recently been popularized through Jon Ronson's book, *The Men Who Stare at Goats*, and the major film by the same name, which traces the program since 1979.[98] But the roots of this secret research go back further, at least to the early 1970s, and it has surprising links to the Church of Scientology. Indeed, several of the key researchers and psychics in the program were advanced Scientologists: Harold E. Puthoff, Ingo Swann, and Pat Price had all reached the upper-OT levels, and all three were key figures in research into the phenomenon known as "remote viewing" or the paranormal ability to "see" from long distances. The very possibility of such a phenomenon was of obvious interest to both the United States and the Soviets during the cold war.

Remote viewing, as we saw in chapter 2, was one of the advanced abilities promised by Scientology training. As Hubbard defined it in the *Dianetics and Scientology Technical Dictionary*, a remote viewpoint is "a viewpoint without the consideration by the thetan that he is located at that point. The thetan may have any number of remote viewpoints."[99] A physicist with a PhD from Stanford University, Harold Puthoff joined Scientology in the late 1960s and quickly advanced to the OT VII level by 1971. In fact, he wrote enthusiastically of his "wins" in Scientology, claiming to have achieved "remote viewing" abilities. In 1974, Puthoff also wrote a piece for Scientology's *Celebrity* magazine, stating that Scientology had given him "a feeling of absolute fearlessness."[100]

In the early 1970s, Puthoff and his collaborator, Russell Targ, joined the Electronics and Bioengineering Lab at Stanford Research Institute (SRI). In addition to their mainstream research, they also began various studies of the paranormal, including testing with a psychic and artist named Ingo Swann, who was an OT IV Scientologist. In July 1973, Swann had in fact presented a paper at a conference in Prague on the subject of the "Scientology paradigm as a model for developing and exploring paranormal abilities."[101] Another gifted psychic who joined the program was Pat Price, a former police officer and a fellow OT IV Scientologist. As cofounder of the SRI program, Russell Targ, notes in his memoir, "Ingo and Pat both felt that they learned certain useful techniques from Scientology that enhanced their already significant psi ability"; however, he goes on to say that many other psychics involved in the program had no Scientology association whatsoever and were equally proficient at remote viewing. "So," Targ concludes, "it is not necessary to give away all your money . . . to develop your ESP."[102] Other key figures in the psychic research had only peripheral Scientology connections. Thus Edwin May, who inherited directorship of the SRI program in 1985, had also been involved in Scientology courses in the early 1970s and initially found them useful. But he eventually grew disillusioned with the high costs of Scientology and finally "said to hell with it" after the FBI raids on the church in 1977.[103]

It does seem, however, that there was a natural sort of affinity between those who were interested in the abilities promised by Scientology and those who would be involved in a secret psychic research program. As Jim Schnabel suggests in his history of the remote viewing program, Scientology had a surprisingly strong foothold among the high-tech professionals on the West Coast during this period, and at SRI, "there seemed to be Scientologists everywhere." "Scientology seemed particularly attractive to people who were both spiritually and technically oriented," Schnabel suggests, "probably because it combined Eastern religious themes of reincarnation and introspection with Western themes of predestination, ethical rigor and self-improvement through science and technology. It was, arguably, a severely mutated form of Protestantism, gone amok in the machine age."[104]

Puthoff later resigned his Scientology membership in the mid-1970s and thereafter lent his support to a group of anti-Scientologists who criticized the church because of its conspiratorial, cultlike atmosphere. Swann, too, eventually resigned from Scientology. Price, meanwhile, died under mysterious circumstances in Las Vegas in 1975. Russell Targ, the cofounder of the psychic research program, claims that Price was in fact "funneling classified remote viewing data to the Scientology Guardian's Office" and suggests that either the CIA or the Russians may have been involved in his death.[105] However, Puthoff and Targ remained convinced that Swann, Price, and others involved in the testing had genuine psychic powers, including the power of remote viewing. The results of their findings were published in 1977 as *Mind-Reach: Scientists Look at Psychic Ability*, which claims for these psychics many of the same powers of remote viewing claimed by Hubbard and OT Scientologists: "The basic phenomenon appears to cover a range of subjective experience variously referred to . . . as astral projection . . . clairvoyance or out-of-body experience . . . exteriorization or dissociation."[106]

Because of its obvious national security potential, the CIA took an active interest in the remote viewing project and began funding its research in the early 1970s. Very much a cold war project, the SRI program was competing with paranormal research laboratories established in the USSR, which were also exploring remote viewing and other psychic abilities. The program continued to be funded by the U.S. government until 1995, when it was terminated due to a lack of evidence that it had any value to the intelligence community. However, if Jon Ronson's account in *The Men Who Stare at Goats* is to be believed, some form of secret psychic research was reactivated shortly after 9/11 as part of the new war on terror. "For everyday agnostics," Ronson concludes, "it is not easy to accept that our leaders . . . sometimes seem to believe that the business of managing world affairs should be carried out within both standard and supernatural dimensions."[107]

Conclusions: Religion and Secrecy Post-9/11—A New Cold War of the Spirit?

L. Ron Hubbard's death occurred in 1986, just a few years before the fall of the Berlin Wall and the collapse of the Soviet Union. From the development of *Dianetics* in the late 1940s until his passing on from the realm of MEST, Hubbard's career closely mirrored the decades of the cold war. Even more clearly, his church's preoccupations with secrecy, surveillance, information control, Communism, nuclear war, and space opera also closely reflected—perhaps in a sort of exaggerated, fun house mirror way—the preoccupations of the FBI, CIA, and other government agencies during these decades. Above all, I would argue, the Church of Scientology reflects, embodies, and epitomizes the cold war obsession with secrecy. From the increasingly esoteric levels of training known as Operating Thetan to its increasingly fantastic war of espionage and counterespionage with various government agencies, the history of the church at times seems like something straight out of a cold war spy novel. Indeed, I have really only scratched the surface of the church's remarkable cold war story and have not even delved into some of the more outlandish allegations that have been made about the church during these decades (such as L. Ron Hubbard Jr.'s remarkable claim that his father was also helping to sell secret information to the Soviet Union, acting as a middle man for the KGB).[108]

Here I would suggest that Scientology also gives us some broader insights into the nature of religious secrecy and its role in culture, politics, and history. On the one hand, the increasingly esoteric levels of Hubbard's OT "advanced tech" clearly served as a kind of "adorning possession," in Simmel's sense—that is, a source of status, prestige, and power that enhances one's character precisely by virtue of what it conceals. Or to borrow a phrase from sociologist Pierre Bourdieu, secrecy can also serve as a form of "symbolic capital," that is, a symbolic resource of distinction, honor, and status that comes from possession of rare, highly valued esoteric knowledge.[109] Yet at the same time, secrecy can also be a profound liability for a religious group. By its very exclusivist nature, the practice of secrecy tends to arouse suspicion among dominant social and political powers, giving rise to all manner of fears: "Freemasons are running the country," "the Mau Mau are ready to revolt," "brainwashing cults are stealing America's youth," etc. And this in turn brings new forms of government surveillance of groups who choose to keep aspects of their beliefs and practices secret. Scientology is a striking embodiment of both these aspects of secrecy, its power and its liability. Indeed, the church soon found itself not just generating large amounts of income through its confidential advanced tech, but also quickly enmeshed in an incredibly complex war of surveillance, information control, and espionage both within its own ranks and with numerous government agencies.

As such, the example of Scientology also has profound implications for the study of religions today, particularly in our own new age of religious secrecy, terrorism, and government surveillance. The case of Scientology during the cold war was at once a kind of prefiguration and a strange mirror of our own generation in the wake of 9/11. As Michael Barkun notes in his study of secrecy and privacy after 9/11, "[D]uring periods of social or political tension, religious secrets, real or imagined, take on a broader and more sinister importance, for they may be seen as evidence that a religious community has unsavory beliefs or behaviors that it must hide. . . . We entered such a period after the September 11, 2001, attacks."[110]

Today, as in the decades of the cold war, we face a host of complex questions as to how to deal with secretive religious groups that might be engaged in subversive, dangerous, and/or illegal activities. Do government agencies have a responsibility to use virtually any and all means at their disposal to monitor secretive groups and protect the public? This seems to have been the logic of the Bush-Cheney administration and their lawyers, who advocated a wide range of new security measures and techniques of surveillance, including the USA PATRIOT Act, a massive program of warrantless wiretapping of U.S. citizens, and the use of harsh interrogation techniques previously considered torture. Or, conversely, are these highly invasive new measures in fact dangerous erosions of basic civil liberties and rights to privacy, reflecting what legal scholars David Cole and James Dempsey call a new "McCarthy-era philosophy"?[111] As Barkun asks, moreover, are such new forms of government surveillance ultimately counterproductive, generating more fear, paranoia, and a "siege mentality," which leads to even more secrecy among marginalized religious groups?[112]

In the case of Scientology, it seems clear that church offices such as the GO did in fact engage in massive, widespread—and really quite astonishing—covert criminal activities. But it also seems clear that Hubbard's obsession with secrecy, surveillance, and Communist threats was very much a product of his time and place. A cold war religion, Scientology embodied all of the most widespread and pernicious cold war anxieties. We might therefore wonder to what degree our own post-9/11 era of surveillance and invasive security might be generating new forms of paranoia, obsessive secrecy, and siege mentality today—in short, a New Cold War of the Spirit.

- FOUR -

THE "CULT OF ALL CULTS"?
Scientology and the Cult Wars of the 1970s and 80s

Scientology is quite likely the most ruthless, the most classically
terroristic, the most litigious and the most lucrative cult the country has
ever known. No cult extracts more money from its members.
—Cynthia Kisser, former director of the Cult Awareness
Network (1991)[1]

Brainwashing is a very simple mechanism. One gets a person to agree
that something *might be* a certain way and then drives him, by
introverting him and through self-criticism, to the possibility
that it is that way.
—L. Ron Hubbard, *All About Radiation* (1957)[2]

Beginning in the 1970s and 80s, Scientology came to the center of yet
another set of volatile and contested debates surrounding religion in the
United States: the "cult" controversies and the anticult movements that
spread rapidly throughout these decades. Particularly in the wake of violent new religious movements such as the Charles Manson Family, with
its murder spree in 1969, and the Peoples Temple, with its mass suicide
of over nine hundred members in 1978, a widespread anxiety about
alternative religious groups began to spread throughout the American
public, the media, and government agencies. These "cult" anxieties were
intimately tied to a wide range of other anxieties, tensions, and obsessions of post-1960s America—not simply the fear of Communism on
U.S. soil, but also the countercultural movement, the sexual revolution,
experimentation in mind-altering drugs, shifting gender roles, and alternative social experiments.[3]

Literature on cults, of course, had been around for some time, at least since the 1920s, with books such as Gaius Atkins's *Modern Religious Cults and Movements* (1923). But the real flood of anticult publications began in the 1960s and 70s—not surprisingly, the very period in which the American spiritual marketplace began to overflow with new religious offerings—with books such as Walter Martin's *The Kingdom of the Cults* (1965), Jan Van Baalen's *Chaos of the Cults* (1962), and countless others.[4] By the early 1960s, anticult paranoia was also combined with growing fears about the alleged phenomenon of "brainwashing" during the cold war. This was particularly the case after the publication of Robert Jay Lifton's widely read book on brainwashing in China, *Thought Reform and the Psychology of Totalism*.[5] Fueled by the anticult literature, the fear was now that brainwashing might take place not just in a faraway Communist state but within alternative religious groups right here on American soil. And by the 1970s, the fear of new religions had blossomed into a widespread "cult scare" and gave rise to a wide array of anticult groups—the Individual Freedom Foundation, Love Our Children, Citizens Freedom Foundation, the Spiritual Counterfeits Project, and Cults Exodus for Christ, among many others—dedicated to saving America's youth from dangerous mind-control groups.[6]

Scientology lay at the center of these debates and was frequently identified as the most deviant, dangerous and destructive of all the many new religious experiments popping up in the United States during these decades. From the first appearance of Dianetics in the early 1950s, the movement was attacked as a dangerous "cult without professional tradition," and critics were shocked to find that "society permits persons without any medical training to treat persons with every kind of mental and physical illness."[7] When Scientology announced itself as a "religion" in 1953, moreover, even some members worried that it had become "cultish." As the independent Scientology journal *Aberree* reported in 1954, "Some were outspokenly antagonistic to the idea. . . . Many from California feared that designating Scientology as a religion would classify it with that state's 9,857,385,237 cults."[8] The cult accusations became only more forceful in the 1970s as the church began to emerge as perhaps the wealthiest, most expensive, and most ostentatious new religion in the

Cover image of *Time*, "Scientology: The Cult of Greed," 5/6/1991 © 1991 Time Inc. Used under license

United States. Beginning in 1969, the church opened a series of "Celebrity Centres" and soon attracted an array of affluent actors and musicians such as John Travolta, Chick Corea, Isaac Hayes, and numerous others who helped propel the movement into its era of most rapid growth and commercial success.[9] By the 1980s, Scientology had become iconic in the American media as the quintessential money- and power-obsessed cult, finally branded the "the cult of greed and power" by *Time* magazine. As Hubbard's own son, L. Ron Jr., put it in a devastating interview with *Penthouse* in 1983, Scientology is a cult that is "as dangerous as drugs. They commit the highest crime: the rape of the soul."[10]

As such, Scientology raises profound questions about the very concept of "cults" and the question of how—and indeed if—such groups can be usefully distinguished from "mainstream religions." These are questions that strike at the heart of the First Amendment and our understanding of religion in a complex democratic society. As David Bromley and Anson Shupe put it in their study of the cult scares of the 1970s, "At stake may not only be their fates but also the shape of religious freedom and civil liberties in the future."[11] On the one side, since the early 1980s, most American scholars of religions have criticized and often vehemently rejected the use of the word *cult*, which they see as so burdened with negative connotations as to be largely useless, if not downright dangerous, when applied to new religious groups. As Catherine Wessinger argues in her study of millenarian movements: "It is important that people become aware of the bigotry conveyed by *cult*. The word *cult* dehumanizes the religion's members. . . . It strongly implies that these people are deviants; they are seen as crazy, brainwashed, duped by their leader."[12] The term "cult," in short, has been defined in direct contrast to "religion" and used to deny religious freedoms to groups labeled as such: "'cult' signifies the absence of 'religion.' 'Cult' . . . is the opposite of religion. The usage of 'cult,' however it might be intended, inevitably resonates with the discourse of an extensive and pervasive anticult campaign that has endeavored to deny the status of 'religion' to a variety of new religious movements."[13]

On the other side, however, more critical authors have argued that there *are* in fact problematic and potentially dangerous groups out there who should *not* be honored with the label or with the benefits and privileges of a "religion." As Canadian sociologist Stephen Kent has argued, the Church of Scientology has been involved in clearly illegal activities and human rights violations. To defend them on the grounds of "religious freedom," Kent suggests, is to naively collude with an organization that causes psychological and physical damage to many individuals. As he wrote in defense of the German government's very critical stance toward Scientology, "By granting Scientology tax exemption, the United States government is cooperating with an organization that appears to put citizens from around the world at significant mental health and perhaps medical risk."[14]

Scientology, I will suggest, highlights these complex debates in excruciating detail. Its complex corporate structure, its obsession with secrecy, and its aggressive tactics against its critics would seem to make Scientology the epitome of the popular image of the "cult." And yet, for that very reason, it also raises profound questions about how such groups should be treated in a society that prides itself on religious freedom, diversity, and tolerance. These questions have only become more intense in the wake of the 9/11 attacks and more recent terrorist attempts, as we struggle to defend rights to religious expression while at the same time policing groups that may be involved in illegal or destructive activities.

A Billion-Year Contract: The Sea Org and the RPF

With its long hours of auditing, its elaborate hierarchy of levels of training, and its pervasive system of surveillance, Scientology has long been attacked with the charge of brainwashing. For critics, the entire trajectory of Scientology, from entry-level courses to the most advanced OT levels, is often seen as a systematic, if rather gradual, process of mind alteration.[15]

Since the late 1960s, however, perhaps the most intense charges of "cult" behavior and brainwashing in Scientology have focused on the group of elite, highly devoted, and disciplined members known as the Sea Organization (Sea Org). With their crisp naval uniforms and remarkable military discipline, the members of the Sea Org became not only the icons of the inner core of the church but also the poster children for anticult activists warning about totalitarian mind control. Formed in

1968, the Sea Org was to be Scientology's elite core of devoted followers, accompanying Hubbard on his voyages on the high seas and dedicated to the highest service of the church. As the church itself describes the Org, it is a "religious order for the Scientology religion" comparable to other "fraternal religious orders."[16] Initially, the Sea Org was housed aboard Hubbard's fleet of ships, most importantly his flagship, the *Apollo*. Hubbard, we should note, had been deported from the United Kingdom as an undesirable alien in 1968, and was facing increasing criticism in other countries such as Australia (where he was the focus of a scathing governmental report in 1965) and the United States (where he was the focus of both government and media criticism throughout the late 1960s). Thus, Hubbard's shift to a sea-based organization during these years was clearly in part a response to his inability to operate freely in many nations. But the Sea Org quickly evolved into an elite "naval" order based on intense devotion to the church and remarkable discipline, uniformed with gold braids, service ribbons, and naval caps.[17] Since 1975, however, the Org has moved ashore and is centered at the Flag Land Base in Clearwater, Florida, now maintaining only one seagoing vessel, the *Freewinds*.

According to the church's *Advance!* magazine in 1969, the Sea Org understood its mission to be a profound one indeed, that of a "heroic band" now "serving Mankind at the time of its most crucial need" and dedicated to nothing less than the creation of a new civilization on earth: "The Sea Org was formed to compose a superiorly disciplined, elite group working directly under Ron to aid the creation of a new civilization on this planet."[18] An advertisement for the Sea Org from 1971 contains an even more dire warning. On the cover lies an image of a mushroom cloud explosion with the words "Join the Sea Org Before it's Too Late." The ad then goes on to warn that the earth faces catastrophic peril unless we join the Sea Org to save the world from total annihilation:

WE MAY NEVER AGAIN HAVE ANOTHER CHANCE!! . . .

Riots, revolt, insanity and war run rampant while world leaders stand helpless. . .

The potential for self-destruction of this world is frightening. Look around and see for yourself.

This planet is on the last downward plunge toward oblivion. If we
don't act NOW tomorrow won't matter. . . .

This is a last ditch stand against the terror or total destruction.

YOU MUST JOIN THE SEA ORG.[19]

Another flyer from 1971 urges the reader to "Join the Sea Org" and
quotes one of Hubbard's most infamous policy letters entitled "Keep
Scientology Working." The KSW letter, as it is known today, warns that
the church's mission is not mere child's play but a deadly serious mission
on which the entire fate of the planet hangs:

We're not playing some minor game in Scientology. It isn't cute. . . .

[T]he whole agonized future of this planet, every Man, Woman and
Child on it, and your own destiny for the next trillions of years, depend
on what you do here and now with and in Scientology.

This is a deadly serious activity.[20]

Adopting naval uniforms and ranks, the Sea Org appeared to be a kind
of idealized re-creation of Hubbard's own World War II naval past combined with a messianic zeal to save the entire planet from imminent
destruction.

In many ways, however, the Sea Org is also reminiscent of the "Soldiers
of Light" in Hubbard's science fiction series "Ole Doc Methuselah"—
that group of intrepid space explorers who travel the galaxies in order to
bring healing to all beings. Indeed, an advertisement for the Sea Org in
1987 shows a *Star-Trek*-like spaceship with the Sea Org logo zooming
through outer space.[21] According to Hubbard's 1973 book, *Mission into
Time*, the Sea Org's mission is "an exploration into both time *and* space,"
as they investigate past lives and secret mysteries throughout the ancient world.[22] As such, the Sea Org also closely resembles the image of
the "Loyal Officers" of the Galactic Confederacy described in the top
secret OT III Xenu story, which we discussed in chapter 3.

The commitment of a Sea Org member is indeed a profound one,
involving a promise to serve Scientology not only in this lifetime but in
myriad future lifetimes as well. According to the CSI publication *Scientology: Theology and Practice of a Contemporary Religion*, "Sea Org
members sign a billion-year covenant, a pledge which has an intensely

personal and deeply religious significance to a Scientologist."[23] The covenant contract includes the promise to "get Ethics in on this planet and the universe" and concludes with the pledge: "THEREFORE, I CONTRACT MYSELF TO THE SEA ORGANIZATION FOR THE NEXT BILLION YEARS."[24]

Not surprisingly, more than a little controversy has surrounded the Sea Org and its billion-year commitments. On the more generous side, several scholars of religion, such as J. Gordon Melton, have argued that the Sea Org is best understood as a form of "ordered religious community," comparable to other ordered communities such as Eastern Orthodox and Roman Catholic monastic orders, Tibetan Buddhist monks, or sannyasin ascetics in India.[25]

On the more critical side, ex-members and some scholars have compared the Sea Org to a totalitarian organization based on intense surveillance and lack of freedom. Robert Vaughn Young, for example, spent twenty-two years in the church and served as its public relations officer. In Young's experience, the Org was reminiscent of the incessant, invasive surveillance of the Thought Police narrated in George Orwell's *Nineteen Eighty-four*: privacy of any kind was highly suspected, while members were "subject to routine and unannounced inspection regardless of whether it is day or night, or if the member is awake, asleep, in the bedroom or the bathroom."[26]

If the Sea Org has been dubbed by many critics as the epitome of the dark "cult within the cult," even more serious criticism has been aimed at the church's RPF or "Rehabilitation Project Force." The RPF grew out of disciplinary programs aboard the Sea Org ships in the late 1960s, such as the "Mud Box Brigade," in which members were assigned to clean the filthier parts of the ships, such as the area where the anchors dragged in mud. By 1973, the more formal RPF was established to discipline members found guilty of deviation from Sea Org norms. Eventually, RPF centers were created at the major Scientology complexes in Los Angeles, Clearwater, London, and Copenhagen. In 1974 Hubbard also introduced the RPF's RPF, an even more disciplinary program for those who were not progressing sufficiently or had not taken their RPF assignment seriously enough. According to official statements by the church, the RPF is designed for individuals "who would otherwise be subject to dismissal for serious and/or continuous ecclesiastical violations." Participants

receive daily religious counseling and work eight hours a day "to improve the church's facilities."[27]

Even more so than the Sea Org itself, the RPF has been the subject
of intense and deeply divided debate. Regarded by more sympathetic
observers as a form of spiritual discipline not very different from cor-
rectional measures found in other religions, the RPF has been widely
attacked by critics as a brutal, psychologically damaging, and even brainwashing system. On the more generous side, scholars such as Juha Pentikäinen, Jurgen F. K. Redhardt, and Michael York argue that the RPF is
comparable to the practices of other ordered religious communities,
such as monastic retreats where the devoted member can find a quiet
respite and deal with spiritual problems: "The programme is . . . directly
comparable to a 'retreat' in the monastic sense, where withdrawal from
the everyday hustle and bustle of life is a requisite in order to resolve
inner conflict."[28] J. Gordon Melton likewise suggests that the program is
not unlike the monastic discipline enforced by rule of St. Benedict in
Christian monasteries or the *vinaya* monastic rules followed by Buddhist communities.[29]

On the other side, however, former members and critics argue that
the RPF bears less resemblance to a monastic retreat than it does to an
unusually brutal prison or even a "Chinese ideological Re-Education
Center."[30] As Gerry Armstrong reflected on his time spent in the Sea
Org, the RPF was "essentially a prison to which crew who were considered non-producers, security risks, or just wanted to leave the Sea Org
were assigned"; RPF conditions aboard ship were "roach-infested, filthy
and unventilated cargo holds," while those in the RPF were required to
run everywhere and subjected to discipline that was "harsh and bizarre"
with essentially "no liberties and no free time."[31] In Armstrong's opinion, the existence of the RPF program is the strongest evidence against
Scientology's claim to "religious" status and an example of the way in
which the church has manipulated religious protections as a means to
cover over its destructive practices:

> The RPF is something Germany and every government should look at
> because the citizens of every country are being assigned to these US-
> based gulags in violation of basic human rights. People assigned are not

free to leave but are held, guarded, and must sign lists of their "crimes" culled from their pc folders before they are routed out. Until . . . the organization abolishes its RPFs, freedom of religion in the US is a lie. The US has created a freedom for unholy corporations to persecute individuals for "religious" reasons. The US has allowed its Constitutional guarantee of religious freedom to be perverted by money-motivated corporate lawyers.[32]

In her recent memoir, former Sea Org and Office of Special Affairs officer Nancy Many also recounts her abusive experience in the RPF. Despite being five months pregnant, she claims, she was forced to sleep in a dirty, non-air-conditioned parking garage, perform manual labor, and eat the leftovers of other staff while in the Clearwater RPF. She also claims that she was threatened with being placed in the RPF's RPF in Clearwater, which she describes as a "dank, humid, dark space" in the boiler room of the Fort Harrison hotel.[33]

Not only ex-Scientologists but also some scholars have described the RPF in extremely harsh terms. Based on his interviews with numerous Scientologists who had been in the program, Stephen Kent argues that the RPF involves human rights violations, including forcible confinement, physical maltreatment, demanding chores, poor diet, and inadequate medical care. As such, Kent concludes, the RPF is less a "religious community" than a form of severe social and ideological control, which puts "coerced participants through regimes of harsh physical punishment, forced self-confessions, social isolation, hard labour, and intense doctrinal study, all as part of leadership-designed efforts to regain members' ideological commitment. The confinement that participants experience, combined with forms of physical maltreatment, intensive ideological study, and forced confessions, allows social scientists to speak of the RPF as a 'brainwashing' program."[34]

In this sense, the case of the Sea Org and the RPF—and Scientology more generally—raises in an especially acute way one of the most contested questions regarding new religious movements: the brainwashing debate. Can a member of a religious (or political or ideological group) actually become brainwashed, that is, lose her or his own ability to think and choose freely, effectively becoming an uncritical and passive member of a community that thinks and chooses for her or him? On one side, some sociologists such as Stephen Kent suggest that Scientology does in fact involve a form of "systematic, scientific, and coercive elimination of the individuality of the mind of another" that can in fact be described as a process of brainwashing.[35] On the other side, perhaps the majority of scholars of new religious movements are far more skeptical of the brainwashing narrative. As authors such as Catherine Wessinger, Lorne Dawson, Dick Anthony, and others argue, the concept of brainwashing is far too simplistic and generally far too biased to account for the real complexity of an individual's involvement in a new religious movement. "Religions have been in the business, throughout the ages, of emotionally prompting and physically and socially supporting the abandonment of old habits of thought and word and deed and inducing new ones," as Dawson observes.[36] So it seems unfair to single out new religions and their conversion tactics as a form of "brainwashing."

Whether or not we choose to describe Scientology as a form of brainwashing, however, there is one important fact to keep in mind: L. Ron Hubbard himself clearly *did* believe that brainwashing was possible, and he also wrote quite a lot about the phenomenon—including (most likely) the alleged Soviet brainwashing manual that we discussed in chapter 3. Like the CIA itself during these decades, Hubbard was actively interested in and exploring the concept of thought reform. In his 1957 book, *All About Radiation*, Hubbard had quite a bit to say about Soviet brainwashing techniques and offered Scientology auditing as the surest way to combat them. Here he suggests that brainwashing is a much simpler process than most brainwashers—including the Soviets—have thus far realized: "Brainwashing is child's play. One shouldn't be very worried about it . . . the people who have used it are not sufficiently acquainted with the mind in order to make it very effective."[37] In one letter to the FBI in 1955, Hubbard even recommended using Communist methods of "psychopolitics" against the Soviets, thereby turning their sophisticated mind-control techniques to our own advantage: "It may well be that we will also use this [Communist manual on psychopolitics] in anti-Communist campaigns. . . . We have been seriously hurt by Communists and Communism and we see nothing wrong in our using their tactics against them."[38] The E-meter and the auditing process, conversely, are presented as the best possible means to undo any sort of brainwashing. With a meter and a trained auditor, Hubbard suggests, one can easily counteract any brainwashing that might have been done by Communists or others working against the freedom of the human mind:

> Any trained Scientologist with an E-Meter could tell if somebody's loyalty had been changed. . . . If one suspects that one of one's associates has been brainwashed, the best thing to do is to get hold of a Scientologist for he can handle the matter with ease.[39]

As Hubbard argued, Scientology as a whole could be described as a process of reverse brainwashing and "unhypnosis." All of us, as thetans trapped in MEST, are brainwashed or hypnotized to a certain degree, and Scientology is the ultimate means to de-hypnotize us and wake us up to our true nature as infinite beings of limitless potential: "Man exists in a partially hypnotized state. . . . The processes of Scientology could be described as methods of 'unhypnotizing' men to their own freer choice and better life."[40]

More cynical critics of the church, however, argue that Hubbard did not actually intend Scientology to be the antidote to brainwashing. Rather, as Brian Ambry and others allege, the "psychopolitics" manual was itself the very *blueprint* for the actual brainwashing that takes place in Scientology. If one simply substitutes "Scientology" for "psychopolitics" in the text, they argue, one has the basic theory and practice of Hubbard's church.[41]

As such, Scientology really complicates the "brainwashing" debate in an interesting way. From Hubbard's perspective, we non-Scientologists are really the ones who have been brainwashed, and auditing is precisely the "deprogramming" we need in order to return to our "true selves." In short, whether we now view it as a form of "brainwashing" or as a form of "unhypnotizing," Scientology was clearly presented by its founder as a powerful kind of "thought reform" that could bring about a radical change in an individual's mental and spiritual existence. It is simply presented as a *good* sort of mental conditioning that might undo the negative forms imposed by the destructive cultures of the cold war.

The Cult of Greed? The Corporate Structure
and the Costs of Scientology

Probably the two most common criticisms of Scientology—and also the reasons many critics dub it a cult rather than a religion—are its elaborate corporate structure and the large amounts of money that it involves. Critics of the church have long described this as primarily a moneymaking racket aimed less at promoting spiritual values than at "squeezing individual Scientologists for as much as they can pay."[42] The church, meanwhile, has countered that many if not most religions accept payment for services, and Scientology is hardly the first religious organization to take in a large amount of money: "[R]eligions have, of necessity, and throughout the ages, been compensated for their worldly services .... The Church of Scientology is ... by no means the only religion which accepts fixed donations for its religious services. Nor are these services as given in any church, rendered any the less religious thereby."[43]

From its very "incorporation" in late 1953, the Church of Scientology has had an extremely complex, protean, and at times bewildering corporate structure. As former Scientologist Robert Vaughn Young put it, "The Scientology world is much larger than merely the 'Church' of Scientology. It is a labyrinth of corporate shells that, like a hall of mirrors, was designed to baffle all but the initiated"; trying to sort out the astonishingly complex relations between Scientology's myriad corporate entities, he suggests, is "like trying to solve a Rubik's Cube."[44] Vicki Aznaran, the former president and chairman of the board of directors of the Religious Technology Center, was equally blunt in her description of the elaborate corporate structure of the church: "[T]he corporations of Scientology are a carefully contrived sham and shell structure intended to confuse and divert litigants, the courts and the I.R.S."[45]

Indeed, the corporate structure of Scientology is both staggering and incredibly confusing—perhaps intentionally so, as Young and Aznaran suggest. Already by the mid-1950s, Scientology had grown into a complex network of interconnected organizations: thus in 1957, the Founding Church of Scientology listed seventeen organizations that it owned or controlled, including the Congress of Eastern Scientologists, the Scientology Consultants to Industrial Efficiency, and even the Freudian

Foundation of America.[46] Most of these organizations were ad hoc and temporary, loosely organized during the 1950s under the umbrella of HASI. In the 1960s, most of the corporate operations of Scientology were brought under the legal auspices of the Church of Scientology of California, which had conveniently retained its tax-exempt status since the mid-1950s. Then in 1981, the Church of Scientology International (CSI)—also known as the "Mother Church"—was formed, followed by the Church of Spiritual Technology (CST) in 1982—which owns all copyrights on the estate of L. Ron Hubbard—and the Religious Technology Center (RTC). While the RTC claims only to be the "holder of the Dianetics and Scientology Trademarks," it is the most powerful executive organization within the Scientology empire, and its current chairman, David Miscavige, is widely recognized as the effective head of the church.[47]

Today, what we call "Scientology" is in reality a remarkably complex network of ostensibly independent but clearly interconnected corporate entities. These include, among many others, the Watchdog Committee (WDC), the Commodore's Messenger Organization (CMO), Author Services Incorporated (ASI), Church of Scientology Religious Education College, Inc. (COSRECI), Bridge Publications, New Era Publications, the "Flag Ship Service Organization" (FSSO), the Advanced Organizations, the Saint Hills, and the many churches (also known as "outer orgs"). In addition, there are various other groups and programs, such as Scientology Missions International (SMI), the World Institute of Scientology Enterprises (WISE), the Association for Better Living and Education (ABLE), the Concerned Businessmen's Association, the Citizen's Commission on Human Rights (CCHR), and a wide variety of schools and educational programs. As such, Scientology is perhaps best understood not simply as "a religion" but rather as an extremely complex "multi-faceted transnational organization," of which religion is one—but only one—aspect.[48]

In this sense, Scientology appears to have been remarkably well adapted to the particular socioeconomic context in which it emerged: twentieth-century American capitalism. Hubbard offered a new spiritual product that was enormously successful both as a religious institution and as a business enterprise. In this sense, Scientology is an especially clear example of the situation that sociologist Peter Berger calls the "market" conditions of contemporary religious life.[49] With its centralized bureaucracy and hierarchical structure, the early Scientology movement might be said to be an ideal embodiment of the modern "Fordist" model of capitalism that predominated in the United States until the 1970s.[50] However, with its increasingly elaborate, multifaceted, and protean corporate structure since the 1980s, Scientology might also be a striking reflection of the new economic structures that have been variously described as "late-capitalism," "post-Fordism," or "disorganized capitalism." Whereas the early modern or Fordist forms of capitalism were characterized by their centralized, hierarchical bureaucratic structures, the newer forms of capitalism emerging since the 1970s are characterized more by their fluidity and flexibility, their protean structure, and their constantly shifting networks of accumulation.[51] Scientology's rapid growth from a fairly esoteric new movement in the 1960s to a powerful transnational organization in the 1970s and 80s almost exactly mirrors this broader global economic transition.

Whether we call it "Fordist" or "late capitalist," however, Scientology had an explicit financial motive and structure from the very outset. Hubbard himself devoted literally thousands of pages and policy letters to the subject of the bureaucracy, corporate management, and finances of Scientology. At times, Hubbard was quite blunt about the fact that Scientology, though it may be a "religious philosophy," is also very much a moneymaking enterprise. "Our campaign is to sell Scientology," he frankly announced in 1957, " . . . We are in the business of Scientology."[52] Moreover, every religious leader who ever lived—including Jesus and Buddha—was doing nothing else than "selling" yet another path to Clear. As he wrote in March 1971,

> What in essence, was some messiah selling way back on the track? He was selling Clear. He was selling being Clear of Earth. . . .
> You are dealing with a commodity which is as old as man is. . . .
> Man can conquer, through Clearing, the goal of every religion.[53]

But perhaps the clearest and most infamous articulation of Hubbard's attitude toward business is stated in a policy letter of March 9, 1972, in which he outlines the church's finance policies. Here we see Hubbard's astonishingly frank assertion—indeed, his *demand*—that one of the primary aims of the church is to make money and to ensure that all orgs are efficiently bringing in revenue:

> The governing policy of Finance is to:
>
> A. MAKE MONEY.
>
> B. Buy more money made with allocations for expense.
>
> . . .
>
> F. Understand money flow lines not only in an org but org to org as customers flow upward.
>
> . . .
>
> I. Police all lines constantly.
>
> J. MAKE MONEY.
>
> K. MAKE MORE MONEY.
>
> L. MAKE OTHER PEOPLE PRODUCE SO AS TO MAKE MONEY.
>
> A small sack of beans will produce a whole field of beans. Allocate only with that in mind and demand money be made.[54]

As infamous as this particular policy letter has become in the anti-Scientology literature, it is by no means the only one and can be corroborated with numerous other letters from the same era. Thus Hubbard wrote in December 1971:

> [T]he only real crime in the West is for a group to be without money. That finishes it. But with enough money it can defend itself and expand.
>
> Yet if you borrow money you become the property of banks. If you make money you become the target of tax collectors.
>
> But if you don't have it, the group dies under the hammer of bankruptcy and worse.
>
> So we always make it the first condition of a group to make its own way and be prosperous.[55]

In this same letter, Hubbard also makes it clear that Scientology is centrally concerned with *marketing*, that is, with identifying a particular desire among consumers and then "increasing" or "widening" that demand through the skillful use of advertising and other sales techniques:

> What people . . . regard as a valuable service is sometimes incredible. . . . This is why one has to use surveys—to find out what people want that you can deliver. . . .

Once you discover what people want that you *can* deliver you can go about increasing the demand or widening it or making it more valuable, using standard public relations, advertising and merchandizing techniques.[56]

Finally, in many letters from the early 1970s, Hubbard was also fairly blunt about the fact that the aim of the church is not simply the spiritual goal of spreading Scientology in order to "clear the planet"; it also includes the bureaucratic goal of expanding the organization and its resources. As he wrote in a policy letter of August 11, 1971, entitled "Infinite Expansion": "In theory there is no limit to the size of an org. . . . For our purposes there is no real limit to expansion. . . . So long as cash bills is kept more cash than bills there is no limit to expansion."[57]

The practice of Scientology was never exactly inexpensive, but it became increasingly less so from the 1950s onward. As we saw in chapter 1, the initial costs of Dianetics auditing in the early 1950s began at $25 an hour, with a $500 fee for auditor training. These costs steadily rose even as the number of levels, grades, techniques, and rundowns proliferated rapidly over the next several decades. Flyers and magazines advertising Scientology services from the late 1960s and early 70s list a wide array of different courses, grades, and auditing levels, ranging from a few hundred to several thousand dollars. These include the "Hubbard Dianetic Auditor's Course," "Dianetic Course plus Hubbard Advanced Auditor Package," "Org Executive Course," "Management Power Rundown," "Exteriorization Intensive," "Power Processing," "Saint Hill Special Briefing Course," "HAS Children's Course," and so on.[58] A Hubbard executive directive of 1978 lists an even more astonishing array of courses, including "New Era Dianetics," "New Drug Rundown," "Sweat Program," "Relief Rundown," "Dianetic Student Rescue Intensive," "Identity Rundown," "Disability Rundown," "Super Power," "Livingness Repair," "Executive or Businessman's Intensive," and "Profession Intensive,"[59] among many others.

Eventually all of these myriad grades, levels, and courses would be organized into an elaborate road map of Scientology called "the Bridge to Total Freedom." This road map traces the trajectory of the Scientologist all the way from entry-level Dianetics courses up through the various grades leading to "Clear" and then up through the advanced OT levels. On the lowest rung of the bridge are beginning books and public films, followed by introductory services such as the Dianetics Route and the Anatomy of the Human Mind route. Above these are the various stages on the way leading up to the state of "Clear," including the Purification Rundown, Happiness Rundown, Grades 0–IV, New Era Dianetics, Expanded Dianetics, and Clear Certainty Rundown. Then, above Clear, there is the Sunshine Rundown, the OT Preparations, and finally the fifteen OT levels (only eight of which have thus far been released).[60] Working one's way up the bridge can take a good deal of time, depending on one's personal situation (and finances, as we will see later). In Cincinnati, for example, I interviewed a Scientologist who had been involved in the church for more than eleven years and was not even yet a third of the way to "Clear." Other individuals, however, appear to move up the bridge a bit more quickly. John Travolta, who was introduced to Dianetics in 1975, reached the "wall of fire," OT III, by 1991, while actor Jason Beghe reached OT V after fourteen years in the church.[61]

Not surprisingly, the most expensive training takes place in the OT grades, where one learns the most confidential "advanced tech." Shortly after their release in the late 1960s, the OT grades ranged from $75 for OT I up to $875 for the more advanced OT III and V.[62] But by the 1990s, these prices had increased to thousands and tens of thousands of dollars. According to a 2009 price list from the Flag Service Organization in Clearwater (where the highest OT grades are offered), auditing below level OT III ranges from $6,800 (per 12.5 hours at the 20 percent discount for International Association of Scientologists members) up to $56,100 (per 150 hours at a 45 percent discount). Auditing above OT III ranges from $7,800 (per 12.5 hours at a 20 percent discount) to $64,350 (per 150 hours at a 45 percent discount). Then the prices for the actual OT grades themselves run as follows:

OT Preparations and Eligibility: $6,800 per 12.5 hours
New OT I: $2,800
OT II: $5,000
OT III: $8,400

Fort Harrison Hotel, Clearwater, FL. Photo by author

New OT IV $7,800 (per 12.5 hours)
New OT V: $7,800 (per 12.5 hours)
New OT VI: $13,600
New OT VII: $2,800
New OT VII eligibility: $7,800 (per 12.5 hours)

Meanwhile, accommodations at the Flag's Fort Harrison Hotel range from $150 a night for a basic room up to $15,000 for the presidential suite, with packages as long as twenty-six weeks ranging from $19,100 up to $191,100.[63]

The total costs to complete OT training will vary depending on the amount of auditing an individual Scientologist requires to get through each level. However, conservative estimates suggest that rising to OT VIII would require a minimum of $300,000 to $400,000.[64] And that is without including the various other courses, books, and materials offered, such as the latest model E-meter (the Mark Super VII Quantum, $4,650) or various texts, recordings, and DVDs ranging in price from several hundred to several thousand dollars.[65]

Readers are probably wondering at this point: where does all the money go, and how wealthy is the Church of Scientology today? Because, as we will see in chapter 5, the church won its battle for tax-exempt status in 1993, that question is now one that only the most senior church accountants and executives can answer. As of 1993, the last year the church had to declare income, the assets of the worldwide church were $398 million, while the amount it earned in that year alone from investments, counseling fees, and book sales totaled $300 million.[66] Even without detailed public records, one can surmise that the church's assets and earnings since 1993 as a tax-exempt religious entity have probably increased substantially.

Not surprisingly, critics of the church have decried these large amounts of money as clear evidence that Scientology is not a religion at all but essentially a for-profit business—and a very successful business at that. As Nancy Many recounts in her memoir, the costs of even the lower levels of Scientology auditing had grown beyond the reach of most middle-class individuals, making it seem less to her like a "religion" than a service for the wealthy few who could afford it: "Because of the prices, it seemed more of an elitist group rather than one that was working to help all mankind."[67] However, as actor and former Scientologist Jason Beghe suggests, one of the main reasons for the expense of Scientology may be precisely because the high cost also adds to its *perceived* value. After all, if someone is paying tens of thousands of dollars to learn the secrets behind the wall of fire, that person has a strong incentive to believe they are extremely valuable: "[T]hat's part of the reason Scientology is expensive, you know. Well, if you're paying a lot of money for it, it makes it more valuable."[68]

The Church of Scientology, conversely, argues that these fees are simply the same sort of "donations" that any church accepts in return for basic spiritual services and by no means contradict its claims to religious status. Surely Scientology is not alone in accepting money from its parishioners—if anything, Scientology looks like a fairly modest operation when compared with Christian televangelist empires like those of Pat Robertson, Rod Parsley, or Joel Osteen.

Whether we view it sympathetically or critically, however, Scientology does appear to have emerged as a unique fusion of religious movement and transnational corporation. As legal scholars N. Passass and M. E. Castillo observe in their study of Scientology's commercial activities, the church does operate in many ways as a commercial enterprise, even as it legally claims to be a religion, not a business. As such, Scientology is perhaps better described as a kind of "deviant business," one whose commercial success ironically *depends on its very claim that it is not commercial*: "Irrespective of its 'real' motives," Passass and Castillo argue, the church "operates as a commercial enterprise"; however, "because it became a religion, a non-profit organization that had to be officially recognized as such . . . much of its success is due to its successful claim that it is not a business. In this respect, the [church] is a deviant business, which has to remain that way. This explains to a large extent why [the church] has been fighting major legal battles around the world to preserve its religious status."[69]

Yet if this ironic status as a "business that is not a business" has often worked to the church's financial advantage, it has also clearly worked to its disadvantage in terms of its public image and media coverage. While many mainstream Christian Evangelical churches bring in billions of dollars without much media scrutiny, Scientology has been perhaps indelibly labeled "the cult of greed" and still today struggles to rebrand itself as a legitimate religion.

The Messianic Project: Marketing a New Messiah?

Surely one of the most remarkable and controversial chapters in the Scientology story is a secret program allegedly devised by Hubbard in the late 1970s known as the "Messianic Project." The details of the program are not well known and have never been confirmed by anyone but a few ex-Scientologists. However, based on what little is known, it is not difficult to see how this story would feed into the popular image of Scientology as a "cult."

The fullest account of the Messianic Project publicly available today is Nancy Many's description in *My Billion Year Contract*. In the late 1970s, Many claims, she was assigned to work on a series of questionnaires ordered by Hubbard called the "Messianic Surveys." The aim of the surveys was to try to identify exactly what it was that people wanted in a good messiah and then, still more audaciously, to *market* Hubbard as just that kind of messianic figure. The goal, she writes, was precisely "to create the image of L. Ron Hubbard as the next messiah, like Christ, Mohammed or Buddha. . . . [T]he direction Hubbard wanted to go with the organization was that of his being the next spiritual messiah, the next savior of mankind."[70] The surveys were supposed to have identified nine key features that people most associated with the spiritual qualities of a messiah (such as honesty, humanitarianism, justice, happiness, and so on); and based on these features, the plan was to then launch an "aggressive campaign that would create L. Ron Hubbard's messianic image across the world." As Many concludes, "Hubbard truly did believe he was as great as Jesus, Buddha and Mohammed. . . . [H]e also had plans and programs in place and in motion to create that image of himself in the world."[71] The plan to promote the new messiah was in fact inspired by influential new research in advertising, such as the revolutionary idea of "positioning" by marketing gurus Al Ries and Jack Trout. Just as an advertising firm could "position" a product such as Coca-Cola in a consumer's mind, so too, the Messianic Project aimed to position Hubbard in the minds of spiritual seekers as the ideal messiah.[72]

For reasons that are not entirely clear, the Messianic Project apparently never went very far and seems to have been dropped by the early 1980s. To this day, however, it remains highly secretive, and most ex-Scientologists I have interviewed are extremely reluctant to talk about it or let it be known that they had any association with the project.

"The Cult of Personality": Project Celebrity and Scientology in Hollywood

While many aspects of Scientology (such as the alleged Messianic Project) are highly secretive, the church also has a much more visible public face. Indeed, probably the one thing most Americans *do* know about Scientology is its long list of very high-profile celebrity spokespersons. Scientology's list of supporters in the entertainment, film, music, and artistic communities is more than impressive, including the likes of Tom Cruise, John Travolta, Kirstie Alley, Isaac Hayes, Chick Corea, Nancy Cartwright, and numerous others. The names of most of these individuals are displayed prominently in Scientology publications, such as its current website, which features glowing testimonials about the impact of the church on their lives and careers.

This connection between Scientology and celebrities, however, is neither accidental nor particularly surprising. First, one can easily see why the basic philosophy of Scientology would be appealing to actors in particular. For Scientology promises nothing less than to unleash the unlimited power of the individual, to liberate the infinite potential of the thetan, indeed, to awaken the ability to *create one's own universe*. If the idea of creating one's own reality was appealing to the science fiction readers of the 1950s, it was perhaps even more appealing to actors, musicians, and artists hoping to unleash their own creative potential. Secondly, of course, there is the money involved. Not everyone can easily spend $400,000 to move up the OT levels, but to a Tom Cruise or John Travolta, that amount of money is probably trivial.

Finally and perhaps most important, from mid-1950s on, Hubbard explicitly targeted celebrities as potential converts and instructed Scientologists to court them. This effort was announced as early as 1955 in *Ability* magazine under the title "Project Celebrity." The article identifies a list of famous celebrities, including Edward R. Murrow, Ed Sullivan, Orson Welles, Ernest Hemingway, Liberace, Jackie Gleason, Vincent Price, Leopold Stokowski, Cecil B. DeMille, Greta Garbo, Bob Hope, Groucho Marx, and even Billy Graham(!). All of these celebrities are labeled "quarry" to be "hunted" as "game" by ambitious Scientologists. Hubbard warns that "these celebrities are well guarded, well barricaded, aloof quarry," but he promises that "if you bring them home, you will get a small plaque as your reward."[73]

While Hubbard does not appear to have snared any of these particular quarry, the church did succeeded in attracting a number of other celebrities from the late 1960s onward. The first Scientology "Celebrity Centre" was established in Los Angeles in 1969, and was followed by similar centers in New York, San Francisco, Boston, Toronto, and other major cities. Perhaps the most famous and opulent of these is a massive 1920s Hollywood manor, originally dubbed the Chateau Elysée. As the church describes its Celebrity Centres, they are designed to aid those few individuals at the forefront of the world's creative, artistic, political, and business advances—the elite men and women who have the vision to make the world a better place but who also suffer the attacks of the media and the uninformed public:

> Hubbard once said, "The world is carried on the backs of a desperate few." Unfortunately, it is these desperate few who are often the most neglected. It is for this reason that L. Ron Hubbard saw to the formation of a special Church of Scientology which would cater to these individuals—the artists, politicians, leaders of industry, sports figures and anyone with the power and vision to create a better world. That Church is Celebrity Centre International.[74]

Skeptics and critics of the church, however, suggest that the aim of the Celebrity Centres has less to do with bettering the world than with advertising the church and raking in large amounts of money from wealthy patrons. As former senior Scientologists such as Robert Vaughn Young have argued, the goal was primarily "to get celebrities active, to convince them to hustle and promote Scientology."[75] Other critics claim that celebrities are basically "manipulated by the fiercely doctrinaire religion," which, "like an octopus," takes over their lives and exploits their fame to its advantage.[76]

In any case, the money and publicity provided by Scientology's celebrity patrons have clearly been of enormous help to the church. Not surprisingly, Scientology's most rapid period of expansion in the 1970s and 80s closely corresponds to the flourishing of the Celebrity Centres during these two decades. And still today, celebrities continue to donate impressive amounts to the church. According to the *New York Post*, Scientology's *Impact* magazine reported that a number of celebrities made large donations to the church in 2007 as part of its "Global Salvage" effort designed to "de-abberrate Earth." Topping the list of donors was Nancy Cartwright (voice of Bart Simpson), who donated $10 million, followed by Tom Cruise and Kirstie Alley at $5 million each, John Travolta and Kelly Preston at $1 million each, and Priscilla Presley at $50,000.[77]

Among Scientology's most dedicated celebrity patrons is Tom Cruise, who first became involved with the church in 1986 through fellow actress and future wife, Mimi Rogers. Although Cruise would divorce Rogers just a few years later, he quickly became Scientology's most outspoken

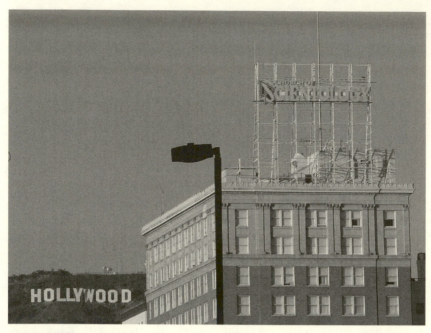

Church of Scientology International with "Hollywood" sign in the background. Photo by author

Scientology Celebrity Centre, Hollywood, CA. Photo by author

and controversial supporter. Among others things, Cruise claims that Hubbard's technology helped him overcome dyslexia and that Narconon is the only successful drug rehabilitation program in the world.[78] A great many rumors surround Cruise's involvement in the church, such as Andrew Morton's allegation that Cruise is in fact Scientology's "second in command in all but name" and that the celebrity has largely financed the church's new Ideal Orgs being planned and built since 2000.[79] Whether or not these rumors are true, Cruise has been a tremendously important spokesman for the church. As we will see in chapter 6, for example, he was featured in a confidential and highly controversial promotional video for Scientologists that was leaked to YouTube in 2008.

After Cruise, Scientology's most prominent celebrity spokesman is John Travolta, who was first introduced to Dianetics in 1975 while working on his first film. According to his own testimony, it was because of Hubbard's technology that he landed a leading role on the sitcom *Welcome Back Kotter* and had a string of successful films: "I have been a successful actor for more than twenty years and Scientology has played a major role in that success. I have a wonderful child and a great marriage because I apply L. Ron Hubbard's technology to this area of my life. . . . Scientology put me into the big time."[80] The church, in turn, has recognized Travolta's work for Scientology, and, as early as 1978, presented him with a "Service Award" for his "major contributions in the dissemination of Dianetics and Scientology."[81]

Perhaps the greatest sign of Travolta's dedication to the church, however, was his close involvement in making the film version of Hubbard's epic science fiction saga, *Battlefield Earth*. For a variety of reasons—including its projected expense, the plot, and its ties to Scientology—major Hollywood studios were unwilling to take on the project, despite Travolta's enthusiasm. As one studio executive put it, "On any film there are ten variables that can kill you. On this film there was an eleventh: Scientology. It just wasn't something anyone really wanted to get involved with." The film was finally taken on by an independent production company, Franchise Pictures, which specializes in rescuing stars' pet projects. Released in May 2000, the film was almost universally panned and widely regarded as one of the worst movies ever made. As film critic Roger Ebert put it, the movie is not just bad but "something

Tom Cruise speaking at a Scientology event. Getty Images

historic, a film that for decades to come will be the punch line of jokes about bad movies"; sitting through it, he laments, is "like taking a bus trip with someone who has needed a bath for a long time. It's not merely bad; it's unpleasant in a hostile way."[82] Ebert's was actually among the more generous reviews of the film, which appears to have inspired almost a competition among critics to write the most colorful and devastating reviews possible.

Much debate has ensued as to whether and to what degree Scientology beliefs played a role overtly or perhaps even subliminally within the film. *Battlefield Earth* was released just three days after the fiftieth anniversary of the publication of *Dianetics*, a major holiday for Scientology, which many believe is not accidental. Hubbard's story is set on Earth in the year 3000, after it has been ruled by a brutal race of aliens called the Psychlos. What remains of the human race has either been enslaved by the Psychlos or live in small tribes outside the Psychlos's power. Terl (played by Travolta) is a Psychlos security chief who has been condemned to an indefinite post on Earth. Meanwhile, a human hero named Jonnie Goodboy Tyler leads a rebel uprising against Psychlos rule. Various observers have suggested that the domineering "Psychlos" appear to be a reference to psychiatry, a longtime enemy of Scientology; and the struggle between the rebel forces and the Psychlos for the freedom of Earth is reminiscent of Scientology's claim to be fighting for the freedom for the planet against destructive forces such as psychoanalysis.[83]

Regardless of the direct influence of Scientology in the film, the narrative is in perfect keeping with the larger "space opera" themes that run continuously from Hubbard's early science fiction through his early Scientology lectures and the OT III materials. Moreover, the fact that an actor as successful as Travolta was willing to stake his reputation on such an unmitigated commercial failure is striking evidence of his unusual dedication to this movement.

"Scientology Is Evil": Government, Media, and Anticult Attacks on the Church in the 1970s And 80s

Scientology's period of rapid growth and prosperity from the late 1960s to the early 1980s also corresponded—not surprisingly—with the most intense scrutiny and criticism of the church by an array of government, media, and anticult sources. Various governmental investigations had already begun in the 1960s, including one of the most damning reports by Kevin Victor Anderson for the state of Victoria, Australia, in 1965. In the most severe and uncompromising terms, Anderson's report condemned Scientology as a frankly evil and dangerous organization:

> There are some features of Scientology which are so ludicrous that there may be a tendency to regard Scientology as silly and its practitioners as harmless cranks. To do so would be gravely to misunderstand the tenor of the Board's conclusions. . . . Scientology is evil; its techniques evil; its practice a serious threat to the community, medically, morally and socially; and its adherents sadly deluded and often mentally ill.[84]

At times, Anderson seems to be almost groping for appropriately colorful adjectives to express his outright revulsion at the practices of this dangerous and degenerate organization:

> If there should be detected in this Report a note of unrelieved denunciation of scientology, it is because the evidence has shown its theories to be fantastic and impossible, its principles perverted and ill-founded, and its techniques debased and harmful. Scientology is a delusional belief system, based on fiction and fallacies and propagated by falsehood and deception. . . . [I]t employs techniques which further its real purpose of securing domination over and mental enslavement of its adherents. It involves the administration by persons without any training in medicine or psychology of quasi-psychological treatment, which is harmful medically, morally and socially.
>
> Its founder, with the merest smattering of knowledge in various sciences, has built upon the scintilla of his learning a crazy and dangerous edifice.[85]

In sum, Anderson concluded, "it is quite clear" that Scientology "does not remotely resemble anything even vaguely religious" but is in fact a sinister cult.[86]

Two decades later, the church was subjected to an equally merciless judgment by a British justice, John Latey. In this case the justice ruled against awarding custody of two children to their father, a member of

Scientology. Latey's language in delivering the decision is even more colorful than Foster's, flatly rejecting the suggestion that Scientology is any form of religion and instead dubbing it an insidious cult that lacks even the slightest redeeming quality:

Mr. Hubbard is a charlatan and worse as are his wife Mary Sue Hubbard . . . and the clique at the top privy to the Cult's activities. In blunt language "auditing" is a process of conditioning, brainwashing and indoctrination.

Scientology is both immoral and socially obnoxious. . . . It is corrupt because it is based on lies and deceit and has as its real objective money and power. . . . It is sinister because it indulges in infamous practices both to its adherents who do not toe the line unquestioningly and to those outside who criticise or oppose it. It is dangerous because it is out to capture people, especially children and impressionable young people, and indoctrinate and brainwash them so that they become the unquestioning captives and tools of the cult. . . .

"A religion"
Scientology approached a large number of theologians and other savants on the question whether Scientology is a religion. . . . Their purpose was to try to obtain acknowledgment that Scientology was a "religion" within the meaning of certain fiscal enactments and so obtain tax immunity. . . .

I have searched and searched carefully for anything good, some redeeming feature, in Scientology. I can find nothing.[87]

Although never subjected to a governmental report in the United States like the Anderson and Foster enquiries, Scientology came under perhaps even more severe criticism by the American media and anticult groups during these decades. Already in November 1968—just seven months before the Manson murders of 1969—*Life* magazine published a damning article entitled "Scientology: a Growing Cult Reaches Dangerously into the Mind."[88] But perhaps the most scathing media account came from Richard Behar in his 1991 cover story for *Time* magazine, entitled simply "The Cult of Greed." With a cover image featuring the volcano from the cover of *Dianetics* with sinister octopus tentacles, the *Time* story offers a merciless critique of the church as a vicious engine of profit and domination. Behar concludes his critique by dismissing

Scientology's claims to "religious" status, suggesting that this is little more than a ploy to distract its real agenda, which is simply greed: "One of Scientology's main strategies is to keep advancing the tired argument that the church is being 'persecuted' by antireligionists. . . . But in the end, money is what Scientology is all about. As long as the organization's opponents and victims are successfully squelched, Scientology's managers and lawyers will keep pocketing millions of dollars by helping it achieve its ends."[89] The *Time* magazine article was perhaps the most damning and visible condemnation of Scientology in the U.S. media up to that point and, not surprisingly, met with a powerful response from the church.

Scientology's Revenge: From the "Cult of All Cults" to the "New Cult Awareness Network"

As we saw in the introduction and in chapter 3, Hubbard was never one to take criticism lightly and had in fact written official policies—such as "fair game"—to respond to any external or internal threats. The church is today infamous for its use of numerous, simultaneous lawsuits and legal threats to challenge and silence its critics. As Hubbard himself put it in 1955, in the most uncompromising terms, "The purpose of the suit is to harass and discourage rather than to win. The law can be used very easily to harass, and enough harassment on somebody who is simply on the thin edge anyway . . . will generally be sufficient to cause his professional decease. If possible, of course, ruin him utterly."[90] The church would eventually bring hundreds of suits against its enemies and by the 1990s was paying an estimated $20 million annually to more than one hundred lawyers.[91] As Behar recounts his experience with Scientology during his research for the *Time* magazine article, he was assaulted by a frightening array of legal and extralegal persecution, including a swarm of lawyers and private detectives: "[A]t least ten attorneys and six private detectives were unleashed by Scientology and its followers in an effort to threaten, harass and discredit me. . . . A copy of my personal credit report—with detailed information about my bank accounts, home mortgage, credit-card payments, home address and Social Security numbers—had been illegally retrieved from a national credit bureau. . . .

[P]rivate investigators have been contacting acquaintances of mine . . . to inquire about subjects such as my health and whether I've ever had trouble with the IRS."[92] Following the publication of the article, Scientology brought a libel suit against Behar and Time Warner, seeking $416 million in damages.[93] Behar, meanwhile, brought his own countersuit against the church, claiming that the Church of Scientology had harassed him with private investigators. All counts of Scientology's suit were eventually dismissed by 1996, but not before Time Warner had spent $3.7 million in legal defense fees.

But surely one of the most remarkable chapters in the history of Scientology's complex road to religious status was its war with the Cult Awareness Network (CAN). As we saw in the quote from Cynthia Kisser in the epigraph to this chapter, CAN had targeted Scientology as the most dangerous, rapacious, and destructive cult in contemporary America, a vicious cult of greed whose primary aim is to extract money from its unfortunate followers. Not surprisingly, the church responded with equally aggressive rhetoric, accusing CAN of criminal activities of its own (such as the controversial anticult technique of "deprogramming") and comparing them with the Nazis and the KKK for the persecution of minority religions. Thus, a 1995 issue of the church's *Freedom* magazine labeled CAN simply as "the Serpent of Hatred, Intolerance, Violence and Death."[94] In the words of Heber Jentzsch, president of the Church of Scientology International, CAN was guilty of "[k]idnapping people, holding them against their will, beating up on people, pistol whipping, safe houses where they hold people against their will, rape of their victims, that sort of thing." As such, the world is better off without such an intolerant, defamatory group: "[I]f you're a Jew, no . . . no Jew is going to cry about the fact that the Nazi Party is gone. If you're an African-American, no one is going to cry that the KKK is gone. . . . They were a vicious group."[95]

Scientology's response to CAN went far beyond strong rhetoric, however. Indeed, the church bombarded CAN with more than fifty lawsuits and launched an aggressive plan to undermine and discredit the network. By 1993, CAN was paying $10,000 a month in legal bills.[96] In the words of former Scientologist Stacy Young, a staff member assigned to CAN, "[O]ur whole orientation was, well, what have you done this week to get rid of CAN, and how, how well have you done to discredit the leaders of CAN? How much progress have you made on disrupting this group?"[97] Other former Scientologists have testified that the attacks on CAN went further still. According to Garry Scarff's testimony from 1994, Scientology had not only launched an array of frivolous lawsuits against CAN, but Scarff himself was personally instructed to kill CAN's head: "I was directed, one, to go to Chicago, Illinois and to murder Cynthia Kisser . . . the Executive Director of the Cult Awareness Network, by a staged car accident."[98]

Finally, in 1996, CAN was forced into bankruptcy. The final blow was the result of a lawsuit by Jason Scott, a member of the Pentecostal "Life Tabernacle Church," who had been forcibly kidnapped and subjected to the controversial technique of "deprogamming" by Rick Ross, a CAN-referred activist. Scott's lawyer in the case was Kendrick Moxon, a prominent Scientology official and lawyer. Moxon, we should note, was also one of the Scientologists named as an unindicted coconspirator after the FBI's investigation of the infamous "Snow White" operation.[99] Scott himself later claimed that he had been manipulated by the Church of Scientology as part of its "vendetta against CAN"; as Scott's mother told the *Chicago Tribune*, "Jason said he was tired of being the poster boy for the Scientologists. . . . When he was approached by Moxon, he was lured by his promises of a $1 million settlement, so he went for it."[100]

The Scott case brought about the end of CAN and marked a significant turning point in the anticult movement in the United States. The final irony, however, took place in bankruptcy court in 1996, as CAN's logo, furniture, and phone number were auctioned off. The individual who arrived to buy the rights to CAN's name, logo, and hotline number was Stephen Hayes, a Scientologist, who outbid Cynthia Kisser herself and won what remained of CAN's assets for $20,000. And perhaps an even more bizarre twist occurred when Scott sold his $1.875 million settlement to Gerry Beany—also a Scientologist and represented by Moxon—for $25,000, making Beany CAN's largest creditor. CAN then reluctantly reached a settlement by agreeing to turn over all of its extensive files and records to Beany, who in turn donated them to "the Foundation for Religious Freedom." This foundation is, not surprisingly, owned by the Church of Scientology. In the words of Ed Lottick, the former director of CAN, "We're talking about a strategic conspiracy of grand proportions, an unabashed tragedy. And now that they've got the files, God only knows the havoc they'll wreak."[101]

Thus, in one of the most remarkable turnabouts in American religious history, the alleged "cult of all cults" became the owner of the Cult Awareness Network (now relabeled New CAN). Today, New CAN continues to function as a source of information on new religions and alternative spiritual movements, but it is, effectively, another entity in the complex network that is the Church of Scientology. As David Bardin, an attorney who represented the Cult Awareness Network, put it, "It kind of boggles the mind. People will still pick up the CAN name in a library book and call saying, 'My daughter has joined the Church of Scientology.' And your friendly CAN receptionist is someone who works for Scientology."[102]

From the perspective of "New CAN," however, the reformed movement is in fact an advocate of religious tolerance and freedom that is undoing the negative biases of anticult groups like the old CAN. Whereas previous anticult groups warned about brainwashing and psycho-cults, New CAN presents itself as a vehicle for accurate information that dispels myths and offers reasoned discussion. According to New CAN's website, "The word cult has too often been twisted into a hate word labeling and marginalizing any group the person using the word doesn't like. . . . The New Cult Awareness Network is using the name to get out factual information about many groups. . . . We try to get people to calm down and respect each other's religious beliefs no matter what their own opinion might be of those beliefs."[103] Even some scholars of new religions have praised New CAN as a positive alternative to the old CAN. As Anson Shupe and Susan E. Darnell argue, New CAN offers a "legitimate clearing house of information" on unconventional religious groups that seeks "dialogue and increasing moderation" rather than "coercive deprogramming."[104]

Here we find one of the most remarkable twists in the long debate over "religion" and its various definitions that we have been tracing in this book: not only has Scientology claimed itself to be a legitimate religion, but it now owns one of the major "cult" networks that has been a

key voice in the debate over the very definition of "religion" in the
United States.

Conclusions: Rethinking the "Cult Wars" Today

In sum, the "cult of all cults" became a key part of the ongoing process
of imagining and reimagining religion in the United States during the
1970s, 80s, and 90s. With the demise of the old CAN and the discrediting of deprogrammers such as Rick Ross, much of the "cult war" in the
United States also came to an end. While widely used during the 1970s
and 80s, the term "cult" fell largely out of favor with most American
scholars of religion by the 1990s and was replaced by a new spirit of religious tolerance and defense of alternative spiritual groups.[105] As Bromley and Shupe argued in their work on the cult scares of the 1970s and
80s, the anticultists threaten to undermine the very foundations of a
pluralistic, tolerant, religious, diverse democracy, which can be preserved only by respecting controversial new movements such as Scientology: "The closer we as citizens move toward considering only the beliefs and practices of certain dominant, established segments of our
society as legitimate, the closer we move toward the destruction of democratic pluralism. Diversity, tolerance, and openness are not easily created and sustained, and democracy is a continuing quest."[106]

But all of this still leaves us with a question: if we agree that the term
"cult" is not useful and that a healthy, pluralistic democracy should celebrate the diversity of its many religious traditions, what then do we do
with a group as problematic as Scientology? We have seen in the preceding chapters ample evidence of illegal, unethical, and extremely disturbing activities undertaken by the church, at times bordering on the surreal. These actions are not merely those of a few rogue Scientologists,
but often directives from the very top of the organization, including
Hubbard himself, who left ample documentation of his fair game policies, RPFs, and "ethics." As we will see in the subsequent chapters, many
critics allege that these activities have continued up to the present time
under Scientology's current head, David Miscavige.[107] It seems no less
problematic to de-emphasize or gloss over these aspects of the church,
as much of the existing scholarship has often done.[108]

Again, I would like to argue for a more balanced approach, maintaining the dual perspective of a hermeneutics of respect and a hermeneutics of suspicion. Recognizing Scientology's rights under the First Amendment surely does not mean that we cannot *also* look critically at the disturbing policies and activities that have been a key part of the church's history for the last sixty years. But of course, this same spirit of respectful suspicion should not be reserved only for controversial new movements such as Scientology; indeed, it can and must also be applied equally to "mainstream" religious organizations as well. And it should be no less critically applied to the anticult groups, such as Rick Ross and the (old) CAN, who have at times engaged in disturbing activities of their own.

As Ivan Strenski has argued in his recent work on religion and politics, we need to move beyond the simplistic view that by calling something "religion" we mean that it is entirely "good" (or conversely, that religion is entirely "bad").[109] Adherents of mainstream religion no less than "cults" are capable of engaging in violent, criminal, and immoral acts. Moreover, even if Scientology's leadership from L. Ron Hubbard down to David Miscavige has engaged in extremely problematic activities, that still does not mean that thousands of ordinary practitioners do not find the church to be quite meaningfully "religious" in their own lives. After all, the fact that Catholic bishops have covered up child sexual abuse does not prevent millions of ordinary believers worldwide from continuing to find Catholicism meaningful in their daily lives.

Here I would suggest we follow Bruce Lincoln's definition of religion that we discussed in the introduction. Religion, in Lincoln's terms, is better understood not as a particular *thing* but rather as a *claim* to a special kind of authority and, specifically, a kind of authority that is believed to be suprahuman, transcendent, and eternal.[110] As such, religious discourse is uniquely powerful and can inspire acts of both great goodness and great evil: it can help lead movements of social justice (the civil rights movement, Gandhi's nonviolent resistance against British colonial rule, Mother Teresa's campaign to help the poor, etc.); but it can also be used to legitimate acts of violence and terror (flying airplanes into skyscrapers, justifying preemptive wars, covering over cases of pedophilia, etc.). So by taking controversial groups such as Scientology seriously as "religions" rather than branding them as "cults," we are not thereby glossing over their negative, darker, or illegal aspects. Rather, we are simply saying: *they are quite as capable of exploiting their claims to religious authority as adherents of any "mainstream" religion.*

In this sense, a balanced, respectful, yet also rigorously critical study of a movement as controversial as Scientology can serve as the model for a more nuanced, complex, and critical study of religion in the twenty-first century.

- FIVE -

"THE WAR" AND THE TRIUMPH OF SCIENTOLOGY
Becoming a Tax-Exempt Religion in the 1990s

> While fighting a cold front with Communists the US is violently
> co-operating with Communist aims by destroying her individual
> confidence and initiative with a Marxist tax reform. The basic principles
> of US income tax were taken from "Das Kapital" and are aimed at
> destroying capitalism. Unless the US ceases to co-operate with this Red
> push, Communism could win in America.
> —L. Ron Hubbard, "Income Tax Reform" (1959)[1]

> It has made a business out of selling religion; it has diverted millions of
> dollars through a bogus trust fund and a sham corporation to key
> Scientology officials; and it has conspired for almost a decade to defraud
> the United States Government by impeding the IRS from determining
> and collecting taxes from it and affiliated churches.
> —Judge Samuel Sterrett, *Church of Scientology of California v.*
> *Commissioner of Internal Revenue Service* (1984)[2]

> On October first, 1993, at 8:37 p.m. Eastern Standard Time, the IRS
> issued letters recognizing Scientology and every one of its organizations
> as fully tax exempt! The war is over!
> —David Miscavige (1993)[3]

The debate over Scientology's status as a "cult" or a legitimate "religion"
is far more than an academic exercise or fodder for sensationalistic jour-
nalism. It is also a question with extremely complicated legal, constitutional, and financial implications. On the one hand, it is a question of
money—indeed, as we saw in the previous chapter, often very, very large

amounts of money—that became an issue particularly during the church's period of rapid growth during the 1970s.[4]

But on the other hand, it is also a question with profound implications regarding the free exercise and establishment clauses of the First Amendment. As Bruce Hopkins points out in his comprehensive study of the law of tax exemption, government agencies and the courts have generally been reluctant to define the terms "religion" or "religious organizations." Indeed, "by reason of the religion clause of the First Amendment, it would be unconstitutional for the federal government to adopt and apply a strict definition of these terms," since any fixed definition would inevitably exclude the beliefs and practices of some faith communities.[5] As the Supreme Court acknowledged as early as 1878 in its discussion of Mormonism, "The word 'religion' is not defined in the Constitution. We must go elsewhere, therefore, to ascertain its meaning."[6] The United States does not register religious groups and has no official hierarchy of religious organizations. And yet, federal income tax law *does* provide exemption for religious organizations, and, therefore, there must be *some* means to determine whether a group claiming to be religious is "genuine" for purposes of tax-exempt status. Ironically, this means that "perhaps the most important decision made on this question in America is that of the tax authorities."[7]

Even the IRS, however, has no fixed, standard definition of a "church" that it uses in tax-exemption requests. As Hopkins notes, "[J]ust as is the case with respect to the term *religious* there is no definition in the Internal Revenue Code or in a currently applicable tax regulation of the term *church*. Again, a rigidly regulatory definition of the term *church* would undoubtedly be unconstitutional."[8] The closest it has is a set of rough criteria and thirteen points common to "religions," which were made public in 1977[9] (the same year, we should note, that the Church of Scientology was investigated by the FBI for infiltrating IRS offices in Washington, DC). But even with the publication of these guidelines, the IRS was careful to say that these are not fixed or absolute criteria but merely general prescriptions. Thus, for the IRS itself, the determination of what is and is not a legitimate "religion" remains a complex, conflicted, and contested one.

Not surprisingly, then, Scientology's greatest battle in the twentieth century has been waged not against the anticult groups or the media but against the Internal Revenue Service. Although the church had been granted tax-exempt status in 1956, that status was revoked in 1967 after an intensive auditing process. What followed was a twenty-six-year war between the church and the IRS that involved literally thousands of lawsuits and an array of illegal activities, as GO operatives infiltrated IRS and other federal offices through an incredibly audacious program of espionage.[10] Indeed, the story of Scientology's war with the IRS could easily serve as the basis for a thriller movie screenplay.

Interestingly enough, in response to the new challenges from the IRS, Hubbard himself began to explicitly invoke the language of the First Amendment and freedom of religious expression in his defense of Scientology. Thus on February 5, 1969, he issued a policy letter entitled "Press Policy: Code of a Scientologist," clearly indicating that its contents were a matter of public image for the church. This revised Code of a Scientologist explicitly emphasizes First Amendment concerns, stating that the Scientologist vows "[t]o work for freedom of speech in the world" and "to support the freedom of religion."[11] Hubbard, in short, was self-consciously pitting the First Amendment against any government agencies such as the IRS (and before them, the FDA) who might challenge the rights and benefits claimed by Scientology. Hubbard's successor, David Miscavige, has made no less explicit invocations of the First Amendment to defend the church and its claims to tax exemption.

At the same time, the church also began even more self-consciously to adopt the outward appearance of a religion, and specifically a sort of vaguely "Christian"-looking one. As we saw in chapter 2, the adoption of religious garb began in the 1950s during Scientology's conflicts with the FDA and its incorporation as a church with a range of more recognizably spiritual beliefs. However, as various former Scientologists have recalled in interviews and in print, this religious image was, in reality, only sporadically if ever put into practice prior to the late 1960s and 70s. As former OSA officer Nancy Many recounts in her recent memoir, Scientology still largely appeared to be a secular therapy and science of the mind until the early 1970s.[12] In the face of its new conflict with the IRS, however, Scientology undertook what the *Los Angeles Times* called its "most sweeping religious make-over," as Hubbard began to deliver quite blunt and explicit directives that "visual evidences that Scientology is a religion are mandatory."[13] As Scientology franchises officially became "missions" and display of clerical collars and crosses became strictly enforced, the "religion angle" was pursued in a far more intensive way. Even so, it would take another two and a half decades and millions of dollars in legal fees before the IRS finally accepted this religious makeover as sincere.

As such, the case of Scientology raises profound questions regarding freedom of religious expression and the very principle of tax exemption. Critics of Scientology have long argued that Hubbard (like other wealthy religious leaders) has simply exploited the convenient tax-exempt loophole to his and the church's lucrative advantage. Defenders of the church and many academic observers, meanwhile, have argued that this is really a fundamental question of religious freedom and that to strip Scientology of tax-exempt status would be an act of intolerance that threatens the very core of the First Amendment.[14] Perhaps the deeper and more profound question in all of this, however, is *why have the IRS and tax-exempt status*—rather than some other authority or criterion—*become the litmus test for "religious status" in the United States*? Scientology's war, in other words, raises a much more fundamental question about exactly how and why "religion" has been legally and bureaucratically defined in this country.

"The War": Scientology v. the Internal Revenue Service

The history of Scientology's quest for tax-exempt status is a long and confusing one—indeed, a labyrinthine and often bewildering story that at times defies the imagination. This history is surely worthy of a book or even a detective novel of its own, but I will do my best to summarize it briefly here. As we saw in chapter 2, the new Scientology organization—or rather the shifting, overlapping network of organizations—was first created in 1952 after the fragmentation of Dianetics and the founding of the Hubbard Association of Scientologists (HAS), an apparently secular organization; this was followed in December 1953 by the incorporation of three "churches," the Church of Scientology, the Church of American Science, and the Church of Spiritual Engineering; and these churches in turn came under the umbrella of the newly renamed HASI, now defined as a "religious fellowship." Various churches then proliferated across the country, among them a church in California, which was founded in February 1954 and changed its name to the "Church of Scientology of California" (CSC) in 1956—a name it holds to this day. Initially, the new Scientology churches had little difficulty obtaining tax-exempt status. Thus, in 1956 the Washington, DC, church was recognized as tax-exempt, and other churches soon followed suit, including the CSC in 1957. Even then, however, Hubbard made it clear that one of the primary reasons for the insistence upon things such as "ministerial ordinations" and "ministerial qualifications" was a matter of tax exemption. As he wrote quite frankly in a policy letter of March 1957, "All Ministerial Ordinations of the Church must be in full force for the current year before Income Tax Provisions can be claimed."[15]

Just a year later, however, in 1958, the IRS sent the Washington church a letter withdrawing its tax-exempt status. Apparently, the service decided that the "tenets set forth in the books of L. Ron Hubbard, and related instruments of instruction relative to 'Scientology' in training courses, clinical courses and otherwise" did not constitute an exclusively religious or educational activity.[16] When the church in turn appealed to the U.S. Court of Claims, the court ruled that exempt status was rightly withdrawn because Hubbard and his wife were benefiting financially from the Church of Scientology beyond reasonable remuneration. Hubbard, the court found, had been given $108,000 by the church between 1955 and 1959, along with a car, while his family withdrew thousands of dollars from church funds. In short, Scientology was found to be a "business, a profit-making organization, run by Hubbard for his personal enrichment."[17]

Clearly upset by this decision, Hubbard issued a bulletin on July 18, 1959, entitled simply "Income Tax Reform," instructing Scientologists to forward a critique of the income tax system to their local news outlets and politicians. In it, he compares the U.S. income tax system to Communism and warns that it threatens to undermine the very fabric of American government, economics and culture:

> Please write the enclosed letter to (1) your leading local paper, and (2) your representatives in Congress. . . .

There comes a time in the history of a country when tax collection activities become a disease that its economy cannot bear. Such a disease is ordinarily heralded by revolt, inflation, or financial collapse. The primary source of disintegration in all governments, whether ancient Egypt or modern America is tax voracity or abuses.

While fighting a cold front with Communists the US is violently cooperating with Communist aims by destroying her individual confidence and initiative with a Marxist tax reform. The basic principles of US income tax were taken from "Das Kapital" and are aimed at destroying capitalism. Unless the US ceases to co-operate with this Red push, Communism could win in America.[18]

From the early 1960s, Hubbard was also fairly clear about the fact that he hoped to use the "religion angle" not simply to evade the scrutiny of the FDA and various medical boards, but also to find a tax-exempt home for his multiple Scientology organizations. He states this quite frankly in a 1962 policy letter entitled "Religion." Here Hubbard makes it clear that he hoped to shift all of Scientology's worldwide entities under the umbrella of a single tax-exempt, nonprofit "church." However, he also notes that such transfer would be *purely bureaucratic and financial* and would mean no substantive changes to the usual activities of Scientology:

> For information of the London and Commonwealth offices, they will soon be transferred to Church status when the Founding Church of Washington DC is given full tax exemption, and HASI Ltd. and HCO Ltd. shares will be converted to equally valuable Church certificates.
>
> Scientology 1970 is being planned on a religious organization basis throughout the world.
>
> This will not in any way upset the usual activities of any organization. It is entirely a matter for accountants and solicitors.[19]

However, Hubbard's plan to shift all of Scientology's various organizations under a single tax-exempt umbrella remained unfulfilled until 1966. While facing increasing skepticism and pressure from governments in the United States, the United Kingdom, South Africa, and Australia, Hubbard apparently realized that he still had a remaining tax-exempt haven in the hitherto minor CSC, which had been given 501 c (3) status in 1957 and had apparently flown under IRS radar to this point. As he explained in a detailed Hubbard Communications Office executive letter entitled "Corporate Status" from March 1966, Hubbard therefore decided to transfer all of HASI's worldwide assets to the CSC, thus getting around these bureaucratic obstacles and shielding the church from government scrutiny. By placing them under the tax-exempt CSC, he could bypass all his other bureaucratic headaches in the United Kingdom and other countries where their tax-exemption was still in question. This revealing letter was quoted in full in Sir John Foster's 1971 report, "Enquiry into the Practice and Effects of Scientology," and makes it clear that Hubbard is well aware of the benefits and privileges that come along with being labeled a "religion" rather than a secular enterprise: "Finally, in January of 1966 while handling another lot of stupidity by Inland Revenue and UK accountants, I was able to sort out the picture. The Church of Scientology of California was willing to take over all US, Commonwealth and South African interests. It is a Federal certified US non-profit corporation and Inland Revenue will apparently accept its certificate." Hubbard concludes by noting that the church's religious status will protect it from government intervention and tax collectors alike: "And good news! As all auditors will be ministers, ministers have in many places special privileges including tax and housing allowances. Of course anything is a religion that treats the human spirit. And also Parliaments don't attack religions."[20]

Hubbard's ingenious move to shift all of Scientology's manifold finances under the CSC was only short-lived in its success, however. Just a year later, in 1967, the IRS decided to strip the CSC of its tax exemption along with all other related Scientology organizations. The Founding Church of Scientology in turn promptly sued, claiming to be exempt from federal income tax on the grounds that it was a corporation organized "exclusively for religious purposes."[21] Indeed, throughout the *Founding Church of Scientology v. United States* suit in 1969, the church relentlessly argued that Scientology should be tax exempt primarily because of its *religious* status. Significantly, however, the court concluded that Scientology's "religious" status was largely irrelevant. Whether or not it was a bona fide religion, Scientology's revenue was *still* primarily benefiting private individuals such as Hubbard and his family:

> [P]laintiff has failed to prove that no part of the corporation's net earnings inured to the benefit of private individuals. . . . The court finds it unnecessary to decide whether plaintiff is a religious or educational organization as alleged, since, regardless of its character, plaintiff has not met the statutory conditions for exemption from income taxation.[22]

The IRS, in turn, undertook a mammoth audit of the church for the years 1970 through 1974. And yet another decade of litigation ensued, as the church continued to challenge the agency's decision. As Judge Samuel Sterrett later summarized (and concurred with) the IRS's reasoning, the service's decision to strip the church's tax exemption had been based on three things—namely, "that the Church's activities were akin to a business, that it was serving the private interests of its members and not the public, and that its income inured to the benefit of Scientology practitioners."[23] Again, Scientology's attempt to have its financial cake and eat it too—by claiming to be a religion yet acting essentially like a for-profit corporation—had proved to be a mixed blessing. While enormously profitable in many ways, it had also led to enormous legal costs in its protracted battle with the IRS. As former OSA and Sea Org member Nancy Many recounts, even Hubbard himself had begun to question the logic of pursuing the "religion angle" and tax exemption, which had perhaps caused as many problems as it had seemingly resolved. Hubbard, she claims, began to wonder whether "going with the whole church angle for Scientology might have been a mistake in the first place. . . . [T]he trouble we were currently having with the IRS would not have existed if he had . . . stayed as a for-profit corporation and just made more money to pay the taxes."[24]

Reasserting the "Religion Angle" in the Late 1960s and Early 1970s

It is no accident that, shortly after the IRS's decision against it, Scientology began to make increasingly explicit claims to its status as a genuine religion. As we saw in chapter 2, Hubbard had already begun to pursue the "religion angle" in the 1950s, in part as a response to criticisms from the FDA and the medical community. Yet this appears to have been more theoretical than practical and not widely put into effect during the 1950s and early 1960s. As Nancy Many recalls, when she first joined the church, she was clearly told that the "religion aspect" was purely for "legal reasons," and attendance at "religious" events such as Sunday church services was minimal to nonexistent.[25] However, a second and even more pronounced effort to adopt the public image of religion began in the late 1960s and early 1970s as the church faced a new threat from the IRS in the United States and from other governments abroad. As Stephen Kent notes, "Cultivating a religious image was particularly important at this time, since his Washington DC church lost its petition to regain its tax-exempt status, while governments in Australia, Great Britain, New Zealand and Rhodesia were restricting, if not banning, its practices or initiating official investigations about it."[26]

We can see this reassertion of the "religious" nature of Scientology throughout Hubbard's bulletins and policy letters of the late 1960s and early 1970s. Perhaps the clearest example is a policy letter of February 1969 entitled simply "Religion," which directs all staff to make certain to display the religious paraphernalia of crosses, clerical collars, and the Scientology Creed. Hubbard also notes that such a display is the best and most necessary defense against Scientology's current wave of critics:

> Visual evidences that Scientology is a religion are mandatory. . . .
>
> Any staff who are trained at any level as auditors . . . are to be clothed in the traditioned [sic] ministerial black suit, black vest white collar silver cross for ordinary org wear.
>
> Creed of the Church is to be done big and plainly and posted in public areas. . . .
>
> The minister's course is a requisite for permanent certification. . . .
>
> This may or not be publicly acceptable. This is NOT the point. It is a requisite defense.[27]

If we look at press photos from this time period, we can clearly see this emphasis on the "visual evidences that Scientology is a religion." Articles on Scientology in the *New York Times* and various other newspapers prominently feature auditors wearing clerical collars and displaying the cross.[28]

A month later on March 6, 1969, the church issued another policy letter entitled simply "Scientology is a Religion," which flatly asserts that "Scientology is a religion in the oldest sense of the word, a study of wisdom. Scientology is a study of man as a spirit, in his relationship to life and the physical universe." More important, however, the letter also directs that all Scientology materials should clearly show that this is in fact a "religion," while any statements to the contrary must be corrected: "It is highly important that all promotional literature and Church literature reflect the fact that Scientology is a religion. . . . If any statements are made in any literature which reflect that Scientology is other than a religious philosophy, an appropriate condition must be assigned to the party so making same."[29] The following year, Hubbard also noted that there had been a "gradual standardization of Sunday Church services and other ceremonies"; hence it was necessary to produce a "standard ministerial and lay reference book for study and corporate prayer" entitled *The Background to the Religion of Scientology and Ceremonies of the Church of Scientology*, which was now to be in the possession of every chaplain in every org.[30]

A former Scientologist (who asked to remain anonymous) told me that he observed most of these changes being enforced at the org that he directed in Michigan. Previously an entirely secular org that made no reference to religion whatsoever, his center was ordered to now display the cross, set up an altar, and wear ministerial collars, while auditors were instructed to read basic texts on world religions such as Huston Smith's *The Religions of Man*. Lacking an actual cross, he recalls having to make one out of paper to display. He also recounts that most of those working at the org were extremely upset and worried that the overt display of religion would actually drive people away.[31] I have heard almost identical stories recounted by numerous Scientologists who were active during this time period.

This "religionization" of Scientology and its direct response to the IRS is also reflected in major church publications from this period. Thus, in May of 1968, the church launched the magazine *Advance!*, whose issues were primarily devoted to religion and to comparing Scientology with various other major world religions. Many issues of *Advance!* feature a cover story on a particular world religion—ranging from Judaism and Jainism to Shinto and Native American religion—in each case concluding that Scientology is the ultimate fulfillment of the spiritual quest embodied in every one of these faiths.[32] Not surprisingly, given Hubbard's preference for the Buddha as a spiritual leader, many issues are devoted specifically to Buddhism and to the argument that Scientology is the fulfillment of Siddhartha's religious quest. Thus in an issue on the Buddha's sermon on Vulture Peak, the magazine concludes that "today, *The BRIDGE to Total Freedom* grade chart by L. Ron Hubbard is the exact path to the fulfillment of those hopes raised on Vulture Peak 2,500 years ago."[33]

Also in 1968, the church published *The Character of Scientology*, which argues that Scientology is in fact a religion following *Webster's* dictionary definition of the term: "the profession or practice of religious beliefs; religious observances collectively; rites." This religion, moreover, is said to have ancient roots, finding its earliest version in the Veda, and developing into an "all denominational" philosophy whose teachings are "fundamental to *religion* rather than to anything which divides religions."[34] The text also contains a photo of a Scientologist wearing a clerical collar and a large cross with the following caption: "Chaplain after Sunday Service with members of the congregation at the door of the beautiful Chapel of Hubbard College."[35] Auditing is now explicitly referred to as a "confessional" and the auditor as a "minister."

An even stronger assertion of Scientology's religious status occurred a few years later in the 1974 book *Scientology: A World Religion Emerges in the Space Age*. The primary aim of the book is not simply to establish the fact that Scientology is a "religious" organization but that it is also the *first major world religion of the twentieth century*. After all, "Men are looking for new answers in the Age of Space, and are finding them in the religion of Scientology."[36] The book begins with eleven definitions of "religion" drawn from a range of scholarly texts; and it proceeds to place Scientology in the historical lineage of the Hindu and Buddhist traditions, outlining its "doctrines and practices," "symbol and scriptures," "charity services," and "ministerial standards."[37] Most important, the book contains a lengthy discussion of religion, the Constitution, and the courts, proudly displaying an image of the Bill of Rights and asserting Scientology's clear status as a legally recognized religion: "In a series of cases involving dis-related circumstances and causes of action, the courts have, via an unbro-ken series of judicial precedents, firmly upheld and sanctified the reli-gious nature and bona fides of the Church of Scientology."[38]

Perhaps even more telling, however, is the fact that the church during this period also *censored* passages from early Hubbard writings that were critical of religion. In later (post-1971) editions of several texts, passages from Hubbard's early works that appear hostile to religion are simply edited out. For example, in his 1952 text *A History of Man*, Hub-bard is clearly critical of religion, which he classifies as superstition along with voodooism and mysticism, and strongly contrasts with Sci-entology auditing:

> Theta clearing is about as practical and simple as repairing a shoe-lace. It is nothing to do with hypnotism, voodooism, charlatanism, monkeyism or theosophy. Done, the thetan can do anything a stage magician can do in the way of moving objects around. But this isn't attained by holding one's breath or thinking "right" thoughts or . . . any other superstitious or mystic practice. So . . . rule out, auditor, any mumbo jumbo or mysticism or spiritualism or religion.[39]

In later editions of the same text, however, we find the exact same pas-sage reproduced almost identically—with the sole exception that the word "religion" has been removed from this list of "mumbo jumbo" that should be ruled out.[40]

Initially, the IRS and the courts were not particularly sympathetic to this assumption of religious garb and religious language by the church. In the *Church of Scientology of California v. Commissioner of Internal Revenue Service* (1984), Judge Sterrett was in fact quite skeptical of the church's attempt to clothe itself in religious rhetoric, which he saw as essentially a cynical ploy to claim tax exemption for what is in reality a highly lucrative big business:

> Practically everywhere we turn, we find evidence of petitioner's commer-cial purpose. Certainly, if language reflects reality, petitioner had a sub-stantial commercial purpose since it described its activities in highly

commercial terms, calling parishioners, "customers"; missions, "franchises"; and churches, "organizations" just to mention a few of the more glaring examples of petitioner's commercial vocabulary.

> [Scientology] used business terminology to describe its operations. . . . Church missions were called "franchises" until 1971 when their designation in the United States was officially changed to "mission." However, even after the name change, petitioner continued to refer to the administrator of the missions as the Franchise Officer.[41]

It would be another nine years before the IRS and the courts were persuaded to adopt a more sympathetic view of the church's claims to religious status.

Operation Snow White: Cold War Espionage Meets the IRS

Perhaps the most astonishing chapter in the already astonishing history of Scientology was the covert operation against the IRS and other federal agencies launched by the Guardian's Office in the mid-1970s. Although the Guardian's Office organized a range of different covert operations, Operation "Snow White" was arguably the most audacious and the one with the most long-term consequences for the church. As former Scientologist Robert Vaughn Young recounted in an interview with the BBC, Hubbard "believed that there was an international cabal that was in control of the attack on him around the world . . . so 'Snow White' was written to find this cabal, find all the connections between these enemy groups, and to expose them, to destroy them. It was done through burglary. It was just pure military intelligence."[42] Most of this incredible story can be followed through the copious FBI files on the church now available through the Freedom of Information Act, which reconstruct the details of this operation and its aftermath.[43]

Planned in 1973, Snow White was a remarkably bold scheme to infiltrate IRS and other government offices in order to gather as much official information, intelligence, and documents on the church as possible. The operation was outlined and orchestrated from the very top of the GO, namely the office's head, Jane Kember, and Hubbard's wife, Mary Sue. Much of the plan was then put into effect by Michael Meisner, who had joined the GO in 1973. Meisner recruited Scientologist Gerald

Wolfe (code name "Silver") to infiltrate the IRS, and Wolfe eventually obtained a job as a clerk-typist in the agency's Washington, DC, offices in November 1974. By May 1975, Wolfe had stolen a ten-foot stack of documents totaling some thirty thousand pages. Also in late 1974, the GO managed to electronically bug the IRS's Chief Counsel Office itself. Knowing that the IRS was about to audit the Church of Scientology of California, Scientologists installed a bug in the office and taped the proceedings from a car using an FM receiver.[44]

It was not until mid-1977 that the spying Scientologists were finally caught. Meisner was eventually apprehended by the FBI and soon persuaded to work with the bureau. On July 7, 1977, the FBI launched one of the largest raids in the bureau's history, targeting the Scientology offices in both Los Angeles and Washington, DC. Indeed, the FBI raid appears to have been at least in part a "show of strength," perhaps responding in kind to the incredible audacity of the spying Scientologists with overwhelming force of its own. Some 134 agents were involved in the raids, armed with crowbars, sledgehammers, and battering rams. The FBI confiscated as many as two hundred thousand documents, along with eavesdropping equipment and burglary tools—so much material that it took a truck to haul it away.[45] Eleven GO officials, including Jane Kember and Mary Sue Hubbard, were apprehended, tried, convicted, and imprisoned, while L. Ron himself was named as an unindicted coconspirator and spent most of his remaining years in hiding.[46]

In its response to the FBI raids, the Church of Scientology once again invoked its religious status in its defense. Decrying the raids as a frightening, abusive, and unnecessarily violent intrusion into a spiritual community, the church claimed that its constitutional rights to both religious freedom and protection from unlawful searches and seizure had been violated.[47] Indeed, the church and its lawyers published an entire volume entitled *The American Inquisition*, which assembles a mass of documents intended to show that Scientology has been for decades subjected to "unconstitutional religious persecution."[48] Church officials repeatedly referred to the FBI investigation as a "Gestapo-like raid" reflecting a "Nazi Mentality."[49] As Heber Jentzsch put it, the FBI raids were nothing less than "fascist attacks" that represented a direct assault on the First Amendment and rights to religious freedom everywhere:

"Religion is under attack. We're not alone. . . . It could result in a vast devastation of an entire society if allowed to proliferate."[50,51] Indeed, in a statement called the "Pledge to Mankind" signed by leading Scientologists, including David Miscavige, the church decried the raid as part of a much larger war waged by intolerance and bigotry against new religions, and thus as a war against freedom itself:

> New religions have been born in blood at the cost of great sacrifice and suffering by adherents. . . . Scientology has survived and expanded because . . . it is a force of goodness and freedom. . . . In the United States . . . we are targets of unprincipled attacks in the court system by those who would line their pockets from our hard won coffers. Bigots in all branches of government . . . are bent on our destruction through taxation and repressive legislation.[52]

However, the church's defense and claim to religious protection did not hold up very well during the trial of Jane Kember, Mary Sue Hubbard, and their coconspirators in the Guardian's Office. The sentencing memorandum for the DC District Court was particularly harsh in its account of Kember's and Mary Sue's activities. The GO's operations, the court concluded, represented nothing less than "brazen, systematic and persistent burglaries of United States Government Offices," whose primary purpose was to "secure exemption from taxation and to protect Scientology's founder, Ron Hubbard." At times, the court seemed at a genuine loss for words to convey its own outrage at the sheer audacity of the GO's operations: "The standards of human conduct embodied in such practices represent no less than the absolute perversion of any known ethical value system."[53]

Still more outrageous to the court, however, was the fact that Scientologists had attempted to use a claim to religious freedom in an effort to shield themselves from the FBI's and the courts' investigations of their crimes:

> [I]t defies the imagination that these defendants had the unmitigated audacity to seek to defend their actions in the name of "religion." That the defendants now attempt to hide behind the sacred principles of freedom of religion, freedom of speech and freedom of privacy—which principles

they repeatedly demonstrated a willingness to violate with impunity—adds insult to the injuries which they have inflicted.

The court was particularly outraged by the Scientologists' apparent hypocrisy in their invocation of religious protection and the First Amendment. While the church tried to defend its actions on First Amendment grounds of religious freedom, the court concluded, its members had also blatantly trampled the First Amendment rights to free speech on the part of its many critics:

> The defendants' contention that they committed the crimes . . . in order to protect their Church from Government harassment collapses when one reviews a sample of the remaining documents seized by the FBI. . . . [T]hese documents established beyond question that the defendants . . . and their unindicted co-conspirators, as well as their organization, considered themselves above the law. They believed that they had *carte blanche* to violate the rights of others, frame critics in order to destroy them, burglarize private and public offices and steal documents outlining the strategy of individuals and organizations that the Church had sued. These suits were filed by the Church for the sole purpose of financially bankrupting its critics and in order to create an atmosphere of fear so that critics would shy away from exercising the First Amendment rights secured them by the Constitution.[54]

In response to these devastating judgments by the court, Scientology in turn launched its own self-described "war." Indeed, this was the start of a massive and aggressive legal campaign waged on numerous fronts that lasted another sixteen years.

The Triumph of Scientology

Shortly after the FBI raids, the church filed two massive suits against the FBI, one for $7.8 million for the Los Angeles raid and one for $1 million for the DC raid.[55] But these were only the beginning of a massive war of litigation that followed throughout the next two decades. As former top lieutenant Marty Rathbun recounted in his interviews with the *St. Petersburg Times* in 2009, the church made its war with the IRS its primary focus during these years, since winning recognition as "religion" and becoming tax exempt were seen as the keys to winning more favorable recognition in the courts more broadly. Indeed, "the number one mission was to obtain tax exemption from the IRS," Rathbun recalls. "It was always perceived that the IRS was the most important thing to handle, because if you have tax exemption, if you have religious recognition, you're treated differently in courts, there's some level of almost immunity, First Amendment immunity."[56] As such, Rathbun claims, he was given the charge of combating the IRS as aggressively as the service had targeted the church, launching hundreds and even thousands of lawsuits: "I was tasked with strategies to overwhelm the IRS the same way they were trying to overwhelm. It was sort of a fight fire with fire situation . . . it was a huge battlefield that was nationwide. There was literally 2700 suits at one point."[57]

Scientology's war with the IRS involved more than just lawsuits, however. According to the *New York Times*, the war also had a "covert side," as church lawyers hired private investigators to look into the lives of IRS officials and to conduct a variety of surveillance operations in the hopes of finding any weaknesses or vulnerabilities: "One investigator said he had interviewed tenants in buildings owned by three IRS officials, looking for housing code violations. He also said he had taken documents from an IRS conference and sent them to church officials and created a phony news bureau in Washington to gather information on church critics."[58] As former Scientologist Stacey Young told the *Times*, the IRS was "considered to be a pretty major enemy. . . . 'What you do with an enemy is you go after them and harass them and intimidate them and try to expose their crimes until they decide to play ball with you.'"[59]

Of course, the Church of Scientology has argued that it too was subjected to covert operations and surveillance by government agencies. From the church's perspective, its use of private investigators is simply a defensive move to protect itself from the invasive scrutiny of the IRS and the many other government agencies attacking it on all sides: "The I.R.S. uses investigators, too," noted one church lawyer, Gerald A. Feffer. "They're called C.I.D. [Criminal Investigation Division] agents . . . and the C.I.D. agents put this church under intense scrutiny for years with a mission to destroy the church."[60] By the 1980s, the war between Scientology and the IRS had escalated into an incredibly costly, complex, and

often bizarre conflict that seemed to leave both sides bloodied but un-
bowed. As an article in *International Scientology News* put it, "It was
becoming a costly war of attrition, with no clear-cut winner in sight."[61]

Up until the early 1990s, the U.S. courts had consistently upheld the
IRS's decision against tax-exempt status for Scientology. Indeed, in 1992,
just a year before the IRS reversed its decision, the U.S. Claims Court
had upheld the service's denial of an exemption for the Church of Spiritual Technology. Among the reasons given for denying the exemption
were "the commercial character of much of Scientology," its "virtually
incomprehensible financial procedures," and its "scripturally based hostility to taxation."[62]

Scientology's war did not finally draw to a close until five years after
Hubbard's death, beginning with an unusual meeting between Rathbun,
Miscavige, and IRS Commissioner Fred T. Goldberg Jr. in late 1991.
What exactly transpired at this meeting may never be publicly known,
but it ultimately resulted in a settlement that ended the church's war
with the service and granted all Scientology entities tax-exempt status in
1993. Indeed, even the terms of the settlement were kept secret, despite
requests from the *New York Times* under the Freedom of Information
Act (and despite the fact that other high-profile religious groups such as
the Jimmy Swaggart Ministries and an affiliate of Jerry Falwell had been
required by the IRS to disclose the details of their tax settlements).[63] It
was not until December 1997 that the terms of the settlement were
leaked to the *Wall Street Journal*, which found that the church had apparently agreed to pay $12.5 million and to drop its myriad lawsuits. In
addition to the payment, "The IRS canceled the payroll taxes and penalties it had assessed against certain church entities and seven church officials, including church leader David Miscavige. . . . The IRS dropped
its audits of 13 Scientology organizations, including the mother church,
the Church of Scientology International, and agreed not to audit the
church for any year prior to 1993."[64] This deal was of obvious benefit
to the church in terms of both finances and public image. As Douglas
Frantz observes, the settlement not only saved the church tens of millions of dollars in taxes, but perhaps more important, it also "provided
Scientology with an invaluable public-relations tool in its worldwide
campaign for acceptance as a mainstream religion."[65]

Indeed, just one week after the IRS decision, David Miscavige delivered a triumphant speech before ten thousand cheering Scientologists in the Los Angeles Sports Arena. Declaring the long-anticipated end of "The War," Miscavige called the church's triumph nothing less than a "historic victory for religious freedom."[66] As Miscavige made clear, moreover, winning tax exemption was hardly a minor legal issue for the church. On the contrary, it was *everything* and perhaps the most important thing the church had fought for over the last two decades:

> On October first, 1993, at 8:37 p.m. Eastern Standard Time, the IRS issued letters recognizing Scientology and every one of its organizations as fully tax exempt!
>
> The war is over! Now your first question is probably—what exactly does this mean?
>
> My answer is: everything. The magnitude of this is greater than you may imagine.[67]

Among other things, Miscavige happily proclaimed, the winning of religious recognition and tax exemption in the United States could be used as powerful evidence to persuade the "suppressive governments" in other countries. If the fact that the United States had not recognized Scientology had been used against the church in the past, now the fact that it had finally recognized its religious character could be the most forceful argument in favor of Scientology's recognition abroad:

> [W]e will waste no time carrying news of this new breakthrough to all foreign countries. Those battles have been held in place by suppressive governments just quoting the IRS. The line has been: "You are an American religion. If the IRS doesn't recognize you, why should we?" The answer is – "They do. And now, you better as well!"[68]

And indeed, the news was soon carried to other countries, both by Scientologists and by the U.S. government.

Just a few months after the church won its exemptions, the U.S. State Department released its 1993 human rights report, an influential annual document that lists countries who abuse their citizens. The 1993 report is the first one to note the harassment and discrimination of Scientologists in Germany.[69] And the department's criticism of Germany became

Chairman of the Religious Technology Center, David Miscavige. Getty Images

more forceful in later reports. In its first report on International Religious Freedom, the department observed that Scientologists were "subjected to intense scrutiny by the Enquette Commission," an "unfortunate trend" that "continued through 1998."[70] The State Department's criticism of the German attitude toward Scientology has continued up through its 2009 report on religious freedom, which states that "there continue to be concerns about societal and governmental (federal and state) treatment of certain religious minorities, notably Scientologists." However, the report also notes that the Federal Conference of Interior Ministers had decided against an all-out "ban" on the church.[71]

The State Department's defense of Scientology, however, appears to have been influenced not simply by the IRS decision in 1993. Taking up Miscavige's call to take the news of Scientology's victory to other nations, a group of prominent celebrity Scientologists such as John Travolta, Isaac Hayes, and Chick Corea also began to lobby on behalf of the church and its mistreatment in European nations, particularly Germany. Appearing before the Commission on Security and Cooperation in Europe in 1997, the celebrities presented "a list of religiously based, alleged human rights complaints."[72] In April 1997, Travolta even met with President Clinton himself to discuss the church's troubles in Europe. The president reportedly assured the actor that "I'd really love to help you with your issue over in Germany with Scientology"[73] and then went "to the extraordinary length of assigning his national security advisor, Sandy Berger, to be the administration's Scientology point person."[74]

To what degree celebrities such as Travolta actually had a role in influencing the State Department's position or Scientology's status in nations abroad remains unclear. But in any case, Miscavige's hope that the IRS decision would help further Scientology's case for religious status abroad has met with at least some success if not an all-out "triumph" outside the United States.

Conclusions: Why Does the IRS Define Religion Anyway?

Scientology's long, convoluted, and at times bizarre war with the IRS really highlights all of the questions that we have been grappling with in this book: how exactly is religion defined, who gets to define it, what are the stakes in laying claim to such status, and what are the legal, intellectual, and ethical implications of denying a particular group such status? Perhaps more important, it raises the complex historical question of why the task of determining a group's "religious" status has fallen to the IRS, rather than to other academic or governmental organizations. As Elizabeth MacDonald summarized in the *Wall Street Journal*, the Church of Scientology is thus a critical example of this difficult question: "Regulating the activities of churches has long been a prickly area for the IRS. The First Amendment generally prohibits the government from determining what is and isn't a valid church; yet the tax-collection agency is charged with making certain that churches don't abuse their tax exempt status, since taxpayers effectively subsidize their operations."[75] As such, the Scientology case is a particularly striking example of how very difficult it is to walk this fine line.

The church's official position, of course, is that this whole debate is not a matter of income tax or finance at all, but rather a matter of religious freedom and First Amendment protections for a marginal but legitimate religion that has been relentlessly harassed by the U.S. government. In the words of Monique E. Yingling, a Washington lawyer who represented Scientology, "This is a church organization that has been subjected to more harassment and more attacks certainly than any religion in this century and probably any religion ever, and they have had to perhaps take unusual steps in order to survive."[76]

From the perspective of Scientology's myriad critics, conversely, the church is by no means a traditional, bona fide religion but rather a kind of simulacrum that has done everything in its power to mask itself in religious trappings in order to win certain benefits such as tax-exemption (and other benefits that we have seen in previous chapters). And we have seen ample evidence in this and in previous chapters that Hubbard gave clear directions to his church that they should go to great lengths to publicly *look* as much like a "religion" as possible. These efforts to highlight the "religion angle" clearly intensified during the very period of Scientology's escalating war with the IRS.

Ironically, then, the conflict between Scientology and the IRS has been a key part of the way in which religion itself has been defined and redefined over the last fifty years. In 1977, as I noted earlier, the IRS made public a general list of criteria and a set of thirteen points it uses to judge the validity of a group's claims to religious status. These thirteen points include a distinct legal existence, a recognized creed and form of worship, a distinct ecclesiastical government, a formal code of doctrine and discipline, a distinct religious history, a membership not associated with any other church or denomination, a complete organization of ordained ministers ministering to their congregations and selected after completing prescribed courses of study, a literature of its own, established places of worship, regular congregations, regular religious services, Sunday schools for the religious instruction of the young, and schools for the preparation of its ministers.[77]

It is probably no accident that the year the IRS introduced these guidelines was the very same year that Scientologists working for the GO were arrested for their covert operations inside the IRS offices as part of their larger war for tax exemption. And this was also during the height of Scientology's efforts to reemphasize its religious profile through the display of crosses, creeds, clerical collars, and religious titles. Indeed, virtually every one of the IRS's thirteen points was self-consciously emphasized in Church of Scientology publications of this time period. As such, the complex legal and extralegal battles between the church and the IRS have been central to the shifting definition of religion itself, as the service has attempted to sort out what is and isn't "religion," and, in turn, Scientologists have tried to fit themselves into whatever definitions of religion have been operative at given moments, creatively (or cynically, one might argue) adapting to the shifting definitions of religion in contemporary America.

As we will see in the following chapter, however, the fact that the church finally won its battle for tax exemption in the United States has by no means ended its war for religious recognition. On the contrary, this war now continues in perhaps even more intense forms both globally and in the far reaches of cyberspace.

- SIX -

SECRETS, SECURITY, AND CYBERSPACE
Scientology's New Wars of Information on the Internet

The Internet is going to be Scientology's Waterloo.

—Robert Vaughn Young[1]

For you cannot unveil the SECRET and have it ever be quite so secret
ever again.

—Hubbard, *Dianetics 55* (1954)[2]

With the rise of new information technologies in the post–cold war era,
Scientology's concerns with secrecy and knowledge control have only
grown more intense. Above all, with the rapid expansion of the Internet,
Scientology faces a whole new series of threats to its exclusive claims to
confidential knowledge such as the OT materials. Since the early 1990s,
a wide array of confidential Scientology documents have been popping
up all over the web, so that now anyone with even the slowest Internet
service can unlock the inner secrets of OT at the click of a mouse. In
turn, the church has adopted an extremely aggressive response toward
any individuals or groups who reproduce its confidential materials online. Indeed, Scientology was among the very first groups to litigate in
the area of Internet copyright violation, and it has done so with an intensity rivaled by few other organizations. As Douglas Cowan notes,
"[I]t is on the Internet that some of Scientology's most significant battles
over public perception are being fought."[3] Beginning in the mid-1990s
with lawsuits against newsgroups such as alt.religion.scientology, the
church has fought a series of major legal battles over confidential Scientology materials posted online and has dedicated its Religious Technology Center to protecting its copyrighted materials, particularly those
circulating in cyberspace.[4]

The presence of Scientology materials on the Internet, however, is far from a simple matter of legal squabbling. Rather, it raises a far more profound set of constitutional and religious debates that strike at the heart of our understanding of religious freedom and privacy in the twenty-first century. These debates center on the interpretation of the First Amendment itself, though read from two very different perspectives. As Alan Prendergrast described this battle in 1995, "Pitting claims of religious rights and copyright protection against claims of free speech, the brawl seems made for the Internet."[5] On the one side, the Church of Scientology has argued that its advanced tech materials are not only copyrighted and trade secrets but also confidential religious texts; therefore, its right to keep them secret is protected by the First Amendment's free exercise of religion clause.[6] On the other side, critics of the church have argued that their right to reveal this information is *also* covered by the First Amendment's freedom of speech clause and that to suppress the dissemination of information on the church is also a profound abridgement of this right.[7]

The rhetoric on both sides has been heated, to say the least. In the words of the church, those who post its materials online are guilty of "terrorist tactics."[8] They have violated the rights of a legitimate religious organization by illegally disseminating its confidential materials, an act as offensive as stealing the esoteric teachings of Australian aboriginal cultures or other religious traditions.[9] Conversely, in Larry Wollersheim's words, Scientology is "an authoritarian political organization structured on the concept of Nazism"[10] that needs to be exposed. Other online critics are even more severe in their assessment of the church; according to Andreas Heldal-Lund, the owner of the extensive anti-Scientology site, Xenu.net, "Scientology is a vicious and dangerous cult that masquerades as a religion."[11] In Heldal-Lund's opinion, revealing the confidential Scientology materials is not only justifiable but a moral obligation so that the public can see for themselves what really lies at the heart of this dangerous organization: "I . . . have reviewed the secret materials of Scientology and after careful consideration have concluded that these materials are being kept secret in order to withhold information from the public with the sole purpose of deceiving the public as to the true nature of Scientology."[12]

Ironically, but not unpredictably, most of Scientology's attempts to control the flow of information online have not only failed but largely backfired. Through its increasingly aggressive attempts to silence critics in cyberspace, the church has become what some say is its own worst enemy, as the call has gone out across the web to duplicate and circulate confidential Scientology materials worldwide. By its very efforts to staunch the virtual flow of its secrets, the church has arguably created its own "worst nightmare, as its 'trade secrets' became far more widely read . . . than they would have been had it done nothing."[13]

Perhaps the most powerful new threat faced by the church in cyberspace, however, has come from an unexpected source: the amorphous, decentralized Internet collective known as Anonymous. Although the many disparate individuals who make up Anonymous share little else in common, they do all appear to agree on the free flow of uncensored information on the Internet; and they have consequently singled out Scientology as perhaps their greatest enemy. Beginning in early 2008, Anonymous targeted the church as the ultimate obstacle to free Internet speech and dedicated itself to a cyber and physical campaign to "destroy" Scientology. Perhaps most significantly, Anonymous also presents itself as the inverse image of Scientology—that is, as a tremendously powerful network, but one that is a decentralized, fluid, shifting, and protean coalition of diverse individuals, set in opposition to the hierarchical, centralized, and conformist corporation of Scientology.

In short, Scientology's wars in cyberspace raise some of the most profound religious and constitutional questions of the twenty-first century. But they may also involve the very future of Scientology itself, in an age when even the best-guarded secrets circulate instantaneously to a global audience that now demands the rapid and free flow of information. As such, they give us critical insights into the changing shape of religion in a strange new world of information. As Lorne Dawson and Douglas Cowan point out, the Internet has opened a variety of remarkable new opportunities for religious groups and individuals, including the possibility to create online communities, cyber rituals, and new forms of "evangelism and proselytization"; but the flip side is that it can just as effectively be used "as an excellent venue for religious antagonism and

Members of Anonymous protesting Scientology. Photo courtesy Rebecca Watson of skepchick.org

countermovement."[14] On a still broader level, however, Scientology's battles in cyberspace also give us key insight into the new wars of information that loom ahead of us in the twenty-first century. As terrorism expert Richard Clarke has recently argued, the most important wars of the future may well be fought not in physical space with bombs but rather in cyberspace with the new weapons of hacking, cyberterrorism, and ever-more sophisticated countermeasures to secure information.[15] The Church of Scientology had already begun to fight its own cyber war in the early 1990s, and it continues to wage war against various enemies online, including even Internet giants such as Google and *Wikipedia*.

Whether Scientology will successfully adapt to these new technologies and survive the powerful new forms of antagonism and countermovement launched by Anonymous and myriad others remains an open question in the years to come.

The Religious Technology Center: Scientology's Guardian in Cyberspace

The backbone of the church's war in cyberspace is the Religious Technology Center (RTC), first created in 1982 in the wake of the FBI investigations and the dismantling of the Guardian's Office. Although the RTC claims that it is "not part of the management structure of the church," it also asserts that the RTC is "the ultimate ecclesiastical authority regarding the standard and pure application of L. Ron Hubbard's religious technologies"[16]; and the RTC's current chairman, David Miscavige, is widely recognized as the de facto "head" of the larger Scientology conglomerate today.

As the RTC describes its mission, it is a "legal mechanism for ensuring that the Scientology religious technologies were orthodox," designed "to prevent anyone from . . . engaging in some distorted misuse of Hubbard's writings."[17] Since the 1990s, however, the RTC has been increasingly focused on policing the flow of information on the Internet, which has become one of the most complex and apparently frustrating new challenges faced by the church. According to Scientology.org, the church now has an extensive and sophisticated presence on the Internet; but it also faces a new host of attacks from cyber critics, who exploit the rhetoric of free speech in order to violate its copyrights and disseminate its confidential materials online:

> During the 1990s the Church of Scientology emerged as an experienced, recognized voice in the debate surrounding the survival of both free speech and intellectual property rights in cyberspace.
>
> The Internet offers a wealth of readily accessible knowledge, but as with any new frontier, the acts of a lawless few can jeopardize the promise of progress and compromise the rights and freedoms of the responsible, law-abiding majority. The Internet can be abused as easily as it can be employed for good. There are those who exploit children through molestation and pornography, commit fraud and other forms of commercial crime, invade zones of personal privacy and infringe the intellectual property rights of artists, musicians and thinkers.[18]

By the mid-1990s, however, the RTC's defense against these abuses of its intellectual property had escalated into a full-scale war in cyberspace against a wide range of individuals, service providers, and anti-Scientology protesters.

Scientology v. FACTNet: The Wollersheim Case

Ironically, Scientology's war in cyberspace began just as its war with the IRS was drawing to a close in the late 1980s and early 1990s. Even as the church was coming to be recognized by U.S. government agencies as a religion, its credibility was being rapidly challenged by the leak of its most confidential OT materials to the Internet, followed by a series of complex lawsuits. Since 1995, according to the RTC's own account, it has engaged in at least seven major lawsuits and a variety of smaller cases over the issue of copyright infringement and trade secret misappropriation on the Internet.[19] For the sake of simplicity here, I will focus on two of the more colorful cases that developed around ex-Scientologists Larry Wollersheim and Stephen Fishman.

Confidential OT materials were first introduced as evidence in court in November 1985 as part of a civil case brought by Wollersheim against the church. A remarkably long and drawn-out ordeal, the Wollersheim suit began in 1980 and initially resulted in an award of $30 million, which was later reduced to $2.5 million on appeal, and finally ended with an $8.6 million settlement in 2002.[20] OT documents, including the most confidential Xenu story, were used as exhibits in the proceedings. Despite the fact that Scientology attorneys argued forcefully that "disclosure of the materials is a violation of the group's religious freedom," Los Angeles Superior Court Judge Alfred Margolis issued an order making the documents public at the clerk's office.[21] In response, some fifteen hundred Scientologists crammed the court buildings, swamping workers with hundreds of requests to photocopy the documents in an attempt to ensure that the materials were not made public. Indeed, "by snaking the line through three courthouse hallways, Scientologists made sure they were the only ones to purchase copies of the materials."[22] Yet in spite of these remarkable efforts, the Los Angeles Times obtained copies of the OT materials and revealed them in an article in November 1985.

In 1993, Wollersheim cofounded the website "Fight Against Coercive Tactics Network" (FACTNet), designed primarily to expose Scientology's activities and provide "resources, support and recovery from the abusive practices of religions and cults."[23] Having amassed some twenty-seven gigabytes of material on Scientology, FACTNet was not surprisingly hit with intense legal threats from the church. The church's argument was that the confidential OT documents were both copyrighted materials and "trade secrets" (that is, information that has economic value from not being generally known); the disclosure of these secrets, it claimed, could cause "irreparable spiritual injury if a rival church . . . were allowed to disseminate them."[24] On August 22, 1995, a federal court ordered a raid on the homes of Wollersheim and another ex-Scientologist, Robert Penny, led by two U.S. Marshals and six RTC representatives. This resulted in the confiscation of all of their computers, software, and dozens of boxes of paper files—a vast amount of materials that, FACTNet charges, far exceeded the scope of the warrant.

The FACTNet raids in turn sparked an intense debate about copyright protection, trade secrets, and free speech, both on the Internet and in demonstrations across the country. The county courthouse in Boulder, Colorado, was surrounded by both protesters and counterprotesters, the former carrying signs that read "Hands Off the Internet" and "Scientology Harasses Critics," and the latter carrying signs that charged "Only criminals spread lawlessness on the Internet."[25]

In September 1995, however, the federal judge in Denver dealt Scientology a severe blow. Ruling that there were in fact no copyright or trade secret violations, the federal district court decided that FACTNet's use of the Scientology materials was simply fair use, and that the church "did not show that the materials in issue are secret or within the definition of trade secrets."[26] The court also ruled that the seizure of FACTNet's materials had been illegal and a violation of free speech. As Judge John L. Kane concluded in his decision, the OT materials were already by this time quite widely disseminated outside the church through multiple sources and therefore "are not secret within the meaning of the Colorado statute." Moreover, Kane also concluded that maintaining the secrecy of these materials was in no way necessary for the free exercise of the church's religious beliefs. He could not, in other words, place the church's claim to free exercise of religion over the defendants' rights to make fair use of the materials:

> RTC claims use of the materials impedes its right to exercise its religious belief that the materials must be kept secret. I am not persuaded that a denial of the injunction sought will deprive followers of the Church of their freedom to exercise their religious beliefs. RTC effectively requests that I advance its religion at the expense of Defendants' lawful rights to use the materials for the purposes of criticism and research. The United States Constitution, common law and the Copyright Act preclude me from doing so.[27]

In sum, Kane's final decision was that openness is preferable to secrecy in this case: "The public interest is best served by the free exchange of ideas."[28]

Even after Judge Kane's decision, however, Scientology's war with FACTNet dragged on for several more years until a settlement was finally reached in 1999. According to the terms of the settlement, if FACTNet is ever found guilty of violating church copyrights, it is permanently enjoined to pay the church $1 million.[29] Moreover, the church also apparently learned its lesson after its failure to defend its "trade secrets" in the FACTNet case. In a case several years later, as Brill and Packard note, the RTC argued that the violation of its trade secrets would lead to serious *economic harm* because it generates so much income from the confidential OT levels:

> The court of appeals held that, under California law, trade secrets were only protected because of their economic value. So, five years later, when the church sued Enid Vien, a former Scientologist who was using OT materials in a scientology-like course, for copyright and trade secret violations, it based its case on a theory of economic harm—and won. Religious Technology Center director Warren McShane testified that the church derives significant revenue from the fixed donations its members pay to study the texts.[30]

Interestingly enough, the church in this case successfully argued that its advanced tech materials are trade secrets *precisely because they are so expensive.*

The Fishman Affidavit and the Secrets of "OT VIII"

A second major war with the Internet began at roughly the same time as the Wollersheim ordeal, as a result of the trial of another former Scientologist, Stephen Fishman. In 1990, Fishman was convicted of mail fraud, a crime that, he alleged, he had been brainwashed into committing in order to pay for his Scientology auditing.[31] Fishman was then quoted in Richard Behar's infamous *Time* magazine article on the "Cult of Greed," where he stated that he had not only been involved in an enormous scam to pay for his Scientology training but that he had even been ordered by the church to kill his own psychiatrist.[32] The church in turn sued Fishman for libel, and, in the course of the trial, Fishman submitted sixty-nine pages of the confidential OT materials, including the Xenu story and secret documents all the way up to OT VIII.

The materials presented in the Fishman case are even more problematic than those from the Wollersheim suit. Among them is a text alleged to be one of Hubbard's own *HCO Bulletins* from 1980 and a key part of the topmost OT VIII materials. Labeled "confidential," the text makes a number of astonishing statements. Among others, it dismisses Jesus as "a lover of young boys and men" who "was given to uncontrollable bursts of temper and hatred that belied the general message of love"; more surprising still, it also identifies Hubbard *both* as the future Buddha Maitreya/Metteyya *and* as Lucifer, the light bearer and anti-Christ(!):

> No doubt you are familiar with the Revelations section of the Bible where various events are predicted. Also mentioned is a brief period of time in which an arch-enemy of Christ, referred to as the anti-Christ, will reign and his opinions will have sway. All this makes for very fantastic, entertaining reading but there is truth in it. This anti-Christ represents the forces of Lucifer (literally, the "light bearers" or "light bringer"), Lucifer being a mythical representation of the forces of enlightenment, the Galactic Confederacy. My mission could be said to fulfill the Biblical promise represented by this brief anti-Christ period. During this period there is a fleeting opportunity for the whole scenario to be effectively derailed, which would make it impossible for the mass Marcabian landing (Second Coming) to take place.[33]

If this document were an authentic text, it would lend strong credibility to the belief among many critics that Hubbard was in fact still immersed in the works of Aleister Crowley and continued to see himself in the lineage of the "Great Beast 666." A number of ex-Scientologists believe this to be the case.[34]

As it happens, the RTC initially claimed copyright of all the OT materials in the affidavit—including this OT VIII text—but later amended its claim to exclude the OT VIII materials, now arguing that they are a forgery. The authenticity of the OT VIII materials therefore remains unclear, though no one to date has ever been identified or come forward as the author of the alleged forgeries.

Copies of these materials were placed in a Los Angeles court file that was to be publicly available for two years. Again, as in the Wollersheim case, church members undertook a remarkable effort to maintain the documents' secrecy throughout that period "by alternately checking out the files each day and retaining them until the clerk's office closed."[35]

Even with these intensive measures by the church, however, copies of the documents were made and, not surprisingly, soon found their way on to the Internet. In October 1994, they appeared on the newsgroup, alt .religion.scientology, which had been formed three years earlier to facilitate critical discussion of the church. The real battle with Scientology began when Dennis Erlich, a former high-ranking Scientologist personally affiliated with Hubbard, began to comment regularly on the site. In January 1995, an attorney for the RTC attempted to have alt.religion .scientology removed from the Internet, and this was followed in February of that same year by an RTC lawsuit against Erlich for copyright violations.[36] A San Jose court issued a temporary restraining order to prevent any further dissemination of Hubbard's copyrighted works. At the same time, it also ordered the seizure of any copyrighted Scientology documents in Erlich's possession, which led to the removal of a vast amount of materials from his home. Thus, on February 13, 1995, "more than 360 computer disks, two 120 MB backup tapes and 29 books were taken from Erlich's residence. Erlich complains that the materials taken from his home and deleted from his hard drive included much more than what was described on the writ of seizure. He also says he was refused the right to look at what was copied from his computer."[37] This massive seizure of materials from Erlich's home, we might note, is ironically reminiscent of the FDA and FBI raids on Scientology offices in the 1960s and 70s.

Despite all of the church's extreme measures, however, the Fishman affidavit, along with all of the confidential OT materials, reappeared on alt.religion.scientology on July 31, 1995. Since then, they have been reproduced on site after site, server after server, in innumerable languages, rendering any concept of confidentiality or secrecy fairly moot in the cyber domain. Dutch journalist Karin Spaink, for example, fought a series of legal battles with the church between 1995 and 2005 over her posting of the Fishman materials online. Finally, after the Netherlands Supreme Court dismissed Scientology's last appeal in December 2005, the Fishman affidavit with all of the OT materials up to OT VIII were allowed to remain freely and legally available.[38] In Spaink's words, "The courts damned Scientology for the secrecy surrounding OT2 and OT3. . . . Scientology—which they call an 'organisation', not a 'church'— uses that secrecy to wield power over its members."[39]

Today, ironically, the Fishman papers are among the first things one encounters when beginning to explore information about Scientology online. As Wollersheim observes, the Fishman materials have been "translated, encrypted and hid just about anywhere you can imagine around the world. They can't stop them fast enough. They tried to put out a fire with matches and gasoline. . . . The first thing you learn when you get on the Internet is where to find the Fishman papers."[40] In this case, as elsewhere, the church's war on the Internet appears to have backfired, and its attempts to staunch the flow of confidential material online have only accelerated their global dissemination.

Scientology v. *Wikipedia* and Google

Scientology's war of information has by no means been limited to a few individual ex-Scientologists and their personal websites. Indeed, the church has targeted some of the largest Internet forces of all, including the web's most powerful search engine, Google, and the hugely popular online encyclopedia, *Wikipedia*. In 2002, Google received a letter from the law firm representing Scientology, Moxon & Kobrin, demanding "removal of Scientology related content from its search engine, complete with a list of allegedly infringing URLs."[41] In particular, the church was concerned with literally hundreds of copyright and trademark infringements on the website "Operation Clambake" (Xenu.net), perhaps the best-known cyber critic of the church. The lawyers demanded that Google either remove or disable all access to Xenu.net.

The church's demands, however, appear to have had only the most marginal effect on one's ability to search for critical information on Scientology. As of February 2010, a Google search for "xenu.net" still produces about 262,000 hits—though the search engine now carries a note at the bottom of the page that reads: "*In response to a complaint we received under the US Digital Millennium Copyright Act, we have removed 1 result(s) from this page. If you wish, you may read the DMCA complaint that caused the removal(s) at ChillingEffects.org.*"

Scientology's war against *Wikipedia*, however, is even more bizarre, and also more ambiguous in its outcome. In May 2009, *Wikipedia*'s arbitration council voted 10–0 (with one abstention) to ban any users coming from all IP addresses owned by the Church of Scientology and its associates. For a site that prides itself for its inclusivity and openness as "the free encyclopedia anyone can edit," this was a truly unprecedented decision.[42] According to *Wired* magazine, the landmark action was taken because the church was found to have repeatedly and deceptively edited hundreds of articles related to the controversial religion, thus "damaging Wikipedia's reputation for neutrality."[43] Apparently, tracking all the edits coming from Scientology machines was particularly difficult because numerous editors worked from a small number of IPs, and the address of each editor was constantly changing. This tactic, known as "sockpuppeting," is not allowed in Wikiland.[44]

As one former member of Scientology's OSA named Tory Christman told the British *Register*, this systematic program of editing and censoring *Wikipedia* pages was hardly anything new but part of a much larger war waged by the church online. According to Christman's account, the OSA had been engaged in "massive efforts to remove Scientology-related materials and criticism" from the web: "The guys I worked with posted every day all day. . . . It was like a machine. I worked with someone who used five separate computers, five separate anonymous identities . . . to refute any facts from the internet about the Church of Scientology."[45]

This was not the first time, of course, that corporations and government agencies had been found "massaging" their own *Wikipedia* pages. But this case was on such a massive scale, and so egregious in the amount and degree of the editing taking place, that the *Wikipedia* council felt compelled to take more drastic action. Given the inherently fluid and anonymous nature of the Internet, however, it remains unclear how successful Wikipedia will be in preventing Scientology from continuing to censor any negative information about the church that appears on the site. There is little to prevent Scientologists from simply switching to new IP addresses and continuing their information war as before.

"We Are Legion": Anonymous v. Scientology

Perhaps the most significant new threat to the church has come from an unlikely source: the faceless, fluid, decentralized, and anarchic network of Internet users that calls itself Anonymous. By no means a coherent or organized movement, Anonymous is more like an Internet *meme*—that is, a concept that spreads from person to person online and then becomes mobilized around loosely agreed-upon causes. Chris Landers of the *Baltimore City Paper* even described Anonymous as "the first internet-based superconsciousness. Anonymous is a group, in the sense that a flock of birds is a group . . . they're travelling in the same direction. At any given moment, more birds could join, leave, peel off in another direction entirely."[46]

Prior to 2008, Anonymous was less known for taking on powerful new religions such as Scientology than for more mundane sorts of cyber warfare, including "technologically sophisticated pranks" such as spamming chat rooms online and "ordering dozens of pizzas for people they don't like."[47] The Anonymous collective only began to mobilize around the Church of Scientology in January 2008 after the leak of a confidential video featuring Tom Cruise. The video in question is a nine-minute promotional interview with Cruise talking about his intense commitment to Scientology and urging other church members to commit themselves just as intensely. In the background, the theme music to *Mission Impossible* plays throughout the video, reaching a climax at the end. In Cruise's words, "I think it's a privilege to call yourself a Scientologist, and it's something you have to earn, because a Scientologist does. He—or she—has the ability to create new and better realities."[48] Cruise is indeed somewhat alarming in his intensity, alternating between moments of deadly seriousness about the challenges facing Scientology and fits of laughter about his own all-or-nothing, just-do-it attitude: "You know, get those spectators either in the playing field or out of the area. That's really how I feel about it. I do what I can. And I do it the way I do everything [laughs]. There's nothing part way about me. It's just *pow!*"[49]

The video was leaked to YouTube on January 15, 2008—the same day that Andrew Morton's *Tom Cruise: An Unauthorized Biography* was released in bookstores worldwide. Viewed literally millions of times (the current incarnation of the video available on YouTube has been viewed over four million times), the video was quickly removed from the site after threat of litigation by the church.[50] And so it was, but not before it had already spread virally to myriad sites throughout the Internet.

Scientology's threats against YouTube became a powerful catalyst for the Anonymous collective, which saw these actions as a dangerous attack on free speech and the open flow of information online. Dubbed "Project Chanology" (from chan message boards), the new Anonymous initiative was aimed at fighting Scientology's intense information control with the anarchic powers of the Internet. Indeed, as one member of Anonymous put it, "The Internet is Serious Business," and Scientology immediately became a kind of icon for all the bullying corporate powers that try to squelch the free circulation of knowledge in cyberspace.[51] On January 21, 2008, Anonymous also released a video entitled *Message to Scientology*, which appeared on YouTube and soon after on countless other websites. The message is an electronically masked voice delivering a merciless critique and a chilling promise to destroy the church, accompanied by ominous industrial music and images of rapidly moving clouds across a dark sky. The message clearly presents Anonymous as the opposite of the church in every way—a loose, fluid, decentralized network of individuals pitted against the hierarchical, totalitarian corporation of Scientology:

Over the years we have been watching you, your campaigns of misinformation, your suppression of dissent, your litigious nature, all of these things have caught our eye. . . . Anonymous has therefore decided that your organization should be destroyed. For the good of your followers, for the good of mankind, and for our own enjoyment, we shall proceed to expel you from the internet and systematically dismantle the Church of Scientology in its present form. . . . You will not prevail forever against the angry masses of the body politic. Your methods, hypocrisy, and the artlessness of your organization have sounded its death knell. You cannot hide; we are everywhere. We cannot die; we are forever. We're getting bigger every day—and solely by the force of our ideas. . . . If you want another name for your opponent, then call us Legion, for we are many.[52]

One of the most interesting aspects of the Anonymous movement is its sophisticated use of various information technologies to attack Scientology, disseminate information and organize events. These technologies have assumed both legal and illegal forms. Shortly after the war between Anonymous and Scientology began in January 2008, a distributed denial of service (DDOS) attack was launched against Scientology websites, temporarily shutting them down with high volumes of traffic (during a DDOS attack, a server is flooded with so many external communications requests that it cannot respond to legitimate requests or responds so slowly that it is rendered effectively unavailable). A year later in May 2009, a nineteen-year old New Jersey man pleaded guilty for his role in the attacks, identifying himself as a member of Anonymous.[53]

More commonly, however, the Anonymous collective has relied on legal and arguably more effective cyber tactics. They make use of a wide array of websites to share guerilla tactics and coordinate protests, including Encyclopedia Dramatica and Facebook, where their page has over eleven thousand fans as of October 2010. As one Anonymous protester who calls herself "Xenubarb" explained to me, they are also fond of filming their various events and then circulating them instantly, along with details of worldwide protests disseminated through Twitter and various other networking tools. They are also notorious for their sense of humor and playfulness, mixing their serious protests with dancing, satire, and at times a party atmosphere:

[M]any anonymous cells have decentralized sites where planning takes place. We also use Skype, IRC and Twitter. . . .

One of the neat things about our global raids is, by the time it's our turn here on the west coast, the Aussies and Kiwis already have their reports and videos up. It's fun to read the accounts from cities all over the world as they come in.

The ability to stage flash raids and global demos, to spread information where it needs to go, to fight a truly horrible cult while maintaining a sense of grace and humor is one of our strengths. It's kind of hard for a police officer to view protesters as "cyberterrorists" when they're eating cake, dancing, and making balloon animals.

Our methods are derived from the flashmob movement, where people will gather to perform a public stunt before dispersing. We've just taken it to the next level.[54]

Here again, we see Anonymous explicitly contrasting its decentralized, playful, chaotic network to the centralized, largely humorless corporate hierarchy of Scientology.

Anonymous's protests, however, have not been limited to cyber attacks. The movement has been active worldwide, protesting physically outside Scientology churches across the globe, from Copenhagen to Clearwater to Columbus, Ohio. Members usually mask themselves, either with bandanas or, more often, with "Guy Fawkes" masks modeled on those in the film *V for Vendetta*. Anonymous protesters typically carry an array of signs bearing slogans such as "Religion is free: Scientology is neither," "$cientology kills," and "Google 'Fair Game.'" One of the more colorful protests even had a pirate theme and was an event called "Operation Sea Arrrgh," highlighting their keen sense of irony and satire.[55]

Not surprisingly, the Church of Scientology has denounced Anonymous in the strongest possible terms. This is, in the church's view, nothing more than "a group of cyber-terrorists who hide their identities" and perpetrate "religious hate crimes against Churches of Scientology and individual Scientologists for no reason other than religious bigotry."[56] Despite its strong rhetoric, however, the church has had little success in silencing the Anonymous protests, in either the physical or the virtual realms. Indeed, Anonymous's inherently decentralized, shifting, and protean (dis)organization makes it more or less impossible to track or confront it in any significant way, making it one of the most potent new threats facing the church in an age of information.

Interview with an Anonymous

On Tuesday, November 10, 2009, I sat in a Columbus bar with a former Ohio State student who has been involved in a five-year conflict with Scientology.[57] This former student, who has now adopted the pseudonym "Chef Xenu," first became the target of Scientology's lawyers in October 2005. As a religious studies major at Ohio State, Chef Xenu had set up a large and detailed website cataloging a wide array of materials on various religions from many traditions. His website, however, also contained a significant collection of Scientology materials. These included many of Hubbard's published works, numerous photographs, and copies of the confidential OT levels. On October 8, 2005, Chef Xenu received an email from the Los Angeles law firm Moxon & Kobrin, which represents the Church of Scientology International and the Religious Technology Center, demanding that he remove all materials relating to Scientology and that he destroy any additional copies he might have. They warned that others had been convicted of copyright violation, some serving jail time and some paying fines and hundreds of thousands of dollars in legal fees for similar infringements. The lawyers had also sent letters to his internet provider, Roadrunner, which promptly terminated his website, Internet access, and email account.[58]

Today, Chef Xenu is an active member of the Anonymous network. Like others who feel that they have been threatened and intimidated by the church, Chef Xenu has made it his mission to spread as much information about Scientology as widely as possible and to combat what he sees as the silencing of free speech and the free exchange of information online. Since early 2008, he has been active in protesting outside the Columbus and other Ohio Scientology centers—though he has also been careful to work openly with the local police, to obtain the necessary permits before any protest, and to follow the letter of the law. In keeping with Anonymous's overall satirical spirit, he typically appears at protests wearing a chef's hat and apron modeled on the character "Chef" from *South Park* (whose voice was played by Scientologist Isaac

Hayes, who quit the show in protest over its satirical episode on the church).

According to Chef Xenu, however, there is some disagreement among those involved with Anonymous about the precise aim of their conflict with Scientology. While some see their mission as a full-scale attempt to destroy Scientology, others such as Chef Xenu see their mission as simply to undermine the current institutional form of Scientology. That is to say, he does not have a problem with individuals who wish to adhere to the beliefs and practices of Scientology, but he does want to disseminate information about what he sees as a destructive and power-hungry institution that reaps billions of dollars and is secretive about its actual aims and activities.

Like other Anonymous protesters, Chef Xenu makes sophisticated use of digital technology in addition to more conventional techniques in his critique of the church. In one amusing anecdote, Chef Xenu was filming a protest outside the Columbus center and was accidentally able to see into the boardroom through the church's front window. Inside the boardroom was a large display showing all the local donors to the church, and the specific amounts of donations happened to be on display. The Chef quickly posted all of the donor information online, where it now circulates with other similar data in various newsgroups and message boards. After this incident, he recounts, the church began putting cardboard over its own front windows (including over its books and other displays) whenever Anonymous came to protest.

In turn, Chef Xenu believes that he has also generated some reaction from the church. Among other things, he claims that he was informed by a local church official that they knew where he lived, and he believes that his place of residence has been visited by Scientologists. He states that the local police believe this to be the case as well. He has also found himself engaged in a sort of game of video "peekaboo," as he put it, trying to film the church's activities even as they tried to covertly catch him on video themselves. For the time being, Chef Xenu remains undeterred. If anything, he seems to find it amusing that Scientology is spending so much of its time worrying about one individual and a small group of protesters in central Ohio. If a few anonymous individuals can become such a thorn in its side, he wonders what a thousand small cells like this all over the country might represent to the church as it faces a new age of skepticism and often open hostility in the digital era.

Given the amorphous and decentralized nature of the Anonymous network, Scientology's response to these attacks has been somewhat muted. At the Columbus, Ohio, church, I was given a short four-page bulletin entitled *Anonymous: Frequently Asked Questions*, which contains various quotes attributed to Anonymous that suggest they are a dangerous, terroristic organization.[59] Scientologists in the Ohio area whom I've interviewed also typically describe Anonymous as a band of criminals, bigots, and hate-mongers who simply "can't stand to see a good thing, something that genuinely helps people, succeed."[60] Of course, the very problem with trying to pin down a group such as Anonymous is that they are—by definition—anonymous, so that anyone from a Project Chanology enthusiast to a Scientology OSA operative to an FBI agent to a run-of-the-mill Internet crank could post a video or a message under the title "Anonymous." By the same token, however, such an amorphous collective is virtually impossible to eradicate—and in every sense of the word "virtually."

Conclusions: Scientology's Waterloo?

If David Miscavige was able to proudly declare victory in the war against the IRS in 1993, the church's war against its enemies in cyberspace is less certain. Both sides in this war, as we saw earlier, have invoked First Amendment rights in their defense: for Scientology, this is a matter of religious freedom, including the right to maintain religious secrets and copyrights; for its online critics, this is matter of free speech, including the right to educate the public with information about an extremely problematic organization.[61] As Brill and Packard note, Scientology's claim that a body of religious knowledge can be *copyrighted* and that its profitability can be protected by law raises a host of unprecedented new questions. Indeed, it highlights fundamental questions about copyright law, religion, and the Internet that we have not yet really begun to sort out:

> The church's attempts to use copyright to protect the secrecy and profit-
> ability of its texts raise interesting theoretical questions about the applica-

tion of copyright law to religious doctrine. For example, the purpose of copyright is to secure the rights of authors to profit from their creative efforts in the hope that a financial incentive will promote the dissemination of knowledge. But should any one person or church be entitled to copyright and profit from divine revelation? If so, what constitutes fair use? ... Finally, if scripture can be owned and sold like any other commodity, what is the value of offering churches tax-exempt status? These are questions that society as a whole will have to debate. At this point they are beyond the bounds of our legal system.[62]

Powerful arguments have been made on all sides of this debate, by Scientologists, ex-Scientologists, courts, legal scholars, and academics alike. On one side, Scientologists and many scholars of religion have argued that the church's rights to religious privacy and confidential information—like those of any religion—should be respected here and that spreading the church's esoteric materials without its permission is highly problematic both ethically and legally. As one respected scholar of new religions, Jeffrey Hadden, put it, "[T]o deny a religious group the right to protect its esoteric knowledge ... constitutes a denial to that group the protection of the Free Exercise Clause of the First Amendment."[63]

On the other side, however, most critics and many legal scholars argue that the church's obsessive secrecy goes against the purpose and historical precedent of copyright law. As Brill and Packard argue, copyright is *not* intended to prevent anyone from access to, discussion of, and critical analysis of particular ideas; rather, it is designed to prevent the *reproduction of specific articulations* of those ideas: "Church secrecy ... prevents the public from having any access to these documents. That violates the purpose of the law. Copyright is intended to protect the expression of ideas, not the ideas themselves. Its purpose is to encourage scholarly and creative contribution to the pool of knowledge. The Supreme Court has made this point numerous times."[64] Moreover, Brill and Packard argue, Scientology also requires members to spend numerous hours of auditing, to pay required donations, and to accept church doctrine before being allowed to even see the OT materials. This too, they suggest, goes against the idea of copyright law, since one must literally *buy* into the doctrine before one has had a chance to view it openly: "[O]ne must buy into the church doctrine literally and figuratively before being allowed to actually read it. That is profoundly in violation of the spirit of the fair use doctrine and the purpose of Copyright law."[65]

Yet ironically, both of these arguments may simply have become moot points amidst the current era of information overload and hyper-accessibility of knowledge. Thus far, Scientology's attempts to staunch the hemorrhaging of information online appear to have not only failed but arguably backfired. The church's wars of "fair game" and "Operation Freakout" were perhaps moderately successful at inhibiting the flow of criticism during the 1960s and 70s, but they are less well adapted to the age of the Internet. "Nobody can sue the Internet," Alan Prendergast notes. "The information it carries doesn't originate in one place, and no one party is responsible for transmitting it."[66] As the cases against FACT-Net and others show, no amount of lawsuits can prevent the Xenu story or the fair game doctrine or the FBI files on Scientology from being viewed and downloaded on to every computer on earth. In many ways, Scientology's difficulties with the Internet are a result of the very nature and architecture of the Internet itself, which is designed to find ways to send information around whatever obstacle might be encountered. As Douglas Cowan observes, "The Internet is designed specifically to route data from one node to another by whatever means are available; it interprets attempts at censorship and control as instances of systemic failure. Blocked on one route, the Internet looks for another."[67]

This new age of media overload may well prove to be the greatest single threat faced by the church in the twenty-first century. It is one thing to combat a print journalist with an identifiable publisher such as Cooper or Behar; but how does one combat ten thousand websites that contain instant links to the confidential OT levels, the *South Park* episode, the Tom Cruise video, the *St. Petersburg Times* exposé, and the myriad Anonymous attacks on YouTube? Indeed, the basic qualities of the Internet—its speed, its fluidity, its relative anonymity—make it tailor-made for those who advocate radical digital free speech and extremely cumbersome for defenders of old-fashioned print-based copyrights and trade secrets: "[T]rying to plug an information leak in the Internet is a losing battle. . . . [T]he church's conduct in trying to silence its critics has alerted Internet users to the possibilities that others may attempt similar measures. And that is something they will fight with their best weapon—the ease and speed at which the Internet can be used to multiply and disseminate information to literally millions of people."[68]

As such, some critics are quite pessimistic about Scientology's ability to survive its new wars in the information age. As Gerry Armstrong commented in an interview with me in August 2009, this may well be "the last generation of Scientologists," since young people today grow up on the Internet, live increasingly in cyberspace, and get all of their information online.[69] It is difficult, he thinks, to foresee great numbers of converts coming from a generation that has ready access not just to the secret OT levels on hundreds of websites but also to countless YouTube videos and *South Park* clips that ridicule the beliefs and practices of Scientology.

It seems to me that the real problem that anyone interested in information about Scientology faces today is surely not how to find the secret OT III documents—something any child of the Internet generation can do in five minutes. Rather, the real problem is *how to sift through the overwhelming barrage of information*—some useful, some simply awful—on movements such as Scientology and come to an informed opinion. As of October 2010, a simple Google search on "OT III" produced a staggering 46,300 hits, while a search on "Xenu" produced another 891,000. Clearly, the RTC is not winning its war of information control in cyberspace. Perhaps the real challenge facing the church today, then, is whether it will continue waging a seemingly quixotic war of secrecy online, or whether it will adapt to a new age of information in which little, if anything, remains secret for very long. Even long before the age of the Internet and its instantaneous access to massive amounts of data, William S. Burroughs had noted that "if the Scientologists persist in self-imposed isolation and in withholding their materials from those best qualified to evaluate . . . them, they may well find themselves bypassed."[70] In the digital age, in which even the most intense efforts of the RTC appear to be largely unsuccessful at staunching the relentless flow of information in cyberspace, Burroughs may well prove to be correct. For, as Hubbard himself remarked in 1954, "you cannot unveil the SECRET" and have it ever be quite so secret ever again.[71]

However, large religious and corporate entities such as Scientology might not be the only ones losing the new wars of information in cyberspace. As terrorism expert Richard Clarke has recently warned, the United States—the nation that first created what we now know as the Internet—itself risks losing the cyber war of the twenty-first century, as its national security faces a whole new wave of sophisticated cyber terrorists, hackers, criminals, and other virtual enemies.[72] In this sense, Scientology's war against the legions of Anonymous might be a prescient foreshadowing of the challenges facing nation-states themselves in the twenty-first century.

- CONCLUSION -

NEW RELIGIONS, FREEDOM, AND PRIVACY IN THE POST-9/11 WORLD

Yes, sir. You're free to worship everything under the Constitution so long
as it's Christian. . . .
[T]he freedom which man is guaranteed in the English-speaking world
today is really not as wide as the freedom which he had as a Roman.
—Hubbard, *Philadelphia Doctorate Course* (1952)[1]

The establishment clause does not cloak a church in utter secrecy, nor
does it immunize a church from all governmental authority.
—Judge Samuel Sterrett, *Church of Scientology of California v.
Commissioner of Internal Revenue Service* (1984)[2]

As I finish writing this book in 2010, Scientology's efforts to assert its status as a "religion" have by no means ended but in many ways have grown
even more intense. Not only have the American media continued to assault the church with a barrage of scathing exposés, such as CNN's week-
long series entitled "Scientology: A History of Violence," but a number of
high-profile members such as Marty Rathbun, Mike Rinder, and director
Paul Haggis have recently exited the church, leaving behind narratives of
scandal and abuse.[3] Meanwhile, various foreign governments have also
continued to target Scientology, such as the French courts, which convicted Scientology of fraud in October 2009.[4] The German government
also continues to regard Scientology with deep suspicion. As recently as
2007, in fact, German federal and state interior ministers undertook a
move to ban the church.[5] And the church, in turn, has continued to argue
that it has been the target of religious bigotry and intolerance, and that
the worldwide hostility to Scientology is a symptom of a much deeper
threat to religious freedom itself. In sum, the war over Scientology's

religious status has by no means subsided but remains a volatile and contested issue even in the second decade of the twenty-first century.

I would therefore like to conclude this book with a sense of humility and a recognition of the limitations of what I have been able to cover in the last several hundred pages. As we have seen throughout the preceding chapters, the story of Scientology is far too vast, complex, and multifaceted to be covered in a lengthy encyclopedia, much less a short book. My history of Scientology here has focused on just one piece of this extremely complex movement—its long, convoluted journey to recognition as a religion in the United States. I could have explored virtually infinite other strange rabbit holes in this book, some of which I have not pursued for legal and ethical reasons. And there are fascinating topics of which I have only scratched the surface but could have explored in more detail, such as Scientology's connection with secret CIA research on the paranormal,[6] Hubbard's pursuit of the "Messianic Project,"[7] the curious intersections between Scientology, Louis Farrakhan, and the Nation of Islam,[8] and the latest allegations of abuse at Scientology's Gold Base in California[9]; and there is the whole question of the church's ongoing battles for religious recognition outside the United States, particularly in countries such as Germany, France, Canada, the United Kingdom, Australia, and Russia.[10] All of these are obviously important aspects of this movement worthy of further investigation, and I hope very much that others—both those *within* the church and critics outside of it—will take these up as research projects in the future.

Yet despite the admitted limitations of this book, I do think it has shed some important light on the complex history of both the Church of Scientology and the changing definition of religion over the last sixty years. Even as L. Ron Hubbard grew from a penny-a-word pulp fiction writer to the leader of the world's most controversial new religion, so too, the very understanding of religion underwent a dramatic transformation during these decades. The comforting triad of "Protestant-Catholic-Jew" rapidly gave way to a radical new diversity of offerings in the American religious marketplace, where Hubbard's new church was just one of many new spiritual commodities. But Hubbard's pursuit of the "religion angle" was by no means a simple or straightforward one. Rather, Scientology's attempts to define itself as a religion were sporadic and situational, responding to the rapidly changing circumstances of American culture, politics, and legal structures over the last six decades. It was really only during its period of all-out war with the IRS that the church adopted a no-holds-barred pursuit of the religion angle. Indeed, by 1993, Scientology was describing itself not simply as "a" religion but in fact as "the fastest growing religion on Earth today."[11] Yet even then, its self-conscious adoption of religious trappings left it open to widespread criticism for its apparent cynicism, opportunism, and dissimulation.

As such, the Church of Scientology is a crucial test case for helping us think about the very concept, categorization, and definition of religion itself in the twenty-first century. The question Scientology raises is not simply "What is religion?" or "How has our understanding of religion changed over the last sixty years?" More important, it raises the critical questions of *who* gets to define religion and *what is at stake* in calling something religion rather than something else (such as a cult, a business, a secular therapy, or a multinational corporation)? As we have seen throughout this book, the definition of religion is hardly an abstract academic game played by a few professors in universities but a far more complex and contested debate between a wide array of actors. These actors range from religious leaders and adherents to government agencies and judges, from journalists and anticult groups to faceless collectives on the Internet. As David Chidester notes, "[T]he very definition of religion . . . continues to be contested in American popular culture."[12] And the stakes in the debate are quite high indeed, ranging from millions of dollars in tax revenues to protections on the national and international stage.

In this conclusion, I will discuss some of the ongoing controversies surrounding Scientology and its religious status in the twenty-first century. Most important, I will suggest that the case of Scientology raises profound questions about religious freedom, secrecy, privacy, and the flow of information in a post-9/11 context.

Scientology in the Twenty-first Century: From the Death of L. Ron Hubbard to the Ascension of David Miscavige

L. Ron Hubbard died on January 24, 1986, in a Blue Bird motor home located at the remote "Emanuel Camp," about five miles East of Creston,

California. Hubbard had been in hiding for years following the FBI raids on the LA and DC centers and the arrest of his wife after Operation Snow White. He appeared to have died eight days after suffering a fatal stroke. According to the coroner's report, Hubbard was found with long, scraggly hair on his scalp and face, and his fingernails and toenails were also "long, unkempt."[13] The toxicology report on his blood specimen showed evidence of the drug hydroxyzine (Vistaril), which is used both as an antihistamine and as a treatment for anxiety due to its sedative, hypnotic, analgesic, and tranquilizing effects.[14] It is not clear why the drug was found in Hubbard's system or whether it contributed to his death.

Overall, Hubbard's death in a remote motor home with his long, unkempt hair and fingernails bears more than a passing resemblance to the deaths of other eccentric billionaires, such as Howard Hughes. The reclusive Hughes, who died just ten years before Hubbard, was also found with long, unkempt hair and fingernails and with suspicious drugs in his system. In any case, Hubbard himself seemed to have known that this might be one fate of the great adventurers that he had admired in works such as Bolitho's *Twelve Against the Gods*. As Bolitho wrote in the introduction to the book, which Hubbard noted that he particularly admired, "The vocation of adventure is as tragic as that of Youth. . . . [A]t a certain point it leads back to the cage again. The greatest adventurer that ever lived ended as a nervous, banal millionaire."[15]

As the church described Hubbard's death, however, the founder had not simply died as an eccentric recluse hiding in the California desert but rather had chosen to move onward to a higher plane and continue his spiritual research "on a planet a galaxy away."[16] As former Scientology PR officer Robert Vaughn Young recounts, "Him dying suddenly made him very mortal. And the last thing we could have was for Hubbard to be mortal. So a story had to be designed, and the story is that he went off to research the next level."[17] Interestingly enough, however, the church has maintained a luxurious mansion for Hubbard at their international headquarters or Gold Base at the former resort of Gilman Hot Springs, California. The mansion is reportedly still staffed and preserved—complete with full water glasses, toothbrushes, and note pads—in the expectation that Hubbard will return in another body.[18]

Following Hubbard's death, leadership of the now vast, multifaceted, and transnational church passed over to its current head, David Miscavige (b. 1960). Having joined the church while not yet even a teenager in 1971, Miscavige rose quickly through the Scientology ranks, from a Commodore's Messenger and assistant to Hubbard to eventual head of the Religious Technology Center. Today, the RTC holds "the ultimate ecclesiastical authority regarding the standard and pure application of L. Ron Hubbard's religious technologies."[19] As of 2010, Miscavige resides at the church's highly secretive and well-guarded Gold Base near Hemet, California.

Exactly how this transition of authority took place, however, is quite unclear. The official church narrative is that Miscavige naturally assumed his position as chairman of the RTC and his current leadership role following Hubbard's death. But many critics—including both those who are hostile to Hubbard's work and those who have left the church but remain loyal to Hubbard's legacy—regard Miscavige's position as the result of an internal coup that ousted leading rivals such as David Mayo, Pat Broeker, and others.[20] This particular story, however, is so complex, controversial, and fraught with legal pitfalls that I will leave it for others to debate.

Yet regardless of the legitimacy of his claims to be Hubbard's successor, Miscavige has clearly generated as much as if not more scandal and media attack than L. Ron himself. Major publications such as *Time* magazine and the *St. Petersburg Times* have described Miscavige as "cunning, ruthless and so paranoid that he kept plastic wrap over his glass of water."[21] More recently, both the *St. Petersburg Times* and CNN's Anderson Cooper 360 series, interviewed former high-level executives who describe Miscavige as an unstable and power-hungry bully who has created a "culture of intimidation and violence" at the very top of the church.[22] Miscavige, in turn, has repeatedly defended his church on the grounds of the First Amendment, arguing that this is and always has been a legitimate religious movement that has been unjustly persecuted by a bigoted, intolerant, and vindictive press.[23]

Today, the Church of Scientology continues to boast massive numbers worldwide and ever-increasing growth of new centers, missions, and organizations, including an impressive series of new Ideal Orgs in Johannesburg, New York, San Francisco, and other major cities worldwide.

According to the church's *Freedom* magazine, this marks Scientology as "the fastest growing religion in the 21st century"; and Scientologists I have interviewed from Ohio to California claim that the church "has never been growing faster."[24] Many scholars and journalists, however, believe that Scientology's numbers are at once much lower than the church claims and apparently on the decline. Thus, the American Religious Identification Survey found that Scientology's numbers in the United States were not only nowhere near the level claimed by the church but also that its numbers had fallen significantly from fifty-five thousand in 2001 to twenty-five thousand in 2008.[25] And even scholars who are sympathetic to the church note that its numbers are probably much exaggerated.[26] In an interview with the *St. Petersburg Times*, former RTC inspector general Marty Rathbun claims that Scientology today is like "the Titanic hitting the iceberg."[27] While the church still has vast monetary reserves and is launching expensive new building projects such as the "Ideal Orgs" and the "Power Center," Rathbun alleges that it has been steadily declining in numbers since 1990: "That's the difference between the old Scientology and the new: the brave new Scientology is all these beautiful buildings and real estate and no people."[28]

Meanwhile, the controversies and scandals surrounding Scientology appear not only to have continued but, if anything, only grown more intense in the last decade. Thus, while its highly controversial Guardian's Office was officially dismantled after the FBI investigations in the 1970s, the church has created an Office of Special Affairs (OSA), which many believe has continued the same sorts of clandestine surveillance and espionage operations, only now in a more sophisticated form. According to the *Los Angeles Times*, the OSA has carried on many of the same undercover operations, though now often farming them out to independent private investigators who cannot be linked directly back to the Church of Scientology: "[P]rivate detectives have simply replaced church members as agents of intimidation. The detectives are especially valued because they insulate the church from deceptive and potentially embarrassing investigative tactics that the church in fact endorses."[29] As we saw in chapter 3, most critics also believe that the church's controversial tactics of "fair game" and "security checks" were never really ended in practice but only abolished in name and that the same hardball measures against suspected enemies have continued to this day. Indeed, if we are to believe accounts of ex-Scientologists such as Marc Headley, the practice of Sec Checking appears to have not only continued but taken on even more aggressive forms in recent years.[30]

Long after its celebrated victory in the war with the IRS, then, the Church of Scientology continues to be surrounded by controversies and accusations of illegal, immoral, and "cultish" behavior. Perhaps the most tragic example is the case of Lisa McPherson, a thirty-six-year-old Scientologist who died at the Flag Service Organization in Clearwater in 1995. This remains one of the most disputed cases in Scientology's already complex and disputed history. According to the initial autopsy report by the district medical examiner, McPherson was found to have died of a thromboembolism caused by severe dehydration, and her body allegedly had multiple bruises and lesions consistent with insect or animal bites. Following the report, the Church of Scientology was indicted on felony charges for abuse of a disabled adult and practicing medicine without a license.[31] The church, in turn, responded by hiring its own team of forensic pathologists, who disputed the medical examiner's report and concluded that McPherson had died from natural causes unrelated to her treatment by Scientology. The original medical examiner was later found to have botched the case beyond repair and subsequently amended the death certificate to state the manner of death as an "accident." Charges against the church were dropped in June 2000.[32]

Despite the apparent exoneration of the church, however, McPherson's case is still commonly cited by critics as one of the clearest examples of the church's dangerous, destructive, and cultlike activities. A watchdog group of critics formed and began hosting annual protests outside the Fort Harrison Hotel in memory of McPherson's death. Likewise, the Anonymous collective, Project Chanology, held worldwide protests against Scientology on the anniversary of McPherson's birthday, February 10, 2008.[33] The dominant theme in their protest, as displayed in countless signs and banners, is that Scientology is not in fact a legitimate religion but a greed-driven, dangerous, destructive, and ultimately deadly cult.

Religion, Cult, Multinational Corporation, or Simulacrum? Rethinking Religion in the Twenty-first Century

So all of this leaves us with the difficult question of what to make of the Church of Scientology. In the pages of this book, we have retraced Hubbard's pursuit of past lives, supernatural powers, space opera narratives, and borrowings from Eastern religions; we have examined his more cynical idea of exploiting the "religion angle" and his explicit attempt to present Scientology in more recognizably religious (i.e., Christian) garb, complete with crosses and ministerial collars; but we have also seen the hostility his movement faced from the media, government agencies, and anticult groups. So how should we describe and define Scientology today, in the twenty-first century? Is it best understood as a legitimate but mistreated religion, as a deceptive cult, as a big business, as a kind of ersatz religion, or as something else altogether? And more important, what is really at stake in these sorts of labels?

The Church of Scientology has in fact worked quite hard to gather support from scholars in the academic community in order to make its case that it should be recognized as a bona fide religion alongside the other great world faiths. Thus, the slickly produced 1998 text, *Scientology: Theology and Practice of a Contemporary Religion*, is explicitly designed to assert the church's status as a genuine religion seated "squarely within the tradition of the world's major religions."[34] The text begins with a classic definition of religion drawn from the University of Chicago scholar Joachim Wach, who describes three primary forms of religious expression: "1) the theoretical forms of religious expression—doctrines, beliefs, myths and sayings; 2) Practical forms of religious expression—services, rites and practices, and 3) sociological forms of religious expressions—organizations, relationships and authority."[35] The book then invokes testimonies from an array of scholars from around the world who defend Scientology's claims to be a true religion. The most impressive of these—which is prominently featured in an appendix to the book—comes from the respected sociologist of religion Bryan S. Wilson. After laying out an inventory of twenty factors common to religions, Wilson concludes definitively that "Scientology is a bona fide religion and should be considered as such."[36]

Moreover, as we noted in chapter 4, even if Scientology's leadership has engaged in extremely problematic and at times illegal activities, that still does not mean that thousands of ordinary practitioners do not find the church to be meaningfully religious in their own lives. Again, the fact that Catholic bishops have covered up child sexual abuse does not prevent millions of ordinary believers worldwide from continuing to find Catholicism meaningful in their daily lives.

Most critics and ex-Scientologists, however, contend that Scientology's appeal to religious status is largely a cynical ploy and an attempt to protect what is essentially a for-profit business from government scrutiny. As I noted in the introduction, even some of my colleagues regard Scientology not as a religion but rather as a simulacrum of a religion. A similar view was expressed by one ex-Scientologist I interviewed. He even quoted a statement allegedly made by Hubbard that "RELIGION IS THE BULLFIGHTER'S CAPE THAT AVOIDS THE GORE." In other words, religion is the distraction that Scientology uses to mislead its enemies and cover over its actual business.[37] Although I cannot verify that Hubbard himself actually made such a statement, I do know that many former Scientologists believe this was his cynical attitude toward the "religion angle" overall. As Gerry Armstrong has argued, for example, Scientology's claim to religious status is a purely cynical and self-serving facade, with no other aim than to reap the material benefits that come with being called a "spiritual" organization. In Armstrong's words,

> Scientology calls itself a "religion" to obtain the benefits, privileges, protections and the benevolent public image that are conferred on religions. Being a religion, the cult claims, makes its aggressive, abusive, dishonest and criminal activities, its war of total attrition of its "enemies," legally protected "religious expression" or "religious freedom."
>
> Scientology is not benevolent, but malevolent. Its ostensibly benevolent activities—its Volunteer Ministers that show up to "help" at disaster sites; its Narconon anti-drug operations; its Way to Happiness booklet campaign, etc.—are to cloak the cult's malevolence.[38]

Significantly, Armstrong also argues that the church's obsessive secrecy and the fact that it *profits* from its secret information also disqualify it from being a legitimate religion. As he argued in his testimony during the RTC's case against Grady Ward in 1997, "Freedom of religion without freedom to discuss religion and religious experience is impossible." An organization, he argues, cannot "have it both ways," that is, claim to be *both* a religion protected by the First Amendment *and* the holder of exclusive secrets that no one else is free to discuss: "Such an entity can be a 'secret-selling company,' or some such, in competition with other secret-selling companies, as long as it does not try to claim that the secrets it sells are 'religious' secrets."[39]

As an alternative to the usual "Scientology is a religion" versus "Scientology is a cult and/or business" debate, the Canadian sociologist Stephen Kent suggests a somewhat more nuanced approach. In his essay "Scientology—Is This a Religion?" Kent argues persuasively that Scientology is really not one entity at all but rather a far more diverse, diffuse, complex *multinational corporation* of which religion is one—but only one—of its various facets. The church is, in short, a "multi-faceted transnational that has religion as only one of its many components. Other components include political aspirations, business ventures, cultural productions, pseudo-medical practices, pseudo-psychiatric claims, and (among its most devoted members who have joined the Sea Organization), an alternative family structure."[40]

My own take on this complex debate is a bit different. Ultimately, I think the question "Is Scientology a religion?" is probably the wrong question to ask in the first place—or at least, it is not the most useful or interesting question we might ask. Again, as Jonathan Z. Smith notes, "The moral . . . is not that religion cannot be defined, but that it can be defined, with greater or lesser success, more than fifty ways."[41] Moreover, as we have seen throughout this book, our definitions of religion are also historically variable, constantly shifting in relation to complex social, cultural, and political dynamics.[42] I will therefore leave it to my readers to decide the "Is it a religion?" question for themselves. After plowing through two hundred pages of Scientology's complex history, lawsuits, and conflicts with various branches of government, readers should be equipped to make up their own minds on this complex debate. This is precisely what I ask my students to do whenever I teach Scientology as an ideal test case in my own introductory classes on religion.

Instead, I think the more profound questions here are (a) *Who gets to define religion?* and (b) *Just what is at stake in calling something "religion"?* If we follow Bruce Lincoln's approach discussed in the introduction, then religion is perhaps better understood not as a "thing" at all, but rather as a particular kind of discourse that makes a claim to a special kind of *authority.* Specifically, it claims a kind of authority that is believed to be suprahuman, transcendent, and/or eternal.[43] In this sense, Scientology clearly worked very hard to use elaborate forms of discourse—such as lectures, journals, books, policy letters, films, websites, and advertisements—designed to make precisely this claim to religious authority. If anything, Scientology is a *self-conscious attempt to make a religion,* that is, *a concerted effort to use explicitly religious sorts of discourse to describe, defend, define, and redefine itself.* But this is perhaps only in keeping with Hubbard's own rather postmodern view of the self and of reality. As we saw in chapter 2, Hubbard believed that we all have the power to create our own reality and to "create our own universe" (much as an author of science fiction has the power to create new worlds of imagination); and for Hubbard, the new universes that we create are *more real* and *more true* than the MEST universe itself. So why not then create a new *religion*? Why not self-consciously construct a new spiritual belief system and then argue that it is in fact *more true* than any existing religion?[44]

However, perhaps an even more interesting question is who then gets to *evaluate and pass judgment* on one's claims to religious status? Is it academics, that is, professors and students at universities? The media? Government agencies such as the IRS, FDA, and State Department? The courts, lawyers, and judges? Ordinary believers? Bloggers and chat room users on the Internet? Or—as I think I have shown in the pages of this book—is it really all of the above in complex, tangled, and interdependent ways?

But the final and most important question in all of this is really *just what is at stake*? What are the potential benefits and risks in making such a claim to religious status, and how have these benefits and risks varied during different periods of American religious history? In some cases, the stakes might seem somewhat frivolous. In the late 1960s, for example, a group called the "Neo-American Church" claimed that LSD was its central sacrament, and its clergy (called "Boo-Hoos") argued in federal court that consumption of the drug was protected under the First Amendment. Noting the Boo-Hoos's official songs such as "Puff the Magic Dragon" and its motto "Victory Over Horseshit," the Supreme Court decided against considering the Neo-American Church a legitimate religion.[45] Yet in other cases, the stakes seem a bit more profound. As I noted in the introduction, the Native American Church has fought a decades-long battle with U.S. state and federal courts over its right to consume peyote as part of its religious rites, which, the NAC claims, have been performed for at least seven thousand years before the U.S. Constitution was even written. When the U.S. Supreme Court ruled against the religious use of peyote in 1990, many saw this as a threat not just to protections for Native American communities but to religious freedom itself, particularly for minority communities such as indigenous peoples. The 1990 Supreme Court decision, they argue, "sent shockwaves through the American religious community as a whole, for the principles that it explicitly directed at a powerless minority religion could be used against any religion should occasion arise."[46]

For the Church of Scientology, the stakes in laying claim to religious status are multiple and have changed significantly over time. These have included not simply the obvious benefit of tax exemption but also protection from FDA scrutiny; control over its copyrighted and highly profitable esoteric materials such as the OT levels; legal defense in a wide array of civil and criminal court cases; recognition from the U.S. State Department; and support overseas in the face of a variety of foreign governments. But at the same time, ironically, the claim to religious status *also* opens the door for other groups to challenge, contest, and undermine that claim. Thus, the more Scientology insists that it is a "bona fide religion," the more the media, anticult groups, Internet activists, and ex-Scientologists can target and subvert its claim to religious status.

In sum, the case of Scientology does not simply raise the basic question of what is and is not religion; rather, it also forces us to fundamentally rethink the very category of religion itself in the twenty-first century. It asks us to examine the deeper questions of, *by whom and how religion is defined, by what intellectual, legal, and cultural processes it is constructed, and what larger economic and political concerns are involved in the very claim to being a religion.* As we have seen in this book, our understanding of religion is not a static thing, but rather the product of an ongoing debate that is also tied to very real relations of power.[47] Therefore, the questions of who gets to define religion, what is at risk in laying claim to being a religion, and the status of groups such as Scientology will never be settled once and for all. Rather, these questions will only continue to be debated and renegotiated in ever more complex ways as we encounter an ever-increasing proliferation of new offerings in the spiritual marketplace.

Religion, Secrecy, and Security in a Post-9/11 Context

Finally, beyond simply the "what is religion" question, the Church of Scientology also raises one other profound set of political, legal, and ethical concerns: namely, how do we deal with secretive, controversial, and potentially dangerous religious movements in a twenty-first-century context, amidst the new wars on terrorism and new concerns over information control, surveillance, and privacy? Again, with its long history of secrecy, its obsession with surveillance and information control, and its complex relations with the FBI, Scientology is in many ways an ideal test case for thinking about these difficult issues. With its cold war–style preoccupation with secrecy, its elaborate clandestine operations, and its history of actual infiltration of government offices, Scientology in many ways long prefigured our own post-9/11 generation and our new wars of information. Indeed, the tactics employed by the FDA and FBI against Scientology in the 1960s and 70s appear rather timid compared with the new measures allowed by the USA PATRIOT Act and other new measures in the war on terror.[48] Perhaps most important, the case of Scientology raises the difficult question of what right to privacy religious movements deserve and how far either government agencies or scholars in the academy should go to penetrate their inner secrets. Do law enforcement agencies, in fact, have some obligation to infiltrate and expose movements that could be dangerous or harmful to their citizens? And what is the role of scholars and students of religion in all of this? Do we have some obligation to expose and unmask such groups, or conversely, to argue for tolerance and respect?

In many ways, the study of new religions today seems caught between two extremes, which are perhaps best illustrated by the cases of the Branch Davidian disaster at Waco in 1993 and the Aum Shinrikyo gas attacks in Tokyo in 1995. On the one hand, many scholars such as Catherine Wessinger, James Tabor, and Eugene Gallagher have made powerful arguments in defense of religious freedom and privacy of these new religions. The BATF's botched raid of the Branch Davidian compound and its disastrous handling of the standoff, they argue, is a stark example of what happens when law enforcement agencies fail to understand these movements as legitimate religions and overstep the limits of the state: "If the purpose of the First Amendment is to protect religions from the state, rather than the state from religion, there is no constitutional basis for enlisting the power of the state in the campaign against so-called cults."[49]

Yet, on the other hand, the case of Aum Shinrikyo would seem to present the opposite problem. In the Aum case, the movement was able to manufacture chemical weapons in large part because of the Japanese government's more hands-off policy in dealing with religious movements. As Wessinger notes, "Aum Shinrikyo had free rein . . . to develop weapons of mass destruction due to lack of scrutiny by law enforcement agents. In reaction to government abuses prior to and during World War II, Japanese law enforcement agencies did not typically investigate religious organizations or conduct covert intelligence gathering."[50] In short, the question we face today is "whether the State and its citizens require greater protection from religious groups, and whether laws need to be brought in or strengthened to allow the State greater surveillance and control over religious groups"[51]; or whether, conversely, minority religious groups in fact require *greater protection from* government intrusion in order to prevent yet another Waco-style disaster.

This difficult question has only become more acute in the wake of 9/11. In the United States, for example, the federal government has introduced extremely invasive new policies and methods of surveillance, such as the USA PATRIOT Act and the NSA's secret program of warrantless wiretapping, which has been used to spy on tens of thousands if not millions of U.S. citizens.[52] In many cases, we now know, this surveillance has been directed specifically at religious groups, including not only Muslim organizations but even Christian peace activists.[53] Indeed, we seem to have entered a new kind of cold war era of secrecy and paranoia in the wake of 9/11, with a new kind of "McCarthy-era philosophy."[54] As Gilbert Herdt observes, "Just as we thought secrecy was about to disappear from the national consciousness . . . the events of September 11, 2001, shattered the present. . . . [T]he U.S. government deployed new and virtually unprecedented measures of secrecy. . . . Secrecy refuses to go away and may become more contested than ever in the life of civil societies."[55]

The Church of Scientology is an extreme example of the complex questions of religious secrecy, privacy, and surveillance in a post-9/11 context. On the one hand, it is clear that Scientology at times engaged in numerous illegal activities—of which the GO's infiltration of the IRS offices was only the most audacious example—as well as repeated attempts to silence critics both within and outside the church. But on the other hand, it seems no less clear that Scientology also emerged within and responded to a larger culture of secrecy, paranoia, and surveillance that only fed its obsessions with information control. As we saw in chapter 3, the FBI and other government agencies were as paranoid about Hubbard as he was about them, and their mutual suspicions created an escalating spiral of secrecy, invasive government assaults, and increasingly audacious counterresponses from the church.

I do not believe there is any easy resolution to this complex issue, any more than I think there is an easy answer to the complex ethical-epistemological double bind of secrecy discussed in the introduction. But I do think it calls for the sort of careful balance between a hermeneutics of respect and a hermeneutics of suspicion that I have argued for throughout this book. We can, I think, respect Scientology's claims to religious status and its members' rights to privacy and freedom of religious expression *while at the same time* looking critically at its long history of problematic, unethical, and illegal activities. But the same attitude of respectful suspicion *also* needs to be applied to government agencies and law enforcement, particularly in a new age of terrorism, as governments are endowed with ever greater powers of surveillance and ever more invasive ways to monitor their citizens. In sum, I would argue, the critical historian of religions today needs to remain at once respectful

and suspicious of *both* religious movements and the governmental powers that would monitor and control them.

These debates are not likely to disappear anytime soon but on the
contrary will likely become more intense as we grapple with ever more
complex questions of information control, secrecy, privacy, and surveillance in the twenty-first century. As such, I expect that the critical study
of religion will also have an increasingly important role to play.

- APPENDIX -

A TIMELINE OF MAJOR EVENTS IN SCIENTOLOGY'S COMPLEX JOURNEY TO BECOMING A "RELIGION"

January 1, 1938: Hubbard claims to have had a near-death experience and writes his "Excalibur" manuscript.

February–March 1946: Hubbard participates in the "Babalon Working" with Jack Parsons.

April 1950: Hubbard and John Campbell form the Hubbard Dianetic Research Foundation.

May 1950: "Dianetics" is published in *Astounding Science Fiction*.

1950: *Dianetics: The Modern Science of Mental Health* is published in book form.

Mid-1950: Dianetics practitioners begin to report memories from past lives.

October 1950: Joseph Winter resigns from Dianetics in part because of auditing of past lives.

Late 1950–1951: Hubbard develops the idea of the thetan and past lives.

January 1951: New Jersey State Board of Medical Examiners accuses the Hubbard Dianetic Research Foundation, Inc., of operating a school for treatment of disease without a license.

1951–1952: Hubbard begins to use the E-meter as part of Dianetics and Scientology auditing.

1952: Hubbard Association of Scientologists (HAS) is formed in Phoenix, Arizona.

1952: Hubbard begins to discuss the "exteriorization" of the thetan in *The Philadelphia Doctorate Course* and *Scientology 8-8008*.

March 1953: Two Dianetics and Scientology practitioners are arrested as part of an investigation into practicing medicine without a license.

April 10, 1953: Hubbard first suggests the "religion angle" in a letter to Helen O'Brien.

Late 1953: A Scientologist in Glendale, California, is jailed for practicing medicine without a license.

December 1953: Three "churches" are incorporated: the Church of American Science, the Church of Scientology, and the Church of Spiritual Engineering.

February 18, 1954: The first Church of Scientology is incorporated in California.

1954: Hubbard's *Phoenix Lectures* identifies Scientology's oldest roots in Indian religions such as the Veda and Buddhism.

August 1954: Hubbard calls for Scientology to "ally itself with religion."

September 1, 1954: HAS becomes HASI (Hubbard Association of Scientologists International).

December 24, 1954: Hubbard asserts that "Scientology is a religion."

1955: Hubbard composes his "Hymn of Asia" identifying himself as the Buddha Maitreya.

1955: Hubbard describes practitioners of Scientology as "ministers."

1955: U.S. District Court for the District of Columbia authorizes Hubbard to celebrate marriages.

1956: California Church changes its name to "Church of Scientology of California" (CSC).

1956: Washington, DC, church is recognized as tax exempt.

1956: "Scientology wedding ceremony" is introduced.

1957: CSC is granted tax-exempt status.

1958: FDA seizes twenty-one thousand tablets of Hubbard's anti–radiation sickness drug, Dianezene.

1958: IRS withdraws Washington, DC, church's tax exemption.

1958: "Hubbard E-meter" is developed and becomes a central part of auditing.

1959: *Ceremonies of the Founding Church of Scientology* is published, including instructions for a church service, wedding, christening, and funeral; the title page states that "the E-meter is not intended or effective for the diagnosis, treatment or prevention of any disease."

June 21, 1960: *HCO Bulletin*, "Religious Philosophy and Religious Practice," states that "Scientology's closest spiritual ties with any other religion are with Orthodox (Hinayana) Buddhism."

October 29, 1962: *HCO Bulletin*, "Religion," states that "Scientology 1970 is being planned on a religious organization basis throughout the world."

January 4, 1963: U.S. Marshals, acting on an FDA warrant, raid the Founding Church of Scientology in Washington, DC.

1965: IRS audit of Scientology begins.

March 12, 1966: *HCO Executive Letter,* "Corporate Status," describes the transfer of all HASI assets to the tax-exempt CSC.

July 1966: Hubbard begins to develop the confidential OT levels.

July 18, 1967: IRS strips CSC of tax exemption.

1968: The Sea Organization forms.

1968: *The Character of Scientology* identifies Scientology as a "religion" according to *Webster's Dictionary* definition.

May 1968: *Advance!* magazine is launched, comparing Scientology with other major religions.

February 12, 1969: *HCO Policy Letter,* "Religion," states that "visual evidences that Scientology is a religion are mandatory."

1969: Founding Church of Scientology sues the IRS.

March 6, 1969: *HCO Policy Letter* entitled "Scientology is a Religion" directs that all Scientology materials should clearly show that this is a "religion."

1973: The E-meter is redefined as a "religious artifact used as a spiritual guide in the church confessional."

April 20, 1973: "Operation Snow White" is devised.

1974–1975: Scientologists infiltrate IRS offices and steal thousands of documents.

1974: *Scientology: A World Religion Emerges in the Space Age* is published.

July 1977: FBI raids Scientology headquarters in Washington, DC, and Los Angeles.

October 1977: Eleven Scientologists, including Mary Sue Hubbard, are convicted of conspiracy; L. Ron Hubbard goes into hiding until his death in 1986.

Late 1970s: "Messianic Project" and "Messianic Surveys" are allegedly launched.

November 1985: Confidential OT materials are leaked to the *Los Angeles Times.*

January 24, 1986: Hubbard dies and moves on "to research the next level."

1987: David Miscavige becomes chairman of the board of the Religious Technology Center.

Summer 1989: Scientology hires private investigators to investigate the personal lives of senior IRS officials.

October 1991: David Miscavige and Marty Rathbun hold an unscheduled meeting with IRS commissioner and offer to drop all lawsuits in exchange for tax exemption.

October 1, 1993: IRS grants tax exemptions to all Scientology organizations in the United States; Scientology agrees to pay IRS $12.5 million in back taxes.

1993: U.S. State Department notes discrimination against Scientologists in Germany.

1996: Cult Awareness Network is driven into bankruptcy, and its name and files are taken over by Scientologists.

1998: *Scientology: Theology and Practice of a Contemporary Religion* is published, with the primary aim of asserting that Scientology is a religion, using testimonies from various scholars of religion.

1999: U.S. State Department report on International Religious Freedom criticizes Germany for unfair scrutiny of Scientology.

January 15, 2008: Tom Cruise's promotional video for Scientology is leaked to YouTube; Scientology demands its removal.

January 21, 2008: Anonymous releases its *Message to Scientology* video.

2009: U.S. State Department report on International Religious Freedom criticizes Germany for its treatment of religious minorities, notably Scientology.

- NOTES -

Introduction: The World's Most Controversial New Religion and Why No One Writes About It

1. L. Ron Hubbard, "The Hope of Man," June 1955, TBDS, vol. 2, 215.
2. Richard Behar, "The Scientologists and Me," *Time*, May 6, 1991, 57.
3. "L. Ron Hubbard: The Founder of Scientology," Aboutlronhubbard.org, 2006, http://www.aboutlronhubbard.org/eng/wis3_1.htm.
4. Federal Bureau of Investigation, airgram, April 17, 1951, Freedom of Information / Privacy Acts Section, Subject: Church of Scientology / L. Ron Hubbard, No. 62-94080. Hereafter cited as FBI.
5. "Mrs. Hubbard Torture Claim," *Los Angeles Examiner*, April 24, 1951, 1.
6. Richard Behar, "Scientology: The Thriving Cult of Greed and Power," *Time*, May 6, 1991, 50–57.
7. Joe Childs and Thomas C. Tobin, "Scientology: The Truth Rundown," *St. Petersburg Times*, June 21, 2009, http://www.tampabay.com/specials/2009/reports/project/. The allegations made by the *Times* article have been repeated by many other sources, such as Laurie Goodstein, "Defectors Say Church of Scientology Hides Abuse," *New York Times*, March 6, 2010, http://www.nytimes.com/2010/03/07/us/07scientology.html; and "Scientology: A History of Violence," *AC360°* (blog), CNN, March 25, 2010, http://ac360.blogs.cnn.com/2010/03/25/scientology-a-history-of-violence/.
8. See Church of Scientology of California, *Press View the FBI Raid* (Los Angeles: Church of Scientology of California, 1977), 1; Robert Gillette and Robert Rawitch, "Church Claims U.S. Campaign of Harassment," *Los Angeles Times*, August 29, 1978, A1.
9. "David Miscavige: The Peacemaker," *Freedom*, 2010, http://www.freedommag .org/david_miscavige_peacemaker.
10. Roy Wallis, *The Road to Total Freedom: A Sociological Analysis of Scientology* (New York: Columbia University Press, 1976); J. Gordon Melton, *The Church of Scientology* (Salt Lake City, UT: Signature Books, 2000); James R. Lewis, ed., *Scientology* (New York: Oxford University Press, 2009). See Harriet Whitehead, *Renunciation and Reformulation: A Study of Conversion in an American Sect* (Ithaca, NY: Cornell University Press, 1987); Hugh B. Urban, "Fair Game: Secrecy, Security and the Church of Scientology in Cold War America," *Journal of the American Academy of Religion* 4, no. 2 (2006): 356–89. Several good articles by Stephen Kent are "The Creation of 'Religious' Scientology," *Religious Studies and Theology* 18, no. 2 (1999): 97–126; and "Scientology's Relationship with Eastern Religious Traditions," *Journal of Contemporary Religion* 11, no. 1 (1996): 21–36.
11. See, among others, Dorthe Refslund Christensen, *Scientology: Fra terapi tel religion* (Copenhagen: Gyldendal, 1997); Friedrich-Wilhelm Haack, *Scientology: Magie des 20. Jahrhunderts* (München: Claudius Verlag, 1991); Oliver Huber, *Scientology: zwischen Verheimlichung und Desinformation* (Hamburg: Institut für Soziologie, 1994).

12. Urban, "Fair Game"; Urban, "The Rundown Truth: Scientology Changes Strategy in War with Media," *Religion Dispatches*, March 17, 2010, http://www.religiondispatches .org/archive/atheologies/2358/the_rundown_truth%3A_scientology_changes_strategy _in_war_with_media_. Many scholars and journalists have recounted being harassed by the church. Among others, see Roy Wallis, "The Moral Career of a Research Project," in *Doing Sociological Research*, ed. Colin Bell and Howard Newby (London: Allen and Unwin, 1976); Behar, "Scientology."

13. Among the popular, nonacademic exposés available, two of the better ones are Jon Atack, *A Piece of Blue Sky: Scientology, Dianetics and L. Ron Hubbard Exposed* (New York: Carol, 1990); and Nancy Many, *My Billion Year Contract* (Bloomington, IN: Xlibris, 2009). Among the better journalistic accounts are Janet Reitman, "Inside Scientology," *Rolling Stone*, February 23, 2006, http://www.rollingstone.com/politics/story/ 9363363/inside_scientology; and Lawrence Wright, "The Apostate: Paul Haggis vs. The Church of Scientology," *New Yorker*, February 14, 2011, http://www.newyorker.com/ reporting/2011/02/14/110214fa_fact_wright?currentPage=all.

14. Here I use the phrase "historian of religions" primarily in the more critical sense outlined by Bruce Lincoln, "Theses on Method," *Method and Theory in the Study of Religion* 8, no. 3 (1996): 225–27. As Lincoln suggests, the task of the historian of religions is to analyze the temporal, material, social, and political aspects of those phenomena that are claimed to be transcendent and eternal: "To practice history of religions . . . is to insist on discussing the temporal, contextual, situated, interested, human, and material dimensions of those discourses, practices, and institutions that characteristically represent themselves as eternal, transcendent, spiritual, and divine." In this sense, my approach here is similar to historians of religions such as Steven Wasserstrom, *Religion after Religion: Gershom Scholem, Mircea Eliade, and Henry Corbin at Eranos* (Princeton, NJ: Princeton University Press, 1999); Tomoko Masuzawa, *The Invention of World Religions: Or How European Universalism was Preserved in the Language of Difference* (Chicago: University of Chicago Press, 2005); Russell McCutcheon, *Manufacturing Religion: The Discourse on Sui Generis Religion and the Politics of Nostalgia* (New York: Oxford University Press, 1997); Ivan Strenski, *Why Politics Can't Be Freed from Religion* (Malden, MA: Wiley-Blackwell, 2010).

15. See chapter 2 below. See also L. Ron Hubbard, *Technique 88: Incidents on the Track Before Earth* (Los Angeles: Golden Era Productions, 2007), 185, 186, 183; Hubbard, *Hubbard Professional Course Lectures* (Los Angeles: Golden Era Productions, 2007), 110.

16. See chapter 5 below. See also Douglas Frantz, "Scientology's Puzzling Journey from Tax Rebel to Tax Exempt," *New York Times*, March 9, 1997, http://www.nytimes .com/1997/03/09/us/scientology-s-puzzling-journey-from-tax-rebel-to-tax-exempt.html? pagewanted=all.

17. Jonathan Z. Smith, *Imagining Religion: From Babylon to Jonestown* (Chicago: University of Chicago Press, 1982), xi.

18. McCutcheon, *Manufacturing Religion*, 3.

19. David Chidester, "The Church of Baseball, the Fetish of Coca-Cola, and the Potlatch of Rock 'n' Roll: Theoretical Models for the Study of Religion in American Popular Culture," *Journal of the American Academy of Religion* 64, no. 4 (1996): 745.

20. Talal Asad, *Genealogies of Religion: Discipline and Reasons of Power in Christianity and Islam* (Baltimore, MD: Johns Hopkins University Press, 1993).

21. See Michael Barkun, "Religion and Secrecy after September 11," *Journal of the American Academy of Religion* 74, no. 2 (2005): 275–301; Hugh B. Urban, "Secrecy and New Religious Movements: Concealment, Surveillance and Privacy in a New Age of Information," *Religion Compass* 2, no. 1 (2007): 66–83.

22. Urban, "Secrecy and New Religious Movements"; Urban, "The Torment of Secrecy: Ethical and Epistemological Problems in the Study of Esoteric Traditions," *History of Religions* 37, no. 3 (1998): 209–48.

23. Andrew Morton, *Tom Cruise: An Authorized Biography* (New York: St. Martin's Press, 2008), 103.

24. Childs and Tobin, "Scientology: The Truth Rundown." The "Bohemian Rhapsody" story is repeated by Marc Headley in his book *Blown for Good: Behind the Iron Curtain of Scientology* (Burbank, CA: BFG Books, 2009) and in Wright's article "The Apostate."

25. See, among others, Melton, *The Church of Scientology*; Lewis, *Scientology*; and Juha Pentikäinen, Jurgen F.K. Redhardt, and Michael York, "The Church of Scientology's Project Rehabilitation Force," CESNUR Center on New Religions, 2002, http://www.cesnur.org/2002/scient_rpf_01.htm.

26. I am adapting the phrase "hermeneutics of suspicion" from Paul Ricoeur, *Freud and Philosophy: An Essay on Interpretation* (New Haven, CT: Yale University Press, 1970), 32, 496.

27. I interviewed Armstrong repeatedly from 2008 to 2010, and he has given me generous feedback on my work. See also Bruce Livesy, "Scientology's Defier," *Maisonneuve*, March 1, 2008, http://maisonneuve.org/pressroom/article/2008/mar/1/scientologys-defier/. Armstrong's allegations against the church were also made in sworn testimony in court—for example, in his Complaint Report of February 16, 2004, http://www.gerryarmstrong.org/50grand/legal/a8/complaint-rpt-doj-2004-02-16.html.

28. "The Foundation," Forgivenessfoundation.org, 2009, http://www.forgivenessfoundation.org/donate.htm.

29. See Urban, "Fair Game"; Douglas E. Cowan, "Researching Scientology: Perceptions, Premises and Problematics," in Lewis, *Scientology*, 53–79.

30. Ann Brill and Ashley Packard, "Silencing Scientology's Critics on the Internet: A Mission Impossible?" *Communications and the Law* 19, no. 4 (1997): 5–8.

31. See Dorthe Refslund Christensen, "Inventing L. Ron Hubbard: On the Construction and Maintenance of the Hagiographic Mythology of Scientology's Founder," in *Controversial New Religions*, ed. James R. Lewis and Jesper Aagaard Petersen (New York: Oxford University Press, 2005), 227–58.

32. For an insider account of Gold Base, see Headley, *Blown for Good*. For the complex debate over the Rehabilitation Project Force, see below, chapter 4.

33. Urban, "Torment of Secrecy."

34. Jeffrey Hadden, quoted in Douglas E. Cowan, "Contested Spaces: Movement, Countermovement and E-Space Propaganda," in *Religion Online: Finding Faith on the Internet*, ed. Lorne L. Dawson and Douglas E. Cowan (New York: Routledge, 2004), 255.

35. Mikael Rothstein, "His Name Was Xenu: He Used Renegades . . . Aspects of Scientology's Founding Myth," in Lewis, *Scientology*, 368. See Cowan, "Contested Spaces," 265.

36. L. Ron Hubbard, *HCO Manual of Justice* (London: Hubbard Communications Office, 1959), 1.

37. Wallis, *Road to Total Freedom*, vi. See Urban, "Fair Game."

38. J. P. Kumar, "'Fair Game': Leveling the Playing Field in Scientology Litigation," *Review of Litigation* 16 (Summer 1997): 747–72. See James Richardson, "Scientology in Court: A Look at some Major Cases from Various Nations," in Lewis, *Scientology*, 283–94.

39. Roy Wallis, "The Moral Career of a Research Project," in Bell and Newby, *Doing Sociological Research*, 158.

40. Behar, "Thriving Cult," 57.

41. Quoted in Robert Vaughn Young, "Scientology from Inside Out" [sidebar], *Quill* 81, no. 9 (1993), http://xenu.net/archive/go/quill.htm.

42. Wallis, *Road to Total Freedom*, vi.

43. Jim Dincalci, email correspondence with author, November 6, 2009.

44. Rothstein, "His Name Was Xenu," 368. See chapter 6 below.

45. Mark Fearer, "Scientology's Secrets," in *Composing Cyberspace: Identity, Community and Knowledge in the Electronic Age*, ed. Richard Holeton (Boston: McGraw-Hill, 1998), 350.

46. Robert S. Ellwood, *The Fifties Spiritual Marketplace: American Religion in a Decade of Conflict* (New Brunswick, NJ: Rutgers University Press, 1997); Wade Clark Roof, *Spiritual Marketplace: Baby Boomers and the Remaking of American Religion* (Princeton, NJ: Princeton University Press, 2001).

47. Jeffrey Kripal, *Esalen: America and the Religion of No Religion* (Chicago: University of Chicago Press, 2007).

48. Hubbard, "Scientology: The Philosophy of a New Age," 1957, TBDS, vol. 3, 153.

49. Dincalci, phone interview with author, November 10, 2009.

50. Ninian Smart, foreword to Peter Connolly, *Approaches to the Study of Religion* (New York: Cassell, 1999), ix.

51. See Robert S. Ellwood, *The Sixties Spiritual Awakening: American Religion Moving from Modern to Postmodern* (New Brunswick, NJ: Rutgers University Press, 1994), 40–43; Will Herberg, *Protestant, Catholic, Jew: An Essay in American Religious Sociology* (Garden City, NY: Doubleday, 1955).

52. Kripal, *Esalen*, 7.

53. Jeffrey Ruff, "The Academic Study of Religion in North America," in *The Encyclopedia of Religion*, vol. 13, ed. Lindsay Jones (New York: Thomson Gale, 2005), 8787.

54. This comment was made during the conference "Religion, Secrecy and Security: Religious Freedom and Privacy in a Global Context," at Ohio State University, April 16–18, 2004.

55. M. Alain Gest, "Rapport fait au nom de la Commission d'Enquête sur les sectes," *Assemblé nationale*, December 22, 1995, http://www.assemblee-nationale.fr/rap-enq/r2468.asp.

56. Asad, *Genealogies of Religion*, 54. See Richard King, *Orientalism and Religion: India, Postcolonial Theory and the "Mystic East"* (New York: Routledge, 1999), 40: "The concept of 'religion' is the product of the culturally specific discursive processes of Christian history in the West and has been forged in the crucible of inter-religious conflict and

interaction. . . . Christianity has generally served as the prototypical example of a religion and thus as the fundamental yardstick . . . for the study of 'other religions.'"

57. David Chidester, *Patterns of Power: Religion and Politics in American Culture* (Englewood Cliffs, NJ: Prentice Hall, 1988), 133.

58. See Huston Smith and Reuben Snake, *One Nation Under God: The Triumph of the Native American Church* (Santa Fe, NM: Clear Light, 1996). For a related discussion of the "religious" status of Native American traditions, see Tisa Wenger, *We Have a Religion: The 1920s Pueblo Indian Dance Controversy and American Religious Freedom* (Chapel Hill: University of North Carolina Press, 2009).

59. See Jan Shipps, *Mormonism: The History of a New Religious Tradition* (Champaign: University of Illinois Press, 1987).

60. See Catherine Wessinger, *How the Millennium Comes Violently: From Jonestown to Heaven's Gate* (New York: Seven Bridges Press, 2000); James D. Tabor and Eugene V. Gallagher, *Why Waco? Cults and the Battle for Religious Freedom in America* (Berkeley: University of California Press, 1995).

61. Jonathan Z. Smith, *Relating Religion: Essays in the Study of Religion* (Chicago: University of Chicago Press, 2004), 192.

62. Hubbard, "Hope of Man," 212.

63. Bruce Lincoln, *Holy Terrors: Thinking about Religion after September 11* (Chicago: University of Chicago Press, 2003), 5–6.

64. *Orientation: A Scientology Information Film*, linked on the *St. Petersburg Times* website, 2009, http://www.tampabay.com/specials/2009/reports/project/.

65. See chapter 6 below. The legal threat came in the form of an email from Ava Paquette of the law firm Moxon & Kobrin, Los Angeles, CA, October 8, 2005.

66. Lincoln, *Holy Terrors*, 5–6.

67. Tabor and Gallagher, *Why Waco?* See Urban, "Fair Game"; and Urban, "Secrecy and New Religious Movements."

Chapter 1: L. Ron Hubbard: American Entrepreneur, Spiritual Bricoleur

1. Friends of Ron, *L. Ron Hubbard: A Profile* (Los Angeles: Bridge Publications, 1995), 4.

2. Hubbard, letter to the U.S. attorney general, May 14, 1951, FBI, 62-94080.

3. Friends of Ron, *L. Ron Hubbard*, 3.

4. See, among myriad other works, Russell Miller, *Bare Faced Messiah: The True Story of L. Ron Hubbard* (New York: Henry Holt, 1988).

5. Quoted in Dennis Wheeler, "Son of Scientology," *News-Herald*, July 7–13, 1982, http://www.lermanet.com/scientologynews/newsherald-DeWolfe07-82.htm. See Wallis, *Road to Total Freedom*, 21.

6. Decision of Judge Paul Breckenridge, *Church of Scientology of California v. Armstrong*, No. C 420153 (Cal. Super. Ct. 1984), 8. For extensive documentation of Armstrong's twenty-year legal battle with Scientology, see the archives on his website: http://www.gerryarmstrong.org/50grand/legal/a1/index.html.

7. Dorthe Refslund Christensen, "Inventing L. Ron Hubbard: On the Construction and Maintenance of the Hagiographic Mythology of Scientology's Founder," in

Controversial New Religions, ed. James R. Lewis and Jesper Aagaard Petersen (New York: Oxford University Press, 2005), 227–58.

8. Robert S. Ellwood, *The Fifties Spiritual Marketplace: American Religion in a Decade of Conflict* (New Brunswick, NJ: Rutgers University Press, 1997), 7. See Wade Clark Roof, *Spiritual Marketplace: Baby Boomers and the Remaking of American Religion* (Princeton, NJ: Princeton University Press, 2001).

9. Ellwood, *Fifties Spiritual Marketplace*, 7.

10. On Dick's mystical experience and its influence on his later fiction, see Lawrence Sutin, *Divine Invasions: A Life of Philip K. Dick* (Cambridge, MA: Da Capo Press, 2005), 208–34; Jeffrey J. Kripal, *The Secret Life of a Superpower: Mythical Themes and Paranormal Currents in American Popular Culture* (Chicago: University of Chicago Press, forthcoming), chap. 6.

11. Hubbard, *Dianetics: The Evolution of a Science* (Los Angeles: Bridge Publications, 2007), 14.

12. Hubbard, *Dianetics: The Evolution*, 9.

13. Ellwood, *Fifties Spiritual Marketplace*, 83.

14. Dick Hebdige, "Subculture: The Meaning of Style," in *Cultural Studies: An Anthology*, ed. Michael Ryan (Malden, MA: Blackwell, 2008), 592. See Wendy Doniger, *The Implied Spider: Politics and Theology in Myth* (New York: Columbia University Press, 1998): "In the ecology of narratives, recycling is a very old process. Myths, like all things in constant use . . . get broken and fixed again, lost and found, and the one who . . . recycles them is what Lévi-Strauss calls a *bricoleur*" (145).

15. Alva Rogers, "Darkhouse," *Lighthouse* 5 (February 1962).

16. Alva Rogers, "Darkhouse," in John Carter, *Sex and Rockets: The Occult World of Jack Parsons* (Los Angeles: Feral House, 1999), 103.

17. George Pendle, *Strange Angel: The Otherworldly Life of John Whiteside Parsons* (Orlando, FL: Harcourt, 2005), 253. In the words of Virginia Downsborough, Hubbard's former personal assistant: "Ron had such an amazing ability for making you feel that you were just so important to him and so valued. So many people wanted to do what he wanted . . . it was 'wait for me, let me come along with this wonderful game you're playing'" (interviewed in the documentary *Secret Lives: L. Ron Hubbard*, Channel 4, November 19, 1997).

18. Nieson Himmel, interview with Ken Urquhart, August 14, 1986. *The Bare-Faced Messiah* Interviews, 1997, http://www.scs.cmu.edu/~dst/Library/Shelf/miller/interviews/himmel.htm. In a letter to Isaac Asimov, L. Sprague de Camp offered the following opinion of Hubbard: "Bob [Robert Heinlein] thinks Ron went to pieces morally as a result of the war. I think that's fertilizer, that he always was that way, but when he wanted to conciliate or get something from somebody he could put on a good charm act. What the war did was to wear him down to where he no longer bothers with the act" (letter of August 27, 1946, in Pendle, *Strange Angel*, 271).

19. Russ Baker, "Clash of the Titans: Scientology vs. Germany," *George*, April 1997, http://www.russbaker.com/archives/George%20Magazine%20-%20Clash%20of%20The%20Titans/Clash%20of%20The%20Titans%20-%20George%20Magazine.htm.

20. Dincalci, phone interview with author, November 10, 2009. Similar accounts can be heard in interviews with Dincalci and others in the documentary *Secret Lives: L. Ron Hubbard*, Channel 4, November 19, 1997.

21. Friends of Ron, *L. Ron Hubbard*, 102.

22. Church of Scientology International, "L. Ron Hubbard: The Founder of Scientology," Whatisscientology.org, 2010, http://www.whatisscientology.org/html/Part01/Chp03/pg0088.html.

23. Church of Scientology International, "L. Ron Hubbard."

24. Hubbard, *Hymn of Asia* (Los Angeles: Golden Era Productions, 2009), n.p.; Church of Scientology International, "L. Ron Hubbard."

25. Hubbard, *Mission into Time* (Los Angeles: American Saint Hill Organization, 1973), 10–11.

26. Graham Smith, "Scientology Founder L. Ron Hubbard Exposed as a Fraud," *Daily Mail*, August 7, 2009, http://www.dailymail.co.uk/news/article-1204715/Scientology-founder-L-Ron-Hubbard-exposed-fraud-British-diplomats-30-years-ago.html.

27. Atack, *A Piece of Blue Sky*, 58, 79–80; Joseph Malia, "Judge Found Hubbard Lied About Achievements," *Boston Herald*, March 1, 1998.

28. Decision of Judge Paul G. Breckenridge Jr., *Church of Scientology of California v. Gerald Armstrong, Superior Court of the State of California*, No. C421053, June 22, 1984, 8.

29. Interviewed in *Secret Lives: L. Ron Hubbard*, Channel 4, November 19, 1997.

30. Jack Williamson, *Wonder's Child: My Life in Science Fiction* (New York: Bluejay Books, 1984), 182. See Kevin J. Anderson, foreword to Hubbard, *The Great Secret* (Hollywood: Galaxy Press, 2008), v.

31. Harriet Whitehead, "Reasonably Fantastic: Some Perspectives on Scientology, Science Fiction and Occultism," in *Religious Movements in Contemporary America*, ed. I. I. Zaretsky and M. P. Leone (Princeton, NJ: Princeton University Press, 1974), 569.

32. John Campbell, "The Place of Science Fiction," *Modern Science Fiction*, ed. Reginald Bretner (New York: Coward-McCann, 1953), 20–21.

33. Anderson, foreword to Hubbard, *Great Secret*, ix.

34. "L. Ron Hubbard: Founder of Dianetics and Scientology," Scientology.org, 2010, http://www.scientology.org/l-ron-hubbard/chronicle/pg004.html.

35. Dincalci, interview with author, November 10, 2009. Likewise, Whitehead recounts that "he used to write his science fiction stories by sitting down in front of a blank wall and 'just typing up the action as it came across the screen'" ("Reasonably Fantastic," 583n).

36. H. H. Holmes (pseudonym), *Rocket to the Morgue* (New York: Duell, Sloan and Pearce, 1942), 84–85.

37. Robert Silverberg, introduction to Hubbard, *Ole Doc Methuselah* (Los Angeles: Bridge Publications, 1992), xii.

38. Pendle, *Strange Angel*, 253.

39. Hubbard, *Fear* (Los Angeles: Bridge Publications, 1991), 141–42.

40. Hubbard, *The Great Secret* (Hollywood: Galaxy Press, 2008), 7, 3.

41. Hubbard, *Ole Doc Methuselah*, xv.

42. Hubbard, *Ole Doc Methuselah*, xv. See also Hubbard's *To the Stars* (Hollywood: Galaxy Press, 2004), which likewise describes space heroes journeying "upward and outward bound on a mission to the ageless stars" (210).

43. William Bainbridge, "The Cultural Context of Scientology," in Lewis, *Scientology*, 37.

44. Hubbard, "The Dianetics Question: Homo Superior, Here We Come!" *Marvel Science Stories* 3 (May 1951): 111–13.

45. Hubbard, *Fear and Typewriter in the Sky* (New York: Popular Library, 1977), 51.

46. "Note on Excalibur," Ron the Philosopher.org, 2009, http://www.ronthephilosopher .org/phlspher/page06.htm.

47. Hubbard, January 1, 1938, Ron the Philosopher.org, 2009, http://www .ronthephilosopher.org/phlspher/page08.htm.

48. Ackerman, interview in *Secret Lives: L. Ron Hubbard*.

49. See Sutin, *Divine Invasions*, 208–37; Kripal, *Secret Life*, chap. 6.

50. Hugh Urban, "The Occult Roots of Scientology? L. Ron Hubbard, Aleister Crowley and the Origins of a Controversial New Religion," *Nova Religio* (forthcoming, 2011); Carter, *Sex and Rockets*, 103–4; Pendle, *Strange Angel*, 253–54.

51. Carter, *Sex and Rockets*, 150. The idea of the moonchild comes from Crowley's novel, *Moonchild* (London: Mandrake Press, 1929). The ritual to attract an elemental is set forth in the OTO treatise *De Nuptiis Secretis Deorum cum Hominibus*. See John Symonds, *King of the Shadow Realm: Aleister Crowley, His Life and Magic* (London: Duckworth, 1989), 563.

52.

53. Jack Parsons, *The Book of B.A.B.A.L.O.N.* (Berkeley: Ordo Templi Orientis, 1982), March 2, 1946, online at http://www.sacred-texts.com/oto/lib49.htm.

54. Jack Parsons, letter to Crowley, March 6, 1946, in Symonds, *King of the Shadow Realm*, 564.

55. Aleister Crowley, letter of April 19, 1946, in Lawrence Sutin, *Do What Thou Wilt: A Life of Aleister Crowley* (New York: St. Martin's Press, 2000), 414.

56. Crowley, letter of May 22, 1946, in Sutin, *Do What Thou Wilt*, 414–15.

57. Alexander Mitchell, "Scientology: Revealed for the First Time," London *Sunday Times*, October 5, 1969, http://www.lermanet.com/scientologynews/crowley-hubbard-666 .htm. See Symonds, *King of the Shadow Realm*, 564.

58. The Church of Scientology, letter to the *Sunday Times*, December 28, 1969.

59. L. Ron Hubbard Jr., "Penthouse Interview," *Penthouse*, June, 1983, 113. "The one super-secret sentence that Scientology is built on is: 'Do as thou wilt'. . . . It also comes from black magic, from Alistair [*sic*] Crowley." Hubbard Jr. argued that his father became involved in magic at age sixteen when he read Crowley's *Book of the Law* and later decided he would take over the mantle of the Beast (ibid).

60. Jon Atack, "Hubbard and the Occult," http://www.religio.de/atack/occl.html; see Atack, *A Piece of Blue Sky: Scientology, Dianetics and L. Ron Hubbard Exposed* (New York: Carol, 1990), 9–93.

61. Wallis, *Road to Total Freedom*, 111n–12n. See John Symonds, *The Great Beast: The Life and Magick of Aleister Crowley* (St. Albans: Mayflower, 1973); Alexander Mitchell, "Scientology: Revealed for the First Time," London *Sunday Times*, October 5, 1969.

62. Wallis, *Road to Total Freedom*, 111; Melton, *Scientology*, 8.

63. See Urban, "Occult Roots." See L. Ron Hubbard, *The Philadelphia Doctorate Course*, vol. 2 (Los Angeles: Golden Era Publications, 2007), 27. In this 1952 lecture, he does explicitly discuss Crowley, even calling him "my very good friend," despite the fact that he had certainly never met the man: "[T]he magic cults of the eighth, ninth, tenth, eleventh, twelfth centuries in the Middle East were fascinating. The only modern work that has anything to do with them is a trifle wild in spots, but it's fascinating work in

itself, and that's work written by Aleister Crowley, the late Aleister Crowley, my very good friend. And he did himself a splendid piece of aesthetics built around those magic cults. It's very interesting reading to get hold of a copy of a book, quite rare, but it can be obtained. The Master Therion, T-h-e-r-i-o-n, The Master Therion by Aleister Crowley. He signs himself 'The Beast,' 'The Mark of the Beast, 666.'"

64. Hubbard, *Dianetics: The Evolution*, 60, 9.

65. Whitehead, *Renunciation and Reformulation*, 52.

66. Pendle, *Strange Angel*, 272.

67. Hubbard, DSTD, 200.

68. Williamson, *Wonder's Child*, 186. See O'Brien, *Dianetics in Limbo: A Documentary about Immortality* (Philadelphia: Whitmore, 1966), 7.

69. Williamson, *Wonder's Child*, 184, 182, 186.

70. Hubbard, *Secrets of the MEST Universe* (Los Angeles: Bridge Publications, 1990), 1, 6.

71. Hubbard, "A Critique of Psycho-analysis 3," *Certainty* 9, no. 7 (1962): 4.

72. "Poor Man's Psychoanalysis," *Newsweek*, October 16, 1950.

73. Williamson, *Wonder's Child*, 183.

74. Wallis, *Road to Total Freedom*, 34.

75. Hubbard, *Dianetics: The Modern Science of Mental Health* (Los Angeles: Bridge Publications, 2007), 397–98.

76. Hubbard, *Dianetics: The Modern Science*, 227. See Hubbard, "Clears in This Society" (1950), RDS, vol. 1, 353.

77. Phone interview with author, March 4, 2010.

78. Phone interview with author, April 7, 2010.

79. Hubbard, *Dianetics: The Evolution*, 103.

80. Hubbard, *Dianetics: The Modern Science*, 113. See Hubbard, *Dianetics: Lectures and Demonstrations* (Los Angeles: Golden Era Productions, 2007), 26–27.

81. *Clear News: The AOLA Weekly Newsletter*, May 11, 1970, 2, UCLA box 3, f.4.

82. *Clear Successes* (Los Angeles: Church of Scientology of California, 1971), 3–4, UCLA box 3, f.5.

83. "William Burroughs: Clear 1163," *Advance!* 2 (1968): 3.

84. Wallis, *Road to Total Freedom*, 68.

85. Frederick Peterson and C. G. Jung, "Psycho-Physical Investigations with the Galvanometer and Pneumograph in Normal and Insane Individuals," *Brain* 30 (1907): 11.

86. Volney Mathison, *Mathison Licensed Electropsychometers* (Los Angeles: International Equipment, 1954), 4, 12.

87. O'Brien, *Dianetics in Limbo*, 54; Whitehead, *Renunciation and Reformulation*, 142–43.

88. Hubbard, *Scientology: A History of Man* (Los Angeles: American Saint Hill Organization, 1968), 7.

89. Hubbard, *Electropsychometric Auditing Operator's Manual* (London: Hubbard Association of Scientologists International, n.d.), 57.

90. Hubbard, "Electronics Gives Life to Freud's Theory," August 1952, TBDS, vol. 1, 269.

91. "Hubbard Electrometer, 1968," *Life*, 2010, http://www.life.com/image/76796742/in-gallery/25371.

92. Martin Gumpert, "The Dianetics Craze," *New Republic*, August 14, 1950.

93. *Los Angeles Daily News*, September 6, 1950.

94. O'Brien, *Dianetics in Limbo*, v–vi.

95. Huxley, unpublished letter in Sybille Bedford, *Aldous Huxley: A Biography*, vol. 2 (London: Chatto and Windus, 1974), 116–17.

96. Whitehead, "Reasonably Fantastic," 578.

97. Albert Q. Maisel, "Dianetics: Science of Hoax?" *Look*, December 5, 1950, 85.

98. Martin Gardner, *Fads and Fallacies in the Name of Science* (New York: Dover, 1957), 263.

99. Russell Miller, "The Messianic Con Man," *Toronto Star*, January 16, 1988, http://www.scientology-lies.com/press/toronto-star/1988-01-16/messianic-con-man.html/.

100. Atack, *A Piece of Blue Sky*, 181.

101. Sue Lindsay, "Scientology Founder Speaks Out," *Rocky Mountain News*, February 20, 1983, 50.

102. William Bolitho, *Twelve Against the Gods: The Story of Adventure* (New York: Simon and Schuster, 1929), 5–6.

103. Bolitho, *Twelve Against the Gods*, 10, 7.

104. Atack, *A Piece of Blue Sky*, 368.

105. Hubbard, "The Circuit Case," 1954, TBDS, vol. 2, 20.

106. Hubbard, "Books Are Disseminations," *HCO Bulletin*, April 28, 1960, UCLA Box 5, f.1.

Chapter 2: Scientology, Inc.: Becoming a "Religion" in the 1950s

1. Hubbard, *The Phoenix Lectures: Freeing the Human Spirit* (Los Angeles: Golden Era Productions, 2007), 59.

2. Hubbard Jr., "Penthouse Interview," 166.

3. Hubbard, "Dianetics and Religion,"1950, TBDS, vol. 1, 38. "What the world of man decrees about religion or what religion decrees about the world of man is well outside the regulation of Dianetics" (ibid.).

4. Hubbard, *Technique 88: Incidents on the Track Before Earth* (Los Angeles: Golden Era Productions, 2007), 185, 186, 183. See Hubbard, *Hubbard Professional Course Lectures* (Los Angeles: Golden Era Productions, 2007), 110: "I see people down here in the church praying and I often ask them what they're praying about. . . . I have a grave suspicion that an Operating Thetan like the Eighth Dynamic just wouldn't really be intrigued with it, if he heard it at all . . . you just couldn't get somebody like God interested in this sort of thing."

5. Hubbard, *HCO Bulletin*, July 18, 1959, TBDS, vol. 3, 494. See Hubbard, "Overt Acts, Motivators and DEDS," 1952, RDS, vol. 10, 729.

6. Eshbach, *Over My Shoulder: Reflections on a Science Fiction Era* (Philadelphia: Oswald Train, 1983), 125.

7. See Williamson, *Wonder's Child*, 185. L. Ron Hubbard Jr. has made similar allegations: "My father started out as a broke science-fiction writer. . . . He told me and a lot of

other people that the way to make a million was to start a religion" ("Penthouse Interview," 110–11).

8. O'Brien, *Dianetics in Limbo*, vii. Likewise, the journal *Aberree* reported: "The news was received with mixed emotions. Some were outspokenly antagonistic to the idea" ("Three Churches Given Charter in New Jersey," *Aberree* 1, no. 1 [1954]: 4).

9. Roof, *Spiritual Marketplace*, 79.

10. Allitt, *Religion in America Since 1945: A History* (New York: Columbia University Press, 2003), xii.

11. Allitt, *Religion in America*, xii.

12. "Wife Accuses Mental Health Expert of Torturing Her," *Times Herald*, April 24, 1951. See Harriet Whitehead, "Reasonably Fantastic: Some Perspectives on Scientology, Science Fiction and Occultism," in *Religious Movements in Contemporary America*, ed. Irving I. Zaretsky and Mark P. Leone (Princeton, NJ: Princeton University Press, 1974), 579.

13. Interviewed in "Secret Lives: L. Ron Hubbard," Channel 4, November 19, 1997.

14. Wallis, *Road to Total Freedom*, 79–80.

15. Hubbard, *Science of Survival* (Los Angeles: Bridge Publications, 2007), 61n. See Whitehead, "Reasonably Fantastic," 579–80.

16. Hubbard, *Dianetics*, 59.

17. "N.J. Starts Actions Against Dianetics," *Elizabeth Daily Journal*, January 15, 1951. See J. Edgar Hoover, letter of March 3, 1953. FBI, no. 62-9408; "Scientology Acts to Legalize as a Religion," *Aberree* 1, no. 1 (1954): 4. See Stephen Kent, "Scientology's Relationship with Eastern Religious Traditions," *Journal of Contemporary Religion* 11, no. 1 (1996): 30.

18. Wallis, *Road to Total Freedom*, 190.

19. Hubbard, "Religion," 1962, OEC, vol. 5, 282.

20. Robert Gillette and Robert Rawitch, "Church Claims U.S. Campaign of Harassment," *Los Angeles Times*, August 29, 1978, A1–18.

21. *United States of America v. Founding Church of Scientology et al.*, 333 F. Supp. 357 (D.D.C. 1971). No. D.C. 1-63, 365.

22. Hubbard, "Dianetic Use," *HCO Bulletin*, April 24, 1969; see Kent, "Scientology's Relationship," 31. Likewise, in an *HCO Policy Letter*, "Legal Statement Concerning Dianetics and Medical Practice Laws," Hubbard emphasizes the difference between the science of Dianetics and the religion of Scientology, stating that a proper adherence to the distinction "will resolve any problems posed by medical practice laws" (UCLA box 1, folio 4).

23. Allen Upward, *The New Word: An Open Letter Addressed to the Swedish Academy in Stockholm on the Meaning of the Word Idealist* (New York: M. Kennerly, 1910), 149. The term "Scientologie" was also used by a German advocate of Aryan racial theory, A. Nordenholz, who defined it as "the system of knowledge and knowing." *Scientologie: System des Wissens und der Wissenschaft* (München: Stückrath, 1937).

24. Hubbard, "What Is Scientology?" 1952, TBDS, vol. 1, 269.

25. Hubbard, "Associate Newsletter," April 23, 1953, 315. See Kent, "Creation of Religious Scientology."

26. Letter from Hubbard to Helen O'Brien, April 10, 1953, provided as evidence in *Church of Scientology of California v. Armstrong*. No. C 420153 (Cal. Super. Ct. 1984),

1977–78. Part of this letter is also quoted in Russell Miller, *Bare-Faced Messiah: The True Story of L. Ron Hubbard* (New York: Henry Holt, 1988), 213.

27. Certificate of Incorporation of the Founding Church of Scientology, Washington, DC, July 21, 1955.

28. "Scientology Acts to Legalize as Religion: Three Churches Given Charters by New Jersey," *Aberree* 1, no. 1 (1954): 4; see Kent, "Scientology's Relationship," 30.

29. "H.A.S. 'Dead'; New Unit Set Up, Successor Organization Is Religious Fellowship," *Aberree* 1, no. 4 (1954): 1.

30. Hubbard, "Six Basic Processes," December 24, 1954, TBDS, vol. 2, 118. See Hubbard, *The Creation of Human Ability: A Handbook for Scientologists* (Los Angeles: Bridge Publications, 2007), 180.

31. Hubbard, "Selling," 1955, TBDS, vol. 2, 266.

32. Hubbard, *Ceremonies of the Founding Church of Scientology* (Washington, DC: Hubbard Communication Office, 1959).

33. Hubbard, *Ceremonies*, 4, 9. "The way to handle an individual minister of some other church" includes agreeing that Jesus Christ was the Savior of Mankind and that "the Bible is a holy work" (Hubbard, "The Scientologist," March 1955, TBDS, vol. 2, 158).

34. Hubbard, *The Phoenix Lectures: Master Directory* (Los Angeles: Golden Era Productions, 2007), 3–4.

35. Urban, "Occult Roots."

36. Hubbard, DSTD, 129.

37. Hubbard, "Why Doctor of Divinity," 1964, TBDS, vol. 2, 72.

38. Hubbard, "The Hope of Man," 215.

39. Hubbard, "Religion," *HCO Policy Letter*, October 29, 1962, OEC 5, 282.

40. Hubbard, "The Parts of Man," 1956, TBDS, vol. 2, 428. See Hubbard, *Science of Survival* (Los Angeles: Bridge Publications, 2007), 4–5.

41. Hubbard, *What Is Scientology?* (Los Angeles: Bridge Publications, 1992), 209.

42. Hubbard, DSTD, 431.

43. Hubbard, *Scientology: A History of Man*, 73.

44. David Bromley, "Making Sense of Scientology: Prophetic, Contractual Religion," in Lewis, *Scientology*, 91.

45. Hubbard, *The Secrets of the MEST Universe* (Los Angeles: Bridge Publications, 1990), 73.

46. Hubbard, *Scientology 8-8008* (Los Angeles: Bridge Publications, 2007), 119, 195; Hubbard, *Secrets of the MEST*, 71.

47. Hubbard, *Scientology 8-80* (Los Angeles: Bridge Publications, 2007), 110–11.

48. Hubbard, "The Scientologist," 152, 158. See Mary Farrell Bednarowski, *New Religions and the Theological Imagination in America* (Bloomington: Indiana University Press, 1989), 34–35. Hubbard's reference to Gnostic religion may just as likely be influenced by the occult ideas of Crowley and the OTO; the OTO was also described as a "neo-Gnostic" religion, and Crowley developed a "Gnostic Mass" for the order. See Urban, *Magia*, chap. 3–4.

49. O'Brien, *Dianetics in Limbo*, 18–19, 43.

50. Dincalci, phone interview with author, November 10, 2009.

51. Hubbard, *Scientology: A History of Man* (Los Angeles: Bridge Publications, 2007), 3. Jim Dincalci suggests that *History of Man* was largely the product of Hubbard giving his son, L. Ron Jr., large amounts of amphetamines: "[H]is dad kept giving him speed and all of a sudden he was talking about his history, when he was a clam and all these different situations in early earth. And out of that came 'History of Man'" (interview in "Secret Lives: L. Ron Hubbard").

52. Hubbard, *Scientology: A History of Man*, 47.

53. Hubbard, *Have You Lived Before This Life? A Scientific Survey* (London: Hubbard Association of Scientologists International, 1958), 21.

54. Hubbard, *Have You Lived*, 22–23, 28–29, 100.

55. Hubbard, *Have You Lived*, 262.

56. Hubbard, *Have You Lived*, 108.

57. Hubbard, *Have You Lived*, 259.

58. Hubbard, *Have You Lived*, 89.

59. Dincalci, phone interview with author, November 10, 2009.

60. As Hubbard wrote in 1957, "Space Opera has again come to a planet on which we live. Always before it meant destruction. Perhaps, this time, due to our efforts a humanitarian world can exist" ("Scientology: The Philosophy of a New Age," TBDS, vol. 3, 154).

61. Allitt, *Religion in America*, 117.

62. Wallis, *Road to Total Freedom*, 56.

63. Williamson, *Wonder's Child*, 185.

64. Hubbard, *Technique 88*, 302–3.

65. "Trapped in the Closet," *South Park*, November 16, 2005.

66. Hubbard, *Technique 88*, 341. See Hubbard, *Mission into Time*, 69.

67. Hubbard, *Technique 88*, 334.

68. Hubbard, *Technique 88*, 2. See Hubbard, *Secrets of the MEST*, 9.

69. Hubbard, *Technique 88*, 338.

70. Hubbard, *Technique 88*, 292.

71. Hubbard, DSTD, 243.

72. Hubbard, *A Series of Lectures on the Whole Track* (Los Angeles: Golden Era Productions, 1985), tape 1.

73. Hubbard, *A Series of Lectures*, tape 1.

74. Hubbard, *A Series of Lectures*, tape 5.

75. Whitehead, "Reasonably Fantastic," 582. "Hubbard is often quoted as having said that most of science fiction is just 'track.' People make the mistake of thinking that they are projecting something into the future where as in fact they are dredging it up from the past" (ibid., 582n).

76. Hubbard, *Secrets of the MEST*, 100.

77. See Annie Besant, *Man and His Bodies* (London: Theosophical Publishing House, 1909); Arthur A. Powell, *The Astral Body and Other Astral Phenomena* (London: Theosophical Publishing House, 1965), 7.

78. Sylvan Muldoon, *The Phenomena of Astral Projection* (New York: Samuel Weiser, 1951), 137; Muldoon, *The Projection of the Astral Body* (New York: Samuel Weiser, 1974), 47.

79. See Urban, "Occult Roots"; Crowley, *Magick in Theory and Practice*, in *Magick Liber ABA*, ed. Hymenaeus Beta (York Beach, ME: Samuel Weiser, 1997), 21–243.

80. Hubbard, *Scientology 8-8008*, 115. See Hubbard, DSTD, 279; Hubbard, *Exteriorization and the Phenomena of Space* (Los Angeles: Golden Era Productions, 1993).

81. Introduction to Hubbard, *The Philadelphia Doctorate Course* (Los Angeles: Golden Era Productions, 2001), vii.

82. Hubbard, *The Creation*, 65–66.

83. Hubbard, *The Creation*, 55. Likewise, *Advance!* magazine invites readers to become an OT and shows a young girl clad in a white angelic gown with her arms stretched forward in Superman style flying through the stars in outer space ("Be an Operating Thetan," *Advance!* 84 [1984]: 6).

84. Hubbard, *Phoenix Lectures*, 472.

85. Hubbard, *Phoenix Lectures*, 471.

86. Hubbard, *Creation*, 64.

87. Williamson, *Wonder's Child*, 186.

88. Hubbard, *Scientology: A History of Man*, 62.

89. "OT Adventures," *Source* 50 (1985): 13.

90. "OT Phenomena," *Advance!* 33 (July 1975): 8.

91. "OT Phenomena Success," *Advance!* 17 (1973): 14–17; "Success Beyond Man's Wildest Dreams," *Advance!* 7 (1969): 3. See Hubbard, DSTD, 345; Whitehead, "Reasonably Fantastic, 584.

92. Hubbard, DSTD, 413.

93. "An Entirely New Universe—Ideal in Every Detail," *Source* 194 (2007): 40–41.

94. Robert Farley, "Scientology Nearly Ready to Unveil Superpower," *St. Petersburg Times*, May 6, 2006.

95. Hubbard, *Philadelphia*, 5.

96. Hubbard, *Philadelphia*, xi. "The secret of the MEST universe is you can create a MEST universe any time you want to" (*Secrets of the MEST Universe*, 13).

97. Hubbard, *Scientology 8-8008*, 175. "Educate the pc by making him create and destroy his own illusions into finally getting a certainty of illusion and from this a certainty of perceiving the real universe with all perceptions (Note: The most real universe is, of course, one's own illusory universe and should be completely rehabilitated before one attempts to perceive or handle or worry about the MEST universe)" (Hubbard, *Secrets of the MEST*, 93–94).

98. Hubbard, *Scientology 8-8008*, 252.

99. Hubbard, *Phoenix Lectures*, 373.

100. Hubbard, *Philadelphia*, 6.

101. Hubbard, *Philadelphia*, 14. See "Mightier than Apollo," *Source* (June/July 1979): 13: "[A] New Era Dianetics for OTs auditor is a powerful and causative being. Apollo had power in the sea, sky and earth. A NED for OTs auditor has the power to help another being become cause over Life. Truly a godlike ability."

102. Cyril Vosper, interview in "Secret Lives: L. Ron Hubbard."

103. Hubbard, *Source of Life Energy*, 264–65.

104. Hubbard, "The Hubbard Certified Auditor Course," June 1957, TBDS, vol. 3, 55. See Hubbard, "The Scientologist," 152.

105. See Thomas Tweed and Stephen Prothero, eds., *Asian Religions in America: A Documentary History* (New York: Oxford University Press, 1998), 178–208.

106. Hubbard, *Phoenix Lectures*, 34. See Hubbard, *The Creation of Human Ability*, 413–16.

107. Hubbard, "Religious Philosophy and Religious Practice," *HCO Bulletin*, June 21, 1960, TBDS, vol. 6, 195. Buddha "pretended to be nothing but what he was, a man inspired with the wisdom which he had gained" (Hubbard, "The Scientologist," 153).

108. Hubbard, "Why Doctor of Divinity," 72.

109. Hubbard, *Phoenix Lectures*, 45; see Paul Carus, *Gospel of Buddha* (Chicago: Open Court, 1898), 111.

110. Hubbard, *Mission into Time*, 21.

111. Hubbard, "OT & Clear Defined," *Advance!* 94 (1987): 6. See Wallis, *Road to Total Freedom*, 112–13.

112. Hubbard, *Hymn of Asia* (Los Angeles: Golden Era Productions, 2009), n.p.

113. Hubbard, "What Are You Trying to Do in Clearing," *HCO Bulletin*, April 6, 1963. Scientology's *Advance!* magazine from 1980 features an image of the Buddha meditating on the front cover. Inside, the cover story recounts the teachings of the Buddha, concluding that they are now fulfilled with the birth of Scientology: "Gautama Siddhartha Buddha predicted that in 2500 years the entire job would be finished in the West. . . .Well, we finished it" ("Descent from Vulture Peak," *Advance!* 84 [1980]: 14).

114. Hubbard, *Scientology 8-8008*, 48.

115. Kent, "Scientology's Relationship," 22

116. Jennifer Osbourne, pseudonym, in Stephen A. Kent, *From Slogans to Mantras: Social Protest and Religious Conversion in the Late Vietnam War Era* (Syracuse, NY: Syracuse University Press, 2001), 105.

117. Wallis, *Road to Total Freedom*, 247–48.

118. Hubbard Jr., "Penthouse Interview," 166.

119. Hubbard, *Mission into Time*, 16.

120. Hubbard, *Philadelphia*, 4.

121. James Phelan, "Have You Ever Been a Boo-Hoo?" *Saturday Evening Post*, March 21, 1963.

122. Wallis, *Road to Total Freedom*, 124. "Hubbard was well aware of the value of corporate structures as weapons in the control of both his movement and its environment. A complex corporate structure maximizes the difficulty of surveillance or investigation of the movement's affairs" (ibid., 128). See Stephen A. Kent, "Scientology—Is This a Religion?" *Marburg Journal of Religion* 4, no. 1 (1999), http://web.uni-marburg.de/religionswissenschaft/journal/mjr/kent.html.

123. Bryan R. Wilson, "Scientology: An Analysis and Comparison of its Religious Systems and Doctrines," in Church of Scientology International, *Scientology: Theology and Practice of a Contemporary Religion* (Los Angeles: Bridge Publications, 1998), 132.

124. Atack, *A Piece of Blue Sky*, 138. Hubbard used the language of "franchises" extensively throughout his policy letters prior to the 1970s; see "Franchise Promotion Musts," November 12, 1969, UCLA Box 1, f.4.

Chapter 3: A Cold War Religion: Scientology, Secrecy, and Security in the 1950s and 60s

1. Hubbard, "Dianetics: The Evolution of a Science," 87.
2. Ted Gunderson, quoted in Behar, "Thriving Cult," 56.
3. Allitt, *Religion in America*, 12, 22.
4. Ellwood, *Fifties Spiritual Marketplace*, 94. See Allitt, *Religion in America*, 116.
5. Miller, *Bare-Faced Messiah*, 160.
6. Susan Raine, "Surveillance in a New Religious Movement: Scientology as a Test Case," *Religious Studies and Theology* 28, no. 1 (2009): 63–94; see Behar, "Scientology."
7. Miller, *Bare-Faced Messiah*, 198.
8. U.S. Ministerial Conference of Scientology Ministers, *The American Inquisition: U.S. Government Agency Harassment, Religious Persecution and Abuse of Power* (Los Angeles: Church of Scientology of California, 1977), 1–27, 38–43, 51–55, 81.
9. Georg Simmel, "The Sociology of Secrecy and Secret Societies," in *The Sociology of Georg Simmel*, ed. K. Wolf (New York: Free Press, 1950). See also Paul Christopher Johnson, *Secrets, Gossip and Gods: The Transformation of Brazilian Candomblé* (New York: Oxford University Press, 2002); Hugh B. Urban, "Secrecy and New Religious Movements," *Religion Compass* 2, no. 1 (2007): 66–83.
10. Hubbard, *Dianetics 55* (Los Angeles: Bridge Publications, 2007), 3.
11. Stephen Whitfield, *The Culture of the Cold War* (Baltimore, MD: Johns Hopkins University Press, 1996), 1. See Ellwood, *Fifties Spiritual Marketplace*, 63.
12. Angus MacKenzie, *Secrets: The CIA's War at Home* (Berkeley: University of California Press, 1997), 201; see Richard Curry, *Freedom at Risk: Secrecy, Censorship and Repression in the 1980s* (Philadelphia: Temple University Press, 1988), 8.
13. Whitfield, *Culture of the Cold War*, 10–11.
14. Whitfield, *Culture of the Cold War*, 83.
15. Whitfield, *Culture of the Cold War*, 10.
16. Whitfield, *Culture of the Cold War*, 81.
17. Allitt, *Religion in America*, 25.
18. "The Secret War at Home," *New York Post*, November 19, 1974.
19. Matthew Etherdon, "*The Day the Earth Stood Still*: 1950s Sci Fi, Religion and the Alien Messiah," *Journal of Religion and Film*, 9, no. 2 (2005), http://www.unomaha.edu/jrf/Vol9No2/EtherdenEarthStill.htm.
20. Rothstein, "His Name Was Xenu," 380.
21. Hubbard, *Dianetics: The Modern Science*, 538.
22. Hubbard, *Scientology: The Fundamentals of Thought* (Los Angeles: Bridge Publications, 1997), 163. "Hundreds of thousands are dead because of the atom bomb. . . . And because of Scientology we may some day win a world without insanity . . . without war" (Hubbard, "Danger: Black Dianetics," 1952, TBDS, vol. 1, 281).
23. Hubbard, "The Radiation Picture and Scientology," 1957, TBDS, vol. 3, 48.
24. Milton Sapirstein, "A Cure for All Ills," *Nation*, August 5, 1950, 130.
25. Hubbard, "The Radiation Picture," 44.
26. Advertisement for *All About Radiation*, TBDS, vol. 3, 49.
27. Hubbard, *All About Radiation*, 75.

28. Hubbard, *All About Radiation*, 154.

29. Robert Gillette and Robert Rawitch, "Church Claims U.S. Campaign of Harassment," *Los Angeles Times*, August 29, 1978, A1.

30. Kevin Victor Anderson, *Report of the Board of Enquiry into Scientology* (Victoria, Australia: State of Victoria, 1965), chap. 28.

31. See Hoover's letters of March 3, 1953, April 9, 1956, January 8, 1958, May 5, 1958, May 26, 1958. FBI, no. 62-94080.

32. Letter from the Hubbard Dianetic Research Foundation to the FBI, March 3, 1951. FBI, no. 62-94080.

33. Hubbard, letter to the attorney general, May 14, 1951. FBI, no. 62-94080.

34. Hubbard, "The War," *Executive Directive*, November 29, 1968, in Wallis, *Road to Total Freedom*, 263–64.

35. F. J. Baumgardner, FBI Office Memorandum, March 7, 1952. FBI, no. 62-94080. See Robert Gillette and Robert Rawitch, "Scientology: A Long Trail of Controversy," *Los Angeles Times*, August 27, 1978, A1.

36. James Phelan, "Have You Ever Been a Boo-Hoo?" *Saturday Evening Post*, March 21, 1964. According to a letter from the Hubbard Dianetic Foundation, Inc., to the attorney general on May 14, 1951: "I found out a method the Russians use . . . to obtain confessions. I could undo that method. My second book was to have shown how the Communists used narcosynthesis and physical torture and why it worked as it did. Further, I was working on a technology of psychological war to present it to the Defense Department" (FBI, no. 62-94080).

37. Hubbard (probable author), *Brain-Washing: A Synthesis of the Russian Textbook on Psychopolitics* (Los Angeles: American Saint Hill Organization, 1955). See Hubbard letter to the FBI, December 16, 1955. FBI, no. 62-94080.

38. See Dick Anthony, "Tactical Ambiguity and Brainwashing Formulations," in *Misunderstanding Cults: Searching for Objectivity in a Controversial Field*, ed. Benjamin Zablocki and Thomas Robbins (Toronto: University of Toronto Press, 2001), 219–20; John Marks, *The Search for the Manchurian Candidate* (New York: Random House, 1980).

39. According to an FBI letter of April 17, 1956, "The authenticity of this booklet seems to be of a doubtful nature since it lacks documentation of source material and communist words" (FBI, no. 62-94080). See Stephen Kent, *Brainwashing in Scientology's Rehabilitation Force Project* (Hamburg: Interior Ministry, 2002), http://www.solitarytrees .net/pubs/skent/brain.htm#endnote05.

40. Hubbard letter to the FBI, December 16, 1955. FBI, no. 62-94080.

41. M. A. Jones, office memorandum to Mr. Nichols, February 27, 1957. FBI, no. 62-94080. In a memo from the same file dated October 11, 1957, H. A. Belmont wrote: "In the past, letters from L. Ron Hubbard . . . have not been acknowledge because of his possible mental instability and rambling and incoherent nature of his letters."

42. F. J. Baumgardner, FBI memorandum to A. H. Belmont, August 11, 1958. FBI, no. 62-94080.

43. Gillette and Rawitch, "Church Claims," A1.

44. William Willoughby, "How to Make the 'Dirty Tricks' List," *Washington Star-News*, December 21, 1974.

45. See Howard Osborn, Memorandum for: Deputy Director of Central Intelligence," November 21, 1967, and Coast Guard files of 1969, both reproduced in *American Inquisition*, 24, 38.

46. Gillette and Rawitch, "Church Claims," A18.

47. Miller, *Bare-faced Messiah*, 229.

48. Wallis, *Road to Total Freedom*, 125. See Lamont, *Religion, Inc.*, 35.

49. D. V. Barrett, *Sects, 'Cults' and Alternative Religions: A World Survey and Sourcebook* (London: Blandford, 1996), 255; Whitehead, *Renunciation*, 130.

50. Afterword to Hubbard, *Have You Lived Before This Life*? 307.

51. "OT Scientologist!" *Advance!* 90 (1986): inside cover advertisement.

52. "State of Operating Thetan," *Scientology Auditing*, 2004, http://www.auditing.org/13-ot.htm.

53. Janet Reitman, "Inside Scientology," *Rolling Stone*, February 23, 2006, http://www.rollingstone.com/politics/story/9363363/inside_scientology.

54. Hubbard, "Advance Course Regulations and Security," *HCO Policy Letter*, January 8, 1981.

55. "Trapped in the Closet," *South Park*, November 16, 2005, http://www.southparkstudios.com/guide/912/.

56. Hubbard, *Ron's Journal 67* (Los Angeles: Golden Era Productions, 1983), side 2.

57. Hubbard, *Have you Lived*, 307. See "OT Successes," *Advance!* 94 (1987): 15.

58. Reitman, "Inside Scientology."

59. Stephen Koff, "Xemu's Cruel Response to Overpopulated World," *St. Petersburg Times*, December 23, 1988. See Atack, *A Piece of Blue Sky*, 173.

60. Joel Sappell, "Scientologists Block Access to Secret Documents," *Los Angeles Times*, November 5, 1985. See Karin Spaink's website, "The Fishman Affidavit," September 1995, http://www.xs4all.nl/~kspaink/fishman/home.html.

61. Whitehead, *Renunciation*, 185.

62. See Hubbard, Class VIII lecture, September 1968, online at http://wikileaks.org/wiki/Scientology_cult_Hubbard_Class_VIII_Xenu_transcripts_1968.

63. See Mark Oppenheimer, "Friends, Thetans and Countrymen," *Telegraph*, September 9, 2007; John Sweeney, "Scientology and Me," *Panorama, BBC*, May 14, 2007.

64. See, for example, Atack, *A Piece of Blue Sky*, 30–32; Margery Wakefield, *The Road to Xenu: A Narrative Account of Life Inside Scientology*, http://www.cs.cmu.edu/~dst/Library/Shelf/xenu. For a scholarly discussion of the OT III narrative and its sources see Rothstein, "They Called Him Xenu."

65. *Religious Technology Center v. F.A.C.T.Net et al.* No. 95-K-2143 (D. Colo. 1995), 229. As McShane argued, "The discussion of the . . . volcanoes, the explosions, the Galactic confederation 75 million years ago, and a gentleman by the name Xemu there. Those are not trade secrets. The officers mentioned there are not. But the . . . parts in there that actually described what happened to the individual and how to handle it . . . that is trade secret."

66. Gerry Armstrong, "Fact-Off: OT III vs. Revolt in the Stars," Suppressive Person Defense League, 2008, http://suppressiveperson.org/spdl/index.php?option=com_content&task=view&id=547&Itemid=1.

67. According to the RTC website, "The bulk of Scientology scriptures are broadly available to anyone seeking spiritual enlightenment. However, the advanced technology . . . is maintained as strictly confidential. Before a parishioner is allowed to use these materials, he or she must meet the highest ethical standards and have completed earlier levels of spiritual release" ("Protecting the Advanced Technology," Religious Technology Center, 2008, http://www.rtc.org/guarant/pg003.html).

68. William S. Burroughs, *Ali's Smile: Naked Scientology* (Bonn: Expanded Media Editions, 1978), 83.

69. See Urban, "Secrecy and New Religious Movements."

70. Margery Wakefield, *The Road to Xenu: A Narrative Account of Life Inside Scientology*, chap. 13, http://www.cs.cmu.edu/~dst/Library/Shelf/xenu/xenu-13.html.

71. Raine, "Surveillance in a New Religious Movement," 87.

72. Hubbard, letter to the attorney general, May 14, 1951. FBI, no.62-94080.

73. Hubbard, "Security Risks Infiltration," *HCO Policy Letter*, October 30, 1962, OEC vol. 5, 359. "Dianetics and Scientology are self protecting sciences. If one attacks them one attacks all the know-how of the mind. . . . It's gruesome to see sometimes. At this instance there are men hiding in terror on Earth because they found out what they were attacking. There are men dead because they attacked us" (Hubbard, *Manual of Justice*, 7).

74. See Hubbard, *Manual of Justice*, 1–10; Hubbard, *Introduction to Scientology Ethics*, 1; MMDT, 179.

75. William S. Burroughs, review of *Inside Scientology* by Robert Kaufman, *Rolling Stone*, October 26, 1972, 68.

76. Hubbard, "Historical Precedence of Ethics," *HCO Policy Letter*, December 29, 1966.

77. Hubbard, "Security Checks," *HCO Bulletin*, May 26, 1960. See "Security Checks," *HCO Policy Letter*, December 13, 1960, OEC, vol. 5, 353.

78. Hubbard, "The Only Valid Security Check," *HCO Policy Letter*, May 22, 1961, quoted in Wallis, *Road to Total Freedom*, 149.

79. Hubbard, "The Only Valid Security Check," quoted in Atack, *A Piece of Blue Sky*, 150–51.

80. Hubbard, "Sec Check Whole Track," *HCO Bulletin*, June 19, 1961, quoted in Atack, *A Piece of Blue Sky*, 151–52.

81. Hubbard, "Security Checks Abolished," *HCO Policy Letter*, August 26, 1969, OEC, vol. 5, 360. On the continuation of security checking, see Raine, "Surveillance in a New Religious Movement," 73; Many, *My Billion Year Contract*, 91; Headley, *Blown for Good*, 75–76.

82. Hubbard, "Attacks on Scientology," *HCO Policy Letter*, February 18, 1966.

83. Hubbard, "Ethics, Suppressive Acts, Suppression of Scientology and Scientologists, the Fair Game Law," *HCO Policy Letter*, December 23, 1965. See MMTD, 196, 509.

84. Hubbard, "Penalties for Lower Conditions," *HCO Policy Letter*, October 18, 1967. This is also cited in Wallis, *Road to Total Freedom*, 144.

85. Hubbard, "Cancellation of Fair Game," *HCO Policy Letter*, October 21, 1968.

86. Declaration of Vicki Aznaran, April 4, 1994. *Church of Scientology International v. Fishman*. No. CV. 91-6426 (C.D. Cal. 1994).

87. Atack, "General Report on Scientology," http://home.snafu.de/tilman/j/general .html.

88. *Church of Scientology of California v. Armstrong.* No. C 420153 (Cal. Super. Ct. 1984), 4080.

89. Omar Garrison, *The Hidden Story of Scientology* (Secaucus, NJ: Citadel, 1974), 80.

90. Margery Wakefield, *Understanding Scientology*, chap. 12, http://www.cs.cmu .edu/~dst/Library/Shelf/wakefield/us-12.html.

91. Sentencing memorandum, *United States of America v. Jane Kember*, 487 F. Supp. 1340 (D.D.C. 1980). No. 78-401 (2) & (3), 20–21.

92. Robert Gillette and Robert Rawitch, "Scientology: A Long Trail of Controversy," *Los Angeles Times*, August 27, 1978, A1.

93. "Mystery of the Vanished Ruler," *Time*, January 31, 1983. http://www.time.com/ time/magazine/article/0,9171,951938-2,00.html.

94. Sentencing Memorandum, *United States of America v. Jane Kember*, 24.

95. Sentencing Memorandum, *United States of America v. Jane Kember*, 23.

96. Ibid., 23.

97. Sentencing Memorandum, *United States of America v. Jane Kember*, 33.

98. Ronson, *The Men Who Stare at Goats* (New York: Simon and Schuster, 2004).

99. Hubbard, DSDT, 345.

100. *Celebrity*, Minor Issue 9 (February 1974).

101. Russell Targ and Harold Puthoff, *Mind-Reach: Scientists Look at Psychic Abilities* (New York: Delacorte Press, 1977), 42. See also Dean I. Radin, *The Conscious Universe: The Scientific Truth of Psychic Phenomena* (New York: HarperEdge, 1997), 25–26; Joseph McMoneagle, *Memoirs of a Psychic Spy: The Remarkable Life of U.S. Government Remote Viewer 001* (Charlottesville, VA: Hampton Roads, 2006), 71; Lyn Buchanan, *The Seventh Sense: Secrets of Remote Viewing as Told by a Psychic Spy for the U.S. Military* (New York: Paraview Pocket Books, 2003), 31–32.

102. Russell Targ, *Do You See What I See? Lasers and Love, ESP and the CIA and the Meaning of Life* (Charlottesville, VA: Hampton Roads, 2010), 148. Targ elaborated on this point further during an interview with me in June 2010.

103. Edwin May, phone interview with author, June 16, 2010.

104. Jim Schnabel, *Remote Viewers: The Secret History of America's Psychic Spies* (New York: Dell, 1997), 199–200.

105. Targ, *Do You See*, 127.

106. Targ and Puthoff, *Mind-Reach*, 5–6; see Schnabel, *Remote Viewers*, 200.

107. Ronson, *Men Who Stare at Goats*, 81. See Targ and Puthoff, *Mind-Reach*, 43.

108. Hubbard Jr., "Penthouse Interview," 170: "What he normally did was allow these strange little people to go into the offices and into his home at odd hours of the night. He told me that he was allowing the KGB to go through our files, and that he was charging 40,000 pounds for it. This was the money he used for the purchase of St. Hill Manor." While there has never been any corroboration for this charge, it clearly adds to the aura of secrecy and espionage that surrounds Scientology.

109. See Urban, "The Torment of Secrecy"; Urban, "Fair Game"; Pierre Bourdieu, "The Forms of Capital," in *Handbook of Theory and Research for the Sociology of Education*, ed. John G. Richardson (New York: Greenwood Press), 241–58.

110. Barkun, "Religion and Secrecy after 9/11," *Journal of the American Academy of Religion* 74, no. 2 (2006): 276.

111. David Cole and James X. Dempsey, *Terrorism and the Constitution: Sacrificing Civil Liberties in the Name of National Security* (New York: New Press, 2002), 153. See Hugh B. Urban, *The Secrets of the Kingdom: Religion and Concealment in the Bush Administration* (Lanham, MD: Rowman and Littlefield, 2007), chap. 2.

112. Barkun, "Religion and Secrecy," 296.

Chapter 4: The "Cult of All Cults"? Scientology and the Cult Wars of the 1970s and 80s

1. Cynthia Kisser, quoted in Behar, "Thriving Cult."

2. Hubbard, *All About Radiation*, 101. See MMTD, 55.

3. See David Bromley and Anson D. Shupe Jr., *Strange Gods: The Great American Cult Scare* (Boston: Beacon Press, 1981), ixx.

4. See Gaius Atkins, *Modern Religious Cults and Movements* (New York: Fleming H. Revell, 1923); Walter Martin, *The Rise of the Cults* (Grand Rapids, MI: Zondervan Publishing House, 1954); Walter Martin, *The Kingdom of the Cults* (Minneapolis: Bethany House, 1965); Jan Van Baalen, *Chaos of the Cults* (Grand Rapids, MI: William B. Eerdmans, 1962).

5. Robert Jay Lifton, *Thought Reform and the Psychology of Totalism* (New York: W. W. Norton, 1961). For an excellent discussion of the brainwashing debates, see Lorne L. Dawson, *Comprehending Cults: The Sociology of New Religious Movements* (New York: Oxford University Press, 2006), 95–124.

6. Eileen Barker, "Watching for Violence: A Comparative Analysis of the roles of Five Types of Cult-Watching groups," in *Cults and Religious Violence*, ed. David G. Bromley and J. Gordon Melton (Cambridge: Cambridge University Press, 2002).

7. Consumers' Union Report, August 1951, quoted in O'Brien, *Dianetics in Limbo*, vi–vii.

8. "Three Churches Given Charter in New Jersey," *Aberree* 1, no. 1 (1954): 4.

9. Robert Gillette and Robert Rawitch, "Scientology: A Long Trail of Controversy" *Los Angeles Times*, August 27, 1978.

10. Hubbard Jr., "Penthouse Interview," 111.

11. Bromley and Shupe, *Strange Gods*, 1.

12. Wessinger, *How the Millennium*, 4; see Tabor and Gallagher, *Why Waco?*

13. Chidester, "Religion of Baseball," 760.

14. Stephen Kent, "Scientology: Is This a Religion?" *Marburg Journal of Religion* 4, no. 1 (1999), http://www.arts.ualberta.ca/~skent/Linkedfiles/Scientology%20--%20Is%20this%20a%20Religion.htm.

15. See Brian Ambrey, "Brainwashing Manual Parallels in Scientology" (2001). Online at http://www.xenu-directory.net/practices/brainwashing1.html. On the brainwashing debates, see Dawson, *Comprehending Cults*, 95–124; Anthony, "Tactical Ambiguity," 215–317.

16. "The Sea Organization," whatisscientology.org, 2010, http://www.whatisscientology.org/html/Part06/Chp26/.

17. Many, *My Billion Year Contract*, 38.

18. "Operation Earth," *Advance!* 7 (1969): 14.

19. Sea Org advertisement (Los Angeles: Church of Scientology of California, 1971), UCLA, box 3, f.5.

20. "Join the Sea Org," Church of Scientology of California, 1971, UCLA Box 3, f.5; see "Keep Scientology Working," *HCO Policy Letter*, February 7, 1965, OEC 5, 47.

21. *Advance!* 94 (1987): back cover advertisement. An article from 1969 also imagines the future world in the year 2010, when the "Space Org" (formerly Sea Org) will bring total freedom to every planet. See "Scientology Mothard," *Advance!* 7 (1969): 11.

22. Hubbard, *Mission into Time*, 22.

23. Church of Scientology, *Scientology*, 69.

24. Many, *My Billion Year Contract*, 39. See Sea Org Application and Routing Form, n.d., circa 1970 (UCLA, box 2 f.7). The full contract reads as follows: "I, _____, DO HEREBY AGREE to enter into employment with the SEA ORGANIZATION and, being of sound mind, do fully realize and agree to abide by its purpose which is to get ETHICS IN on this PLANET AND THE UNIVERSE and, fully and without reservation, subscribe to the discipline, mores and conditions of this group and pledge to abide by them. THEREFORE, I CONTRACT MYSELF TO THE SEA ORGANIZATION FOR THE NEXT BILLION YEARS."

25. J. Gordon Melton, "A Contemporary Ordered Religious Community: The Sea Organization," CESNUR Center on New Religions, 2001, http://www.cesnur.org/2001/london2001/melton.htm.

26. Raine, "Surveillance in a New Religious Movement," 84. See Young, "On Lack of Privacy," http://www.xenu.net/entheta/entheta/1stpersn/rvy/1997-014.html.

27. Alana Semuels, "From the Outside looking in," *Pittsburgh Post-Gazette*, July 25, 2005, http://www.post-gazette.com/pg/05205/542899.stm. See MMTD, 441.

28. Juha Pentikäinen, Jurgen F. K. Redhardt, and Michael York, "The Church of Scientology's Project Rehabilitation Force," CESNUR Center on New Religions, 2002, http://www.cesnur.org/2002/scient_rpf_01.htm. See also Melton, "Contemporary Ordered Religious Community."

29. Melton, "Contemporary Ordered Religious Community."

30. Atack, *A Piece of Blue Sky*, 206.

31. Ibid.

32. Gerry Armstrong, "Gerry Armstrong Describes Experiences on the RPF," Scientology-lies.com, 1999, http://www.scientology-lies.com/gerryarmstrong5.html.

33. Many, *My Billion Year Contract*, 89–99, 108. See Laurie Goldstein, "Defectors Say Church Hides Abuse," *New York Times*, March 6, 2010, http://www.nytimes.com/2010/03/07/us/07scientology.html?pagewanted=4.

34. Stephen Kent, "Brainwashing in Scientology's Rehabilitation Project Force," 1997, http://www.arts.ualberta.ca/~skent/Linkedfiles/Brainwashing%20in%20Scientology%27s%20Rehabilitation%20Project%20Force%20%28RPF%29.htm.

35. Kent, "Brainwashing."

36. Dawson, *Comprehending Cults*, 115; see Wessinger, *How the Millennium*, 6.

37. Hubbard, *All About Radiation*, 101. See MMTD, 55. On CIA brainwashing research, see Anthony, "Tactical Ambiguity," and Mark, *Search for the Manchurian Candidate*.

38. Hubbard, letter to the FBI, December 16, 1955. FBI no. 62-94080.

39. Hubbard, *All About Radiation*, 103–4.

40. Hubbard, *Creation of Human Ability*, 352.

41. Ambrey, "Brainwashing Manual Parallels in Scientology," 2001. Online at http://www.xenu-directory.net/practices/brainwashing1.html. I have heard more than one ex-Scientologist say this as well.

42. Lamont, *Religion, Inc.*, 37.

43. *Scientology: A World Religion*, 69.

44. Robert Vaughn Young, "Scientology from Inside Out," *Quill* 81, no. 9 (1993), reproduced online at http://xenu.net/archive/go/quill.htm.

45. Declaration of Vicki Aznaran, April 4, 1994. *Church of Scientology International v. Fishman*, No. CV. 91-6426. (C.D. Cal. 1994).

46. Wallis, *Road to Total Freedom*, 128–29.

47. See Childs and Tobin, "Truth Rundown."

48. Kent, "Scientology—Is This a Religion?"

49. Berger, "Secularism and Pluralism," *International Yearbook for the Sociology of Religions* 2 (1966): 73–84.

50. See Wallis, *Road to Total Freedom*, 248.

51. For a good discussion of the differences between modern or "Fordist" capitalism and late or post-Fordist capitalism, see David Harvey, *The Condition of Postmodernity* (Oxford: Blackwell, 1989), 128–17; Fredric Jameson, *Postmodernism: or, The Cultural Logic of Late Capitalism* (Durham, NC: Duke University Press, 1991).

52. Hubbard, "The Radiation Picture and Scientology," 1957, TBDS, vol. 3, 47.

53. Hubbard, "The Result of Clearing," advertisement, March 1971, UCLA box 3, f.5.

54. Hubbard, "Income Flows and Pools," MS, 384.

55. Hubbard, *HCO Policy Letter*, December 3, 1971, MS, 413.

56. Hubbard, *HCO Policy Letter*, December 3, 1971, MS, 413.

57. Hubbard, "Infinite Expansion," MS, 346.

58. Flyers from 1967 and 1971, UCLA box 3, ff.2, 4, 5.

59. Hubbard, "Ron's Journal 30," *Executive Directive*, December 17, 1978, UCLA box 5.

60. "The Bridge to a Better Life," Whatisscientology.org, 2010, http://www.whatis scientology.org/html/Part02/Chp06/pg0181_1.html/.

61. Catherine Beyer, "John Travolta," alt.religion.about.com, 2010, http://altreligion .about.com/od/artandculture/ig/Scientologist-Celebrities/John-Travolta.htm; Roger Friedman, "Actor Jason Beghe," Foxnews.com, April 16, 2008, http://www.foxnews.com/story/0,2933,351426,00.html.

62. *Advance!* 6, no. 1 (1969): 13.

63. "Donation and Registration Rates," Church of Scientology Flag Service Organization, 2009.

64. This was Behar's estimate back in 1991 in "Thriving Cult."

65. "American Saint Hill Organization Foundation Services Price List" (Los Angeles, 2006).

66. Joseph Mallia, "Inside the Church of Scientology," *Boston Globe*, March 1, 1998.

67. Many, *My Billion Year Contract*, 189.

68. Beghe, "Jason Beghe Interview," Xenu TV, April 21, 2008, http://xenutv.wordpress
.com/2008/04/21/jason-beghe-interview/.

69. N. Passass and M. E. Castillo, "Scientology and its 'Clear' Business," *Behavioral
Sciences and Law* 10, no. 103 (1992): 110.

70. Many, *My Billion Year Contract*, 165.

71. Many, *My Billion Year Contract*, 166–67. See Gerry Armstrong, "The Way to
Happiness," *Scientology v. Armstrong*, February 11, 2010, http://www.gerryarmstrong
.org/archives/4703.

72. Ries and Trout's idea of positioning was first published in *Advertising Age* in
1972 and then in book form as *Positioning: The Battle for Your Mind* (New York:
McGraw-Hill, 1981).

73. "Project Celebrity," *Ability Minor* 2 (1955): 2.

74. "Church of Scientology Celebrity Centre International," Scientology Celebrity
Centre, 2010, http://www.scientology.cc/en_US/about/index.html. See *Advance* 6, no. 1
(1969): 9; Myron Ruderman, "What Is a Celebrity Centre?" *Celebrity Centre Poets: A
Magazine of Poetry* 2 (1971): n.p.

75. Richard N. Leiby, "One Theory on Michael-Lisa," *Seattle Times*, August 9, 1994.

76. Morton, *Tom Cruise*, 113.

77. David K. Li, "The Church of $impsontology," *New York Post*, January 31,
2008, http://www.nypost.com/seven/01312008/news/nationalnews/the_church_of
_impsontology_366572.htm.

78. "Cruise Credits Scientology for His Success," *Access Hollywood*, May 25, 2005,
http://www.msnbc.msn.com/id/7968809/. See Morton, *Tom Cruise*, 99–127.

79. See Morton, *Tom Cruise*, 255; Headley, *Blown for Good*.

80. "Successes of Scientology," What Is Scientology, 2010, http://www.whatis
scientology.org/html/Part05/Chp19/pg0308.html.

81. "John Travolta," *Source* 17 (August/September, 1978): 7.

82. Ebert, Review of Battlefield Earth, *Chicago Sun Times*, May 12, 2000, http://
rogerebert.suntimes.com/apps/pbcs.dll/article?AID=/20000512/REVIEWS/5120301/
1023.

83. Thomas C. Tobin, "Battlefield of Dreams," *St. Petersburg Times*, May 12,
2000, http://www.sptimes.com/News/051200/news_pf/Floridian/Battlefield_of_dreams
.shtml.

84. Anderson, *Report of the Board of Enquiry into Scientology* (State of Victoria, Australia, 1965), preferatory note.

85. Anderson, *Report of the Board of Enquiry*, chap. 30.

86. Anderson, *Report of the Board of Enquiry*, chap. 31.

87. Judgement of Justice Latey, Re: B & G (Minors) (Custody) Delivered in the High
Court (Family Division), London, July 23, 1984, http://www.xenu.net/archive/audit/
latey.html#1.

88. Alan Levy, "Scientology: A Growing Cult Reaches Dangerously into the Mind,"
Life, November 15, 1968, 99.

89. Behar, "Thriving Cult," 56.

90. Hubbard, "The Scientologist," 1955, TBDS, vol. 2, 157. See also Hubbard, *HCO
Manual of Justice*, 1, 7; Kumar, "Fair Game," 747–72.

91. Behar, "Thriving Cult," 57.

92. Ibid.

93. "Time takes a critical look at Scientology," *St. Petersburg Times*, April 30, 1991, 3B.

94. Ron Russell, "Scientology's Revenge," *Los Angeles Sun Times*, September 9, 1999, http://www.lermanet.com/scientologynews/newtimesla-can.htm.

95. Heber Jentzsch, interview with *60 Minutes*, "The Cult Awareness Network," December 28, 1997, http://rickross.com/reference/scientology/scien427.html.

96. Russell, "Scientology's Revenge."

97. Young, interview with *60 Minutes*, "Cult Awareness Network."

98. Declaration of Graham E. Berry Re Deposition Testimony of Garry Scarff, *Church of Scientology International v. Fishman*, No. CV. 91-6426. (C.D. Cal. 1994).

99. Susan Hansen, "Did Scientology Strike Back?" *American Lawyer* (June 1997): 62–70.

100. Ray Quintilla, "Scientologists now Run Barrington Based Organization," *Chicago Tribune*, February 2, 1997, 1.

101. Ron Russell, "Scientology's Revenge," *Los Angeles New Times*, September 9, 1999; Hansen, "Did Scientology Strike Back?" 62.

102. Laurie Goldstein, "Lawyer Buys Rights to Anti-Cult Organization," *Los Angeles Times*, December 1, 1996.

103. "Who We Are," The New Cult Awareness Network, 2001, http://www .cultawarenessnetwork.org/WhoWeAre.html.

104. Anson Shupe and Susan E. Darnell, *Agents of Discord: Deprogramming, Pseudo-Science and the American Anticult Movement* (New Brunswick, NJ: Transaction Publishers, 2006), 191.

105. See, for example, Wessinger, *How the Millennium*, 4; Massimo Introvigne, "Cults and Sects," *Encyclopedia of Religion*, ed. Lindsay Jones (New York: Thomson Gale, 2005), 3:2084.

106. Bromley and Shupe, *Strange Gods*, 220.

107. Among myriad other works see Headley, *Blown for Good*, Many, *My Billion Year Contract*, the numerous exposés in the *St. Petersburg Times*, etc.

108. For example, Melton, "Scientology"; Pentikäinen, Redhardt, and York, "Church of Scientology's Project Rehabilitation Force."

109. Ivan Strenski, *Why Politics Can't Be Separated from Religion* (Wiley-Blackwell, 2010), 14–18.

110. Lincoln, *Holy Terrors*, 5.

Chapter 5: "The War" and the Triumph of Scientology: Becoming a Tax-Exempt Religion in the 1990s

1. Hubbard, "Income Tax Reform," July 18, 1959, TBDS, vol. 3, 495.

2. *Church of Scientology of California v. Commissioner of Internal Revenue*. No. 3352-78 (D.D.C. 1984), 467.

3. Miscavige, "International Association of Scientologists Speech," October 8, 1993, http://www.cs.cmu.edu/~dst/Cowen/essays/speech.html.

4. Robert Gillette and Robert Rawitch, "Scientology: A Long Trail of Controversy," *Los Angeles Times*, August 27, 1978, A16.

5. Bruce Hopkins, *The Law of Tax-Exempt Organizations* (Hoboken, NJ: John Wiley and Sons, 2003), 227. See Derek H. Davis, "The Church of Scientology: In Pursuit of Legal Recognition," 2004, http://www.umhb.edu/files/academics/crl/publications/articles/the_church_of_scientologypursuit_of_legal_recognition.pdf: "The operative word of the religion clause—religion—was left undefined by the framers. . . . To define the term would have placed a permanent imprimatur upon only those forms of faith and belief that conformed to their definition. The framers instead chose to leave the term undefined, thereby protecting diversity of beliefs."

6. *Reynolds v. United States*, 98 U.S. 145 (1878), 162.

7. James T. Richardson, "Scientology in Court: A Look at Some Major Cases," in *Scientology*, ed. James R. Lewis (New York: Oxford University Press, 2009), 287–88.

8. Hopkins, *Law of Tax-Exempt Organizations*, 237.

9. The thirteen points are a distinct legal existence, a recognized creed and form of worship, a definite and distinct ecclesiastical government, a formal code of doctrine and discipline, a distinct religious history, a membership not associated with any other church or denomination, a complete organization of ordained ministers ministering to their congregations and selected after completing prescribed courses of study, a literature of its own, established places of worship, regular congregations, regular religious services, Sunday schools for the religious instruction of the young, and schools for the preparation of its ministers (Hopkins, *Law of Tax-Exempt Organizations*, 238–39).

10. Most of these covert operations by the GO have been extensively documented by the FBI and in court. See the sentencing memorandum for Jane Kember cited on page 110 and FBI files on Scientology numbers 47-5669, 47-56689, etc.

11. Hubbard, "Press Policy: Code of a Scientologist," *HCO Policy Letter*, February 5, 1969.

12. Many, *My Billion Year Contract*, 189. Gerald Armstrong also confirmed exactly this point in an interview with me on February 14, 2009, as did an anonymous former Scientologist in an interview on March 4, 2010.

13. Joel Sappell and Robert W. Welkos, "Shoring up its Religious Profile," *Los Angeles Times*, June 25, 1990, http://www.latimes.com/news/local/la-scientology062590a,0,3090542.story. See Judge Sterrett's decision in *Church of Scientology of California v. Commissioner of Internal Revenue Service*, No. 3352-78 (D.DC, 1984): "Church missions were called 'franchises' until 1971 when their designation in the United States was officially changed to 'mission.'"

14. See Bromley and Shupe, *Strange Gods*.

15. Hubbard, "Ministerial Ordination," March 20, 1957, OEC, vol. 5, 281.

16. Garrison, *Hidden Story*, 179.

17. Atack, *A Piece of Blue Sky*, 142–43.

18. Hubbard, "Income Tax Reform," *HCO Bulletin*, July 18, 1959, TBDS vol. 3, 495.

19. Hubbard, "Religion," *HCO Policy Letter*, October 29, 1962, OEC 5, 282.

20. Hubbard, *HCO Executive Letter*, March 12, 1966, quoted in Foster, *Enquiry into the Practice and Effects of Scientology*, chap. 3, http://www.xenu.net/archive/audit/foster03.html#org.

21. See *Church of Scientology of California v. Commissioner of Internal Revenue Service*, No. 3352-78 (D.DC, 1984), 386.

22. *Founding Church of Scientology v. United States*, 133 U.S. App. D.C. 229, 409 F.2d 1146 (1969), 1200.

23. *Church of Scientology of California v. Commissioner of Internal Revenue Service*, No. 3352-78 (D.DC, 1984), 451.

24. Many, *My Billion Year Contract*, 74.

25. Many, *My Billion Year Contract*, 189.

26. Kent, "Scientology's Relationship," 32. "So began Scientology's most sweeping religious make-over. . . . Scientology ministers (formerly 'counselors') started to wear white collars, dark suits and silver crosses. Sunday services were mandated and chapels were ordered erected in Scientology buildings. It was made a punishable offense for a staffer to omit from church literature the notation that Scientology is a 'religious philosophy'" (Sappell and Welkos, "Shoring up its Religious Profile").

27. Hubbard, "Religion," *HCO Policy Letter*, February 12, 1969, OEC 6, 119.

28. See Edward B. Fiske, "Scientologists and F.D.A. Clash in Court," *New York Times*, June 8, 1971; Bruce Nelson, "Scientology Offers New Faith in Man," *St. Paul Sunday Pioneer Press*, May 7, 1972; and "Ordination Rites Set for Three By Scientology," *Westlake Post*, April 13, 1972; all of which are featured in the appendix to Church of Scientology Information Service, *Scientology: A World Religion Emerges in the Space Age* (Hollywood, CA: Church of Scientology Information Service, 1974).

29. Hubbard, "Scientology Is a Religion," *HCO Policy Letter*, March 6, 1969, OEC 5, 289–90.

30. Hubbard, *HCO Policy Letter*, October 27, 1970, OEC 5, 294.

31. Phone interview, March 4, 2010.

32. See for example *Advance!* issues 33 (July 1975), 42 (September/October 1976), and 52 (May/June 1978).

33. Hubbard, "Descent from Vulture Peak," *Advance!* 84 (1984): 14.

34. Church of Scientology of California, *The Character of Scientology* (East Grinstead: Department of Publications World Wide, 1968), 9.

35. Church of Scientology of California, *Character of Scientology*, 34.

36. Church of Scientology Information Service, *Scientology*, xvi.

37. Church of Scientology Information Service, *Scientology*, 3–30, 35–52, 69–75.

38. Church of Scientology Information Service, *Scientology*, 92. See also Church of Scientology of California, *Introducing Scientology* (Los Angeles: Church of Scientology of California, 1976), 3: "Scientology is a religion in the oldest and fullest sense of the word: a study of wisdom."

39. Hubbard, *Scientology: A History of Man* (Los Angeles: American Saint Hill Organization, 1968), 56.

40. Hubbard, *Scientology: A History of Man* (Los Angeles: Bridge Publications, 2007), 98.

41. *Church of Scientology of California v. Commissioner of Internal Revenue Service*, No. 3352-78 (D.DC, 1984).

42. Robert Vaugh Young, interviewed in "Secret Lives: L. Ron Hubbard."

43. See FBI, no. 47-56689.

44. See John Burrus, "Scientologists Rap FBI Search," *San Diego Union*, July 19, 1977, A1.

45. Timothy S. Robinson, "Scientology Raid Yielded Alleged Burglary Tools," *Washington Post*, July 14, 1977, A13.

46. *United States of America v. Henning Heldt et al.*, United States Court of Appeals for the District of Columbia, October 2, 1981, no. 79-2442.

47. Robert Rawitch, "Church Sues FBI Agents," *Los Angeles Times*, July 19, 1977.

48. U.S. Ministerial Conference of Scientology Ministers, *American Inquisition*, 81.

49. "Scientology Church Sues on FBI Raid," *San Diego Union*, July 19, 1977.

50. Robert Rawitch, "Use of Seized Church Papers Barred by Judge," *Los Angeles Times*, August 9, 1977; Robert Gillette and Robert Rawitch, "Church Claims U.S. Campaign of Harassment," *Los Angeles Times*, August 29, 1978, A1.

51. Church of Scientology of California, *Press View the FBI Raid*, (Los Angeles: Church of Scientology of California, 1977), 1.

52. "Pledge to Mankind," October 9, 1984, in Atack, *A Piece of Blue Sky*, 345.

53. Charles F. C. Ruff et al., "Sentencing Memorandum of the United States of America," *United States of America v. Jane Kember*, United States District Court, District of Columbia, Criminal No. 78-401 (2) & (3).

54. Ruff et al., "Sentencing Memorandum."

55. "Scientology Church Sues on FBI Raid," *San Diego Union*, July 19, 1977.

56. Marty Rathbun, interview with Tampabay.com, 2009, http://www.tampabay.com/specials/2009/reports/project/rathbun.shtml.

57. Rathbun, interview with Tampabay.com, 2009.

58. Douglas Frantz, "Scientology's Puzzling Journey from Tax Rebel to Tax Exempt," *New York Times*, March 9, 1997, http://www.nytimes.com/1997/03/09/us/scientology-s-puzzling-journey-from-tax-rebel-to-tax-exempt.html?pagewanted=all.

59. Frantz, "Scientology's Puzzling Journey."

60. Ibid.

61. Ibid.

62. Frantz, "Scientology's Puzzling Journey." See *Church of Spiritual Technology v. the United States*, United States Court of Appeals, Federal Circuit, March 29, 1993, 991 F.2d 812.

63. Frantz, "Scientology's Puzzling Journey."

64. Elizabeth MacDonald, "Scientologists and the IRS Settled for $12.5 Million," *Wall Street Journal*, December 30, 1997, http://www.cs.cmu.edu/~dst/Cowen/essays/wj301297.html.

65. Frantz, "Scientology's Puzzling Journey." See also "IRS-Scientology Pact Prompts Withdrawal of 45 FOIA Lawsuits," *Privacy Times*, October 26, 1993, http://www.cs.cmu.edu/~dst/Cowen/essays/pt261093.html.

66. Church of Scientology International, *Scientology: Theology and Practice of a Contemporary Religion* (Los Angeles: Bridge Publications, 1998), 236–37.

67. Miscavige, "International Association of Scientologists Speech."

68. Ibid.

69. U.S. Department of State, "Germany Human Rights Practices, 1993," January 31, 1994, http://www.usask.ca/relst/jrpc/article-scientology.html.

70. U.S. Department of State, "Final Report of the Advisory Committee on Religious Freedom Abroad," May 17, 1999, http://www.state.gov/www/global/human_rights/990517_report/execsumm_iv.html#exec.

71. U.S. Department of State, "Germany: International Religious Freedom Report," 2009, http://www.state.gov/g/drl/rls/irf/2009/127312.htm.

72. Stephen A. Kent, "Hollywood's Celebrity Lobbyists and the Clinton Administration's American Foreign Policy Toward German Scientology," *Journal of Religion and Popular Culture* 1 (2002), http://www.usask.ca/relst/jrpc/article-scientology.html.

73. Travolta quoting Clinton in Josh Young, "Bill Clinton's Grand Seduction," *George*, March 1998, 106. See Kent, "Hollywood's Celebrity Lobbyists."

74. Young, "Clinton's Grand Seduction," 138.

75. MacDonald, "Scientologists."

76. Frantz, "Scientology's Puzzling Journey."

77. See note 9 above; Hopkins, *Law of Tax-Exempt Organizations*, 238–39.

Chapter 6: Secrets, Security, and Cyberspace: Scientology's New Wars of Information on the Internet

1. John Cook, "Cult Friction," *Radar*, April 2008, http://radaronline.com/from-the-magazine/2008/03/scientology_anonymous_protests_tom_cruise_01.php.

2. Hubbard, *Dianetics 55* (Los Angeles: Bridge Publications, 2007), 7.

3. Cowan, "Contested Spaces," 261. See Massimo Introvigne, "So Many Evil Things: Anti-Cult Terrorism via the Internet," in *Religion on the Internet: Research Prospects and Promises*, ed. Jeffrey K. Hadden and Douglas E. Cowan (New York: JAI, 2000), 277–308; Wendy M. Grossman, "The Mills of Xenu Grind Exceedingly Slow," *Inquirer*, September 12, 2003, http://www.theinquirer.net/inquirer/news/912/1040912/the-mills-of-xenu-grind-exceeding-slow.

4. "The Guarantor of Scientology's Future," *Religious Technology Center*, 2008, http://www.rtc.org/guarant/index.html.

5. Alan Prendergrast, "Stalking the Net," *Denver Westworld*, October 4, 1995, http://www.westword.com/1995-10-04/news/stalking-the-net/full.

6. See "Church of Scientology: Copyright and Trade Secrets on the Internet," Theta.com, 2003, http://www.theta.com/copyright/index.htm.

7. Mike Fearer, "Scientology's Secrets," 350: "Both sides see the case as a First Amendment issue, but for entirely different reasons. CoS argues that it is a freedom-of-religion issue to protect its secrets, while CoS's critics see it as a freedom-of-speech issue to expose what they claim are unscrupulous church tactics and doctrine."

8. "The Church of Scientology . . . and its critics have liberally traded accusations of 'copyright terrorism.' For the Church of Scientology, terrorism is the systematic copyright infringement, while for its opponents the real 'terrorism' lies in Scientology's use of the copyright law for the purpose of silencing its critics" (Introvigne, "So Many Evil Things," 287).

9. See Rothstein, "His Name Was Xenu," 368; Frank K. Flinn, "Confidential Scriptures in Religions," Church of Scientology: Copyright and Trade Secrets on the Internet, 1994, http://www.theta.com/copyright/flinn.htm.

10. Fearer, "Scientology's Secrets," 350.

11. Heldal-Lund, "What Is Scientology," Operation Clambake, http://www.xenu.net/roland-intro.html.

12. "Some Copyright Considerations," Operation Clambake, www.xenu.net/copyright.html.

13. Fearer, "Scientology's Secrets," 351.

14. Lorne L. Dawson and Douglas E. Cowan, eds., *Religion Online: Finding Faith on the Internet* (New York: Routledge, 2004), 7.

15. Richard Clarke, *Cyber War: The Next Threat to National Security and What to Do About It* (New York: Ecco, 2010).

16. "Mr. David Miscavige," Religious Technology Center, 2008, http://www.rtc.org/david-miscavige.htm.

17. "Religious Technology Center: Holder of the Dianetics and Scientology Trademarks," Scientology.org, 2009, http://www.scientology.org/WORLD/WORLDEND/corp/rtc.htm.

18. "What Has Been the Church's Role in Protecting Free Speech and Intellectual Property Rights on the Internet?" Scientologynews.org, 2011, http://www.scientologynews.org/faq/what-has-been-the-church-role-in-protecting-internet-free-speech.html.

19. Church of Scientology International, "Briefing Re: The Church of Scientology and the Internet," provided for the University of Virginia Religious Movements Page, 2000, http://religiousmovements.lib.virginia.edu/nrms/scientology_briefing.html. For a good summary of the major lawsuits of the 1990s, see Ann Brill and Ashley Packard, "Silencing Scientology's Critics on the Internet: A Mission Impossible?" *Communications and the Law* 19, no. 4 (1997): 3.

20. Richard Leiby, "Ex-Scientologist Collects $8.7 Million in 22-Year-Old Case," *Washington Post*, May 10, 2002, A3.

21. Joel Sappel and Robert Welkos, "Scientologists Block Access to Secret Documents," *Los Angeles Times*, November 5, 1985, http://pqasb.pqarchiver.com/latimes/access/64568420.html?dids=64568420:64568420&FMT=ABS&FMTS=ABS:FT.

22. Sappel and Welkos, "Scientologists Block Access."

23. "Fight Against Coercive Tactics Network," 2010, http://www.factnet.org/.

24. Brill and Packard, "Silencing Scientology's Critics," 5. "[T]he church not only sued for copyright infringement but for trade secret misappropriation. Copyright infringement occurs when someone violates the exclusive rights of a copyright owner to reproduce, distribute, perform, display, or make derivative works based on a copyrighted work. A trade secret is information that has economic value from not being generally known. A trade secret is misappropriated when it is disclosed or used by another without the consent of the trade secret rights holder" (ibid., 3–4).

25. James Brooke, "Scientologists Lose a Battle on the Internet," *New York Times*, September 14, 1995, http://www.nytimes.com/1995/09/14/us/scientologists-lose-a-battle-on-the-internet.html.

26. Fearer, "Scientology's Secrets," 352.

27. *Religious Technology Center v. F.A.C.T.Net et al.*, 945 F. Supp. 1470 (D. Colo. 1995). No. 95-K-2143.

28. James Brooke, "Scientologists Lose a Battle."

29. Courtney Macavinta, "Scientologists Settle Legal Battle," CNET, March 30, 1999, http://news.com.com/Scientologists+settle+legal+battle/2100-1023_3-223683.html ?tag=item.

30. Brill and Packard, "Silencing Scientology's Critics," 5. See Fearer, "Scientology's Secrets," 352.

31. "Declaration of Steven Fishman," *Church of Scientology v. Steven Fishman.* United States District Court for the State of California, March 1, 1993. No. CV 91 6426 HLH (Tx).

32. Behar, "Thriving Cult."

33. *Church of Scientology International v. Fishman.* No. CV. 91-6426. (C.D. Cal. 1994). Reproduced online at Karen Spaink, "The Fishman Affidavit," 1995, http://www .xs4all.nl/~kspaink/fishman/ot8b.html.

34. See Atack, *A Piece of Blue Sky*, 89–102.

35. Brill and Packard, "Silencing Scientology's Critics," 9–10.

36. Brill and Packard, "Silencing Scientology's Critics," 11.

37. Ibid.

38. Spaink, "The Fishman Affidavit," 1995, http://www.xs4all.nl/~kspaink/fishman/ home.html.

39. Grossman, "The Wheels of Xenu Grind Exceedingly Slow," *Inquirer*, September 12, 2003, http://www.theinquirer.net/inquirer/news/1040912/the-mills-xenu-grind-exceed ing-slow.

40. Prendergast, "Stalking the Net."

41. Chris Sherman, "Google Airs Scientology Infringement Demand," Internetnews .com, April 15, 2002, http://www.internetnews.com/bus-news/article.php/1009321/ Google+Airs+Scientology+Infringement+Demand.htm. The letter to Google can be found at Chillingeffects.org: http://www.chillingeffects.org/dmca512/notice.cgi ?NoticeID=232.

42. Cade Metz, "Wikipedia Bans Church of Scientology," *Register*, May 29, 2009, http://www.theregister.co.uk/2009/05/29/wikipedia_bans_scientology/. See "Wikipedia Bans Scientology Edits," UPI.com, May 31, 2009, http://www.upi.com/Top_News/ 2009/05/31/Wikipedia-bans-Scientology-edits/UPI-34941243746054/.

43. Ryan Singel, "Wikipedia Bans Church of Scientology," *Wired*, May 29, 2009, http://www.wired.com/epicenter/2009/05/wikipedia-bans-church-of-scientology/.

44. Metz, "Wikipedia Bans."

45. Ibid.

46. "Serious Business: Anonymous Takes on Scientology," *Baltimore City Paper*, April 2, 2008, http://www.citypaper.com/columns/story.asp?id=15543.

47. Andrea Seabrook, "Hackers Target Scientology Websites," *All Things Considered*, National Public Radio, January 1, 2008.

48. "Where in the World Is the Internet's Most Popular Video?" FactNet.org, 2008, http://factnet.org/?p=225. See also *Tom Cruise Scientology Video*, YouTube.com, 2008, http://www.youtube.com/watch?v=UFBZ_uAbxS0.

49. *Tom Cruise Scientology Video.*

50. Robert Vamosi, "Anonymous Hackers Take on Scientology," CNET, January 24, 2008, http://news.cnet.com/8301-10789_3-9857666-57.html.

51. Chris Landers, "Serious Business," *Baltimore City Paper*, April 2, 2008, http://www.citypaper.com/news/story.asp?id=15543.

52. "Message to Scientology," Anonymous (Group), Wikisource.org, http://en.wikisource.org/wiki/Message_to_Scientology.

53. "Anonymous Hacker Pleads Guilty to 2008 Attack on Scientology Sites," *Los Angeles Times*, May 11, 2009, http://latimesblogs.latimes.com/technology/2009/05/perpeterator-of-2008-cyberattack-on-scientology-pleads-guilty.html.

54. Xenubarb, email interview with author, February 22, 2010.

55. Gabriel McKee, "Taking It to the Streets," *Religion Dispatches*, June 11, 2008, http://www.religiondispatches.org/archive/mediaculture/294/taking_it_to_the_streets% 3A _anonymous_vs._scientology.

56. "Who Are These Masked Men?" *U Weekly*, March 26, 2008, 6.

57. Chef Xenu, interview with author, Columbus, OH, November 10, 2009.

58. Email from Ava Paquette of Moxon & Kobrin, Los Angeles, CA, October 8, 2005.

59. *Anonymous, Frequently Asked Questions*, booklet distributed in Columbus, OH, October 2, 2010.

60. Interview with author, Columbus, OH, October 2, 2010.

61. Fearer, "Scientology's Secrets," 350.

62. Brill and Packard, "Silencing Scientology's Critics," 22–23.

63. Hadden, in Cowan, "Contested Spaces," 255.

64. Brill and Packard, "Silencing Scientology's Critics," 19.

65. Brill and Packard, "Silencing Scientology's Critics," 22.

66. Alan Prendergast, "Stalking the Net," *Denver Westword News*, October 4, 1995, http://www.westword.com/1995-10-04/news/stalking-the-net/full.

67. Cowan, "Contested Spaces," 267.

68. Brill and Packard, "Silencing Scientology's Critics," 22.

69. Armstrong, phone interview with author, August 10, 2009.

70. Burroughs, *Ali's Smile*, 87.

71. Hubbard, *Dianetics 55*, 7.

72. Clarke, *Cyber War*.

Conclusion: New Religions, Freedom, and Privacy in the Post-9/11 World

1. Hubbard, *The Philadelphia Doctorate Course*, vol. 2 (Los Angeles: Golden Era Productions, 2007), 491–92.

2. *Church of Scientology of California v. Commissioner of International Revenue Service*, No. 3352-78 (D.DC, 1984), 462–63.

3. "Scientology: A History of Abuse," *AC360°* (blog), CNN, March 25, 2010, http://ac360.blogs.cnn.com/2010/03/25/scientology-a-history-of-violence/. For interviews with former high-ranking members who have left the church, see Childs and Tobin, "The Truth Rundown"; Marty Rathbun, *Moving On Up a Little Higher* (blog), http://markrathbun.wordpress.com/; "John Sweeney Revisits the Church of Scientology," *BBC News Panorama*, September 26, 2010, http://news.bbc.co.uk/panorama/hi/front_page/newsid_9032000/9032278.stm.

4. "French Court Convicts Church of Scientology of Fraud," *CNN*, October 27, 2009, http://www.cnn.com/2009/WORLD/europe/10/27/france.scientology.fraud/index.html. See "Scientologists Convicted of Fraud," *BBC News*, October 27, 2009, http://news.bbc .co.uk/2/hi/8327569.stm.

5. "Scientology—Zweifel an Verbotsplänen," *Tagesspiegel*, December 7, 2007, http://www.tagesspiegel.de/zeitung/scientology-zweifel-an-verbotsplaenen/1116020.html. See Andrew Purvis, "Germany's Battle Against Scientology," *Time*, December 17, 2007, http://www.time.com/time/world/article/0,8599,1695514,00.html.

6. See endnotes 98–107 of chapter 3 above and Schnabel, *Remote Viewers*, 199–200.

7. See endnotes 70–72 of chapter 4 above and Many's discussion in *My Billion Year Contract*, 165.

8. On this unusual linkage, see Robert Farley, "Scientology Awards Reach out to Black Community," *St. Petersburg Times*, February 18, 2006, http://www.sptimes.com/2006/02/18/Worldandnation/Scientology_awards_re.shtml. See also the materials collected at "Scientology and Nation of Islam Connections," Whyweprotest.net, 2010, http://wiki.whyweprotest.net/Scientology_and_Nation_of_Islam_connections.

9. See, for example, the allegations in Headley, *Blown for Good*, and Reitman, "Inside Scientology."

10. On the conflicts over religious status in France and Germany, see Purvis, "Germany's Battle," and the CNN, "French Court."

11. Church of Scientology International, *Scientology: Improving Life in a Troubled World* (Church of Scientology International, 1993), 3.

12. Chidester, "Religion of Baseball," 760.

13. Karl E. Kirschner, "Report on Post-Mortem Examination No.86-A-015," Office of the Sheriff-Coroner, San Luis Obispo, CA, January 25, 1986.

14. Karl E. Kirschner, "Toxicology Report," San Luis Obispo, CA, January 27, 1986.

15. Bolitho, *Twelve Against the Gods*, 7.

16. Joel Sappell and Robert W. Welkos, "The Mind Behind the Religion," *Los Angeles Times*, June 24, 1990, http://www.latimes.com/news/local/la-scientology062490,0,5784378.story.

17. Young, interviewed in "Secret Lives: L. Ron Hubbard."

18. Sue Lindsay, quoted in Atack, *A Piece of Blue Sky*, 353.

19. "Mr. David Miscavige," Religious Technology Center, 2008, http://www.rtc.org/david-miscavige.htm.

20. See Marty Rathbun interview with the *St. Petersburg Times*, 2009, http://www.tampabay.com/specials/2009/reports/project/rathbun.shtml. See also Atack, *A Piece of Blue Sky*, 308–13, 360–61.

21. Behar, "Thriving Cult," 51. For similar allegations regarding Miscavige, see Childs and Tobin, "The Truth Rundown"; Goodstein, "Defectors Say Church of Scientology Hides Abuse."

22. Childs and Tobin, "The Truth Rundown." Goodstein, "Defectors Say Church of Scientology Hides Abuse"; "Scientology: A History of Violence," AC360.blogs.cnn.com, March 25, 2010, http://ac360.blogs.cnn.com/2010/03/25/scientology-a-history-of-violence/.

23. "David Miscavige: The Peacemaker," *Freedom*, 2010, http://www.freedommag .org/david_miscavige_peacemaker.

24. Interview in Columbus, OH, October, 2010. See "Islands of Friendliness: Ideal Orgs Around the World," *Freedom*, 2010, http://www.freedommag.org/scientology _Islands_of_Friendliness_Ideal_Orgs_around_the_World.

25. Laurie Goodstein, "Defectors Say Church of Scientology Hides Abuse," *New York Times*, March 6, 2010, http://www.nytimes.com/2010/03/07/us/07scientology .html?pagewanted=2. See "About the Church of Scientology," Religious Tolerance.org, 2009, http://www.religioustolerance.org/sciennews09.htm.

26. As J. Gordon Melton notes, the church's numbers include "anyone who ever bought a Scientology book or took a basic course. Ninety-nine percent of them don't ever darken the door of the church again." If the church did have four million members in the United States, as it claims, "they would be like the Lutherans and would show up on a national survey" (Elaine Jarvik, "Scientology: Church Now Claims More Than 8 Million Members," *Desert Morning News*, September 20, 2004, http://web.archive.org/ web/20071212145039/http://deseretnews.com/dn/view/0,1249,595091823,00.html).

27. Rathbun, interview with the *St. Petersburg Times*, 2009, http://www.tampabay .com/specials/2009/reports/project/rathbun.shtml.

28. Rathbun, quoted in Goodstein, "Defectors."

29. Joel Sappell and Robert W. Welkos, "On the Offensive Against an Array of Suspected Foes," *Los Angeles Times*, June 29, 1990, http://www.latimes.com/news/local/ la-scientology062990x,1,5622544,full.story?coll=la-news-comment. See also Joe Childs and Thomas C. Tobin, "Chased by their Church," *St. Petersburg Times*, October 21, 2009, http://www.tampabay.com/news/scientology/article1048134.ece; and Many's account of the OSA in *My Billion Year Contract*.

30. Headley, *Blown for Good*, 75–76.

31. Douglas Frantz, "Distrust in Clearwater," *New York Times*, December 1, 1997, http://www.nytimes.com/1997/12/01/us/distrust-clearwater-special-report-death-sci entologist-heightens-suspicions.html?pagewanted=1?pagewanted=1. See Joan E. Wood, District Medical Examiner, "Report of Autopsy," Largo, FL, December 7, 1995.

32. Douglas Frantz, "Florida Drops Charges Against Scientology in 1995 Death," *New York Times*, June 13, 2000, http://www.nytimes.com/2000/06/13/us/ florida-drops-charges-against-scientology-in-1995-death.html.

33. Jonathan Abel, "New Foe Emerges Against Scientology," *St. Petersburg Times*, February 8, 2008, http://www.sptimes.com/2008/02/08/Northpinellas/New_foe_emerges _again.shtml.

34. Church of Scientology International, *Scientology: Theology and Practice of a Contemporary Religion* (Los Angeles: Bridge Publications, 1998), v.

35. Church of Scientology International, *Scientology*, 5. For Wach's forms of religious expression, see *The Comparative Study of Religions* (New York: Columbia University Press, 1963), 59–143.

36. Wilson, in Church of Scientology International, *Scientology*, 145. Wilson's twenty points are: (1) belief in agencies that transcend normal sense perception; (2) belief that such agencies affect and/or create the natural world; (3) belief that at some times supernatural intervention in human affairs has occurred; (4) belief that supernatural agencies have superintended human history; (5) belief that man's fortune depends on

relationships with these agencies; (6) belief that the individual may influence his experience by behaving in prescribed ways; (7) prescribed actions for individual or collective
performances; (8) actions performed to seeks special assistance from supernatural
sources; (9) expressions of devotion, gratitude or obedience; (10) sacralization of language, objects, places, and edifices; (11) regular performances of ritual commemorating
important events; (12) worship and exposition of teachings that produce the experience
of community and common identity; (13) moral rules; (14) seriousness of purpose and
lifelong devotion; (15) accumulation of merit or demerit to which a moral economy of
reward or punishment is attached; (16) a special class of religious functionaries who
serve as custodians of sacred objects, scripture, etc. (17) payment to such specialists for
their services; (18) the claim that religious knowledge provides solutions for all problems and explains the meaning of life; (19) claim of legitimacy for religious knowledge
by reference to revelation and tradition; (20) claims to truth that are not subject to em-
pirical test, since goals ultimately are transcendent (116–17).

37. Email interview with author, March 10, 2010.

38. Armstrong, "Scientology: The Dangerous Environment racket," Suppressive Person Defense League, 2008, http://suppressiveperson.org/spdl/index.php?option=com
_content&task=view&id=544&Itemid=1.

39. Testimony of Gerald Armstrong in *Religious Technology Center v. Grady Ward*,
United States District Court for the Northern District of California, No. C-96-20207,
January 26, 1997.

40. Kent, "Scientology—Is This a Religion?"

41. Smith, *Relating Religion*, 193.

42. See Asad, *Genealogies*, 29; King, *Orientalism*, 40.

43. Lincoln, *Holy Terrors*, 5–6.

44. Hubbard, *The Phoenix Lectures: Freeing the Human Spirit* (Los Angeles: Golden
Era Productions, 2007), 59.

45. Hopkins, *Law of Tax-Exempt Organizations*, p. 239. See *United States v. Kuch*,
288 F. Supp. 439, 443–44 (D.D.C. 1968).

46. Smith and Snake, *One Nation*, 136.

47. As Asad suggests, "there cannot be a universal definition of religion, not only
because its constituent elements and relationships are historically specific, but because
that definition is itself the product of discursive processes" (*Genealogies*, 29).

48. See Urban, *Secrets of the Kingdom*; Urban, "Fair Game"; Cole and Dempsey, *Terrorism*, 153.

49. Tabor and Gallagher, *Why Waco?* 184.

50. Wessinger, *How the Millennium*, 150; see D. A. Metraux, *Aum Shinrikyo's Impact
on Japanese Society* (Lewiston, ME: Edwin Mellon Press, 2002).

51. Ian Reader, *Religious Violence in Contemporary Japan* (Richmond, VA: Curzon
Press, 2000), 255. See Edge, *Legal Responses*, 393.

52. See Urban, *Secrets of the Kingdom*, 80–87.

53. See Barkun, "Religion and Secrecy," 275–301; Urban, *Secrets of the Kingdom*, 81.

54. Cole and Dempsey, *Terrorism*, 153.

55. Gilbert Herdt, *Secrecy and Cultural Reality: Utopian Ideologies of the New Guinea
Men's House* (Ann Arbor, MI: University of Michigan Press, 2003), xiii.

- SELECTED BIBLIOGRAPHY -

Abbreviations

DSTD   Hubbard, L. Ron. *The Dianetics and Scientology Technical Dictionary.* Los Angeles: Publication Organizations, 1975.

FBI   Federal Bureau of Investigation Freedom of Information / Privacy Acts Section. Subject: *Church of Scientology/L. Ron Hubbard,* 1951–1991.

MMTD   Hubbard, L. Ron. *Modern Management Technology Defined.* Los Angeles: Church of Scientology of California, 1976.

MS   Hubbard, L. Ron. *The Management Series, 1970–1974.* Los Angeles: Church of Scientology of California, 1975.

OEC   Hubbard, L. Ron. *The Organization Executive Course: An Encyclopedia of Scientology Policy.* Los Angeles: American Saint Hill Organization, 1974.

RSD   Hubbard, L. Ron. *The Research and Discovery Series: A Running Record of Research into the Mind and Life.* Los Angeles: Bridge Publications, 1994–1997.

TBDS   Hubbard, L. Ron. *The Technical Bulletins of Dianetics and Scientology.* Los Angeles: Scientology Publications, 1976.

UCLA   University of California Los Angeles Library, Department of Special Collections. "Material Related to the Church of Scientology," 1960–1982.

Recorded Lectures and Published Works of L. Ron Hubbard

Hubbard, L. Ron. *Electropsychometric Auditing Operator's Manual.* London: Hubbard Association of Scientologists International, n.d.

———. "Terra Incognita: The Mind." *Explorer's Journal* 28, no. 1 (1950).

———. "Dianetics: The Evolution of a Science." *Astounding Science Fiction* 45, no. 3 (1950): 43–87.

———. "The Dianetics Question: Homo Superior, Here We Come!" *Marvel Science Stories* 3 (May 1951): 111–13.

———. *Final Blackout.* Providence, RI: Hadley Publishing, 1948.

———. *Have You Lived Before This Life? A Scientific Survey.* London: Hubbard Association of Scientologists International, 1958.

———. *HCO Manual of Justice.* London: Hubbard Communications Office, 1959.

———. *The E-Meter Essentials.* Phoenix: Hubbard College of Scientology, 1967.

———. *Introduction to Scientology Ethics.* Edinburgh: Publications Organization Worldwide, 1968.

———. *Scientology: A History of Man.* Los Angeles: American Saint Hill Organization, 1968.

Hubbard, L. Ron. *Mission into Time*. Los Angeles: American Saint Hill Organization, 1973.

——. *Modern Management Technology Defined: Hubbard Dictionary of Administration and Management*. Los Angeles: Church of Scientology of California, 1976.

——. *Fear and Typewriter in the Sky*. New York: Popular Library, 1977.

——. *Battlefield Earth: A Saga of the Year 3000*. New York: St. Martin's Press, 1982.

——. *Ron's Journal 67*. Los Angeles: Golden Era Productions, 1983.

——. *A Series of Lectures on the Whole Track*. Los Angeles: Golden Era Productions, 1985.

——. *All About Radiation*. Los Angeles: Bridge Publications, 1989.

——. *Secrets of the MEST Universe*. Los Angeles: Bridge Publications, 1990.

——. *Fear*. Los Angeles: Bridge Publications, 1991.

——. *Ole Doc Methuselah*. Los Angeles: Bridge Publications, 1992.

——. *Exteriorization and the Phenomena of Space*. Los Angeles: Golden Era Productions, 1993.

——. *Scientology: The Fundamentals of Thought*. Los Angeles: Bridge Publications, 1997.

——. *The Philadelphia Doctorate Course*. Los Angeles: Golden Era Productions, 2001.

——. *The Command of Theta*. Los Angeles: Golden Era Productions, 2001.

——. *To the Stars*. Hollywood: Galaxy Press, 2004.

——. *Scientology 8-8008*. Los Angeles: Bridge Publications, 2006.

——. *Scientology 8-80*. Los Angeles: Bridge Publications, 2007.

——. *Dianetics: The Modern Science of Mental Health*. Los Angeles: Bridge Publications, 2007.

——. *Dianetics: The Original Thesis*. Los Angeles: Bridge Publications, 2007.

——. *Dianetics 55*. Los Angeles: Bridge Publications, 2007.

——. *Dianetics: Lectures and Demonstrations*. Los Angeles: Golden Era Productions, 2007.

——. *Hubbard Professional Course Lectures*. Los Angeles: Golden Era Productions, 2007.

——. *The Creation of Human Ability*. Los Angeles: Bridge Publications, 2007.

——. *Technique 88: Incidents on the Track Before Earth*. Los Angeles: Golden Era Productions, 2007.

——. *Phoenix Lectures: Freeing the Human Spirit*. Los Angeles: Golden Era Productions, 2007.

——. *Professional Course Lectures*. Los Angeles: Golden Era Productions, 2007.

——. *Self Analysis*. Los Angeles: Bridge Publications, 2007.

——. *Source of Life Energy*. Los Angeles: Golden Era Productions, 2007.

——. *Science of Survival*. Los Angeles: Bridge Publications, 2007.

——. *The Philadelphia Doctorate Course*. Vol. 2. Los Angeles: Golden Era Productions, 2007.

——. *The Great Secret*. Hollywood: Galaxy Press, 2008.

——. *Hymn of Asia*. Los Angeles: Golden Era Productions, 2009.

Hubbard, L. Ron (probable author). *Brain-Washing: A Synthesis of the Russian Textbook on Psychopolitics*. Los Angeles: American Saint Hill Organization, 1955.

Other Church of Scientology Documents

Church of Scientology International. *Scientology: Improving Life in a Troubled World.* Church of Scientology International, 1993.

——. *Scientology: Theory and Practice of a Contemporary Religion.* Los Angeles: Bridge Publications, 1998.

——. "Briefing re: The Church of Scientology and the Internet." Provided for the University of Virginia Religious Movements Page, 2000.

——. *What is Scientology?* Los Angeles: Bridge Publications, 1998.

Church of Scientology of California. *Introducing Scientology.* Los Angeles: Church of Scientology of California, 1976.

——. *Press View the FBI Raid.* Los Angeles: Church of Scientology of California, 1977.

Friends of Ron. *L. Ron Hubbard: A Profile.* Los Angeles: Bridge Publications, 1995.

Hubbard, Diana. "A Prayer for 'Total Freedom.'" *Advance!* 8 (1970): 11.

U.S. Ministerial Conference of Scientology Ministers. *The American Inquisition: U.S. Government Agency Harassment, Religious Persecution and Abuse of Power.* Church of Scientology of California, 1977.

Selected Periodicals

Aberree   *Celebrity Centre Poets*   *Journal of Scientology*
Ability Minor   *Celebrity*   *Scientology*
Advance!   *Clear News*   *Source*
Auditor   *Freedom*
Certainty   *Freewinds*

Major Court Cases

Church of Scientology of California v. Armstrong. No. C 420153. (Cal. Super. Ct. 1984).

Church of Scientology of California v. Armstrong, 232 Cal. App. 3d 1060 (Cal. 2nd Ct. App. 1991). Nos. B025920, B038975.

Church of Scientology of California v. Internal Revenue Service. 569 F. Supp. 1165 (D. D.C. 1983). No. 80-3239.

Church of Scientology International v. Fishman. No. CV. 91-6426 (C.D. Cal. 1994).

Founding Church of Scientology v. United States. 133 U.S. App. D.C. 229, 409 F. 2d 1146 (1969).

Religious Technology Center v. F.A.C.T.Net et al. 945 F. Supp. 1470 (D. Colo. 1995). No. 95-K-2143.

Religious Technology Center v. F.A.C.T.Net, Inc. 901 F. Supp. 1519 (D. Colo. 1995). No. 95-B-2143.

Scott v. Cult Awareness Network. 151 F. 3d, 1247 (9th Cir. 1998). No. 96-35050.

United States of America v. Founding Church of Scientology et al. 333 F. Supp. 357 (D.D.C. 1971). No. D.C. 1-63.

United States of America v. Jane Kember. 487 F. Supp. 1340 (D.D.C. 1980). No. 78-401 (2) & (3).

Secondary Sources

Allitt, Patrick. *Religion in America Since 1945.* New York: Columbia University Press, 2003.

Anderson, Kevin Victor. *Report of the Board of Enquiry into Scientology.* Victoria, Australia: State of Victoria, 1965.

Anonymous. *Message to Scientology.* YouTube.com, January 2008. http://www.youtube .com/watch?v=fSpZp6sWhgM.

Anthony, Dick. "Tactical Ambiguity and Brainwashing Formulations: Science or Pseudo-Science?" In *Misunderstanding Cults: Searching for Objectivity in a Controversial Field,* ed. Benjamin Zablocki and Thomas Robbins, 215–317. Toronto: University of Toronto Press, 2001.

Armstrong, Gerry. "Gerry Armstrong: Scientology's Salmon Rushdie." GerryArmstrong .org, 2002. http://www.gerryarmstrong.org/50grand/introduction.html#_ednref2.

Atack, Jon. *A Piece of Blue Sky: Scientology, Dianetics and L. Ron Hubbard Exposed.* New York: Carol, 1990.

Bainbridge, William Sims, and Rodney Stark. "Scientology: To Be Perfectly Clear." *Sociological Analysis* 41, no. 2 (1980): 128–36.

Barkun, Michael. "Religion and Secrecy after September 11." *Journal of the American Academy of Religion* 74, no. 2 (2006): 275–301.

Behar, Richard. "The Thriving Cult of Greed and Power." *Time,* May 6, 1991, 50–57.

Bolitho, William. *Twelve Against the Gods: The Story of Adventure.* New York: Simon and Schuster, 1929.

Brill, Ann, and Ashley Packard. "Silencing Scientology's Critics on the Internet: A Mission Impossible?" *Communications and the Law* 19, no. 4 (1997): 1–23.

Bromley, David, and Anson D. Shupe Jr. *Strange Gods: The Great American Cult Scare.* Boston: Beacon Press, 1981.

Burroughs, William S. *Ali's Smile: Naked Scientology.* Bonn: Expanded Mind Editions, 1978.

Carter, John. *Sex and Rockets: The Occult World of Jack Parsons.* Los Angeles: Feral House, 1999.

Chidester, David. "The Church of Baseball, the Fetish of Coca-Cola, and the Potlatch of Rock 'n' Roll: Theoretical Models for the Study of Religion in American Popular Culture." *Journal of the American Academy of Religion* 64, no. 4 (1996): 744–65.

Childs, Joe, and Frank C. Tobin, "Scientology: The Truth Rundown." *St. Petersburg Times,* June 2009. http://www.tampabay.com/specials/2009/reports/project/.

Christensen, Dorthe Refslund. "Inventing L. Ron Hubbard: On the Construction and Maintenance of the Hagiographic Mythology of Scientology's Founder." In *Controversial New Religions,* ed. James R. Lewis and Jesper Aagaard Petersen, 227–58. New York: Oxford University Press, 2005.

———. *Scientology: Fra terapi tel religion.* Copenhagen: Gyldendal, 1997.

Cowan, Douglas E. "Contested Spaces: Movement, Countermovement and E-Space Propaganda." In *Religion Online: Finding Faith on the Internet,* ed. Lorne L. Dawson and Douglas E. Cowan, 233–49. New York: Routledge, 2004.

———. "Researching Scientology: Perceptions, Premises and Problematics." In *Scientology,* ed. James R. Lewis, 53–79. New York: Oxford University Press, 2009.

Davis, Derek, and Barry Hankins, eds. *New Religious Movements and Religious Liberty in America*. Waco, TX: Baylor University Press, 2002.

Dawson, Lorne L. "The Sociocultural Significance of Modern New Religious Movements." In *The Oxford Handbook of New Religious Movements*, ed. James R. Lewis, 68–99. New York: Oxford University Press, 2004.

———. *Comprehending Cults: The Sociology of New Religious Movements*. New York: Oxford University Press, 2006.

Dawson, Lorne L., and Douglas E. Cowan. *Religion Online: Finding Faith on the Internet*. New York: Routledge, 2004.

Edge, Peter W. *Legal Responses to Religious Difference*. New York: Kluwer Law International, 2002.

Ellwood, *The Fifties Spiritual Marketplace: American Religion in a Decade of Conflict*. New Brunswick, NJ: Rutgers University Press, 1997.

Eshbach, Lloyd. *Over My Shoulder: Reflections on a Science Fiction Era*. Philadelphia: Oswald Train, 1983.

Garrison, Omar. *Playing Dirty: The Secret War Against Beliefs*. Los Angeles: Ralston-Pilot, 1980.

———. *The Hidden Story of Scientology*. Secaucus, NJ: Citadel Press, 1974.

Haack, Friedrich-Wilhelm. *Scientology: Magie des 20. Jahrhunderts*. München: Claudius Verlag, 1991.

Hadden, Jeffrey K., and Douglas E. Cowan, eds. *Religion on the Internet: Research Prospects and Promises*. New York: JAI, 2000.

Hanegraaff, Wouter J. *New Age Religion and Western Culture: Esotericism in the Mirror of Secular Thought*. Albany: SUNY Press, 1996.

Hansen, Susan. "Did Scientology Strike Back?" *American Lawyer*, June 1997.

Headley, Marc. *Blown for Good: Behind the Iron Curtain of Scientology*. Burbank, CA: BFG Books, 2010.

Hemminger, Hansjörg: *Scientology. Der Kult der Macht*. Stuttgart: Quell, 1997.

Holmes, H. H. (pseudonym). *Rocket to the Morgue*. New York: Duell, Sloan and Pearce, 1942.

Horrowitz, Paul. "Scientology in Court: A Comparative Analysis and Some Thoughts on Issues in Law and Religion." *DePaul Law Review* 85 (1997): 86–160.

Hubbard, L. Ron, Jr. "Penthouse Interview." *Penthouse*, June 1983, 111–13, 166, 170–75.

Huber, Oliver. *Scientology: zwischen Verheimlichung und Desinformation*. Institut für Soziologie, Universität Hamburg, 1994.

Introvigne, Massimo. "So Many Evil Things: Anti-Cult Terrorism via the Internet." In *Religion on the Internet: Research Prospects and Promises*, ed. Jeffrey K. Hadden and Douglas E. Cowan, 277–308. New York: JAI, 2000.

Kaufman, Robert. *Inside Scientology: How I Joined Scientology and Became Superhuman*. London: Olympia Press, 1972.

Kent, Stephen A. "Scientology—Is This a Religion?" *Marburg Journal of Religion* 4, no. 1 (1999).

———. "The Creation of 'Religious' Scientology." *Religious Studies and Theology* 18, no. 2 (1999): 97–126.

Kent, Stephen A. "The Globalization of Scientology: Influence, Control and Opposition in Transnational Markets." *Religion* 29 (1999): 147–69.

———. *From Slogans to Mantras: Social Protest and Religious Conversion in the Late Vietnam War Era.* Syracuse, NY: Syracuse University Press, 2001.

———. "Hollywood's Celebrity-Lobbyists and the Clinton Administration's American Foreign Policy Toward German Scientology." *Journal of Religion and Popular Culture* 1 (Spring 2002).

King, Richard. *Orientalism and Religion: India, Postcolonial Theory and the "Mystic East."* New York: Routledge, 1999.

Kisser, Cynthia. Interview with *60 Minutes*, "The Cult Awareness Network." December 28, 1997.

Kleinmann, Eberhard, ed. *Psychokonzern Scientology.* Abi Aktion Bildungsinformation, 2004.

Kripal, Jeffrey J. *Esalen: America and the Religion of No Religion.* Chicago: University of Chicago Press, 2007.

———. *The Secret Life of a Superpower: Mythical Themes and Paranormal Currents in American Popular Culture.* Chicago: University of Chicago Press, forthcoming.

Kumar, J. P. "Fair Game: Leveling the Playing Field in Scientology Litigation." *Review of Litigation* 16 (Summer 1997): 747–72.

Levy, Alan. "Scientology: A Growing Cult Reaches Dangerously into the Mind," *Life*, November 15, 1968, 99.

Lewis, James R., ed. *Scientology.* New York: Oxford University Press, 2009.

Lincoln, Bruce. "Theses on Method." *Method and Theory in the Study of Religion* 8 (1996): 225–27.

———. *Holy Terrors: Thinking about Religion After September 11.* Chicago: University of Chicago Press, 2003.

Lindsay, Sue. "Scientology Founder Speaks Out." *Rocky Mountain News*, February 20, 1983, 50.

Many, Nancy. *My Billion Year Contract: Memoir of a Former Scientologist.* Bloomington, IN: Xlibris, 2009.

Marks, John. *The Search for the Manchurian Candidate.* New York: Random House, 1980.

Masuzawa, Tomoko. *The Invention of World Religions: Or How European Universalism Was Preserved in the Language of Difference.* Chicago: University of Chicago Press, 2005.

Mathison, Volney. *Mathison Licensed Electropsychometers.* Los Angeles: International Equipment, 1954.

McCutcheon, Russell. *Manufacturing Religion: The Discourse on Sui Generis Religion and the Politics of Nostalgia.* New York: Oxford University Press, 1997.

Melton, J. Gordon. *The Church of Scientology.* Salt Lake City: Signature Books, 2000.

Miller, Russell. *Bare-Faced Messiah: The True Story of L. Ron Hubbard.* New York: H. Holt, 1988.

Mitchell, Alexander. "Scientology: Revealed for the First Time." London *Sunday Times*, October 5, 1969.

Morton, Andrew. *Tom Cruise: An Authorized Biography.* New York: St. Martin's Press, 2008.

Muldoon, Sylvan. *The Phenomena of Astral Projection*. New York: Samuel Weiser, 1951.

Nordhausen, Frank, and Liane von Billerbeck. *Scientology: Wie die Sektenkonzern die Welt erobern will*. Christoph Links Verlag, 2008.

O'Brien, Helen. *Dianetics in Limbo: A Documentary about Immortality*. Philadelphia: Whitmore, 1966.

Parsons, Jack. *Book of B.A.B.A.L.O.N.* Berkeley: Ordo Templi Orientis, 1982.

Passass, N., and M. E. Castillo, "Scientology and its 'Clear' Business." *Behavioral Sciences and Law* 10, no. 103 (1992).

Pendle, George. *Strange Angel: The Otherworldly Life of John Whiteside Parsons*. Orlando: Harcourt, 2005.

Potthoff, Norbert. *Im Labyrinth der Scientology*. Lübbe, 1997.

Raine, Susan. "Surveillance in a New Religious Movement: Scientology as a Test Case." *Religious Studies and Theology* 28, no. 1 (2009): 63–94.

Reitman, Janet. "Inside Scientology: Unlocking the Complex Code of America's Most Mysterious Religion." *Rolling Stone*, February 23, 2006.

Rogers, Alva. "Darkhouse." *Lighthouse* 5 (February 1962).

Ronson, Jon. *The Men Who Stare at Goats*. New York: Simon and Schuster, 2004.

Roof, Wade Clark. *Spiritual Marketplace: Baby Boomers and the Remaking of American Religion*. Princeton, NJ: Princeton University Press, 2001.

Sappell, Joel, and Robert W. Welkos. "The Scientology Story." *Los Angeles Times*, June 24–29, 1990. http://www.latimes.com/news/local/la-scientology-sg,0,4617583.storygallery.

Schnabel, Jim. *Remote Viewers: The Secret History of America's Psychic Spies*. New York: Dell, 1997.

Singel, Ryan. "War Breaks Out Between Hackers and Scientology." *Wired*, January 23, 2008.

Smith, Jonathan Z. *Imagining Religion: From Babylon to Jonestown*. Chicago: University of Chicago Press, 1982.

———. *Relating Religion: Essays in the Study of Religion*. Chicago: University of Chicago Press, 2004.

Strenski, Ivan. *Why Politics Can't Be Freed from Religion*. Malden, MA: Wiley-Blackwell, 2010.

Sutin, Lawrence. *Do What Thou Wilt: A Life of Aleister Crowley*. New York: St. Martin's Press, 2000.

———. *Divine Invasions: A Life of Philip K. Dick*. Cambridge, MA: Da Capo Press, 2005.

Tabor, James D., and Eugene Gallagher. *Why Waco? Cults and the Battle for Religious Freedom in America*. Berkeley: University of California Press, 1995.

Targ, Russell, and Harold Puthoff. *Mind-Reach: Scientists Look at Psychic Abilities*. Delacorte Press, 1977.

Thiede, Werner. *Scientology, Religion oder Geistesmagie?* Neukirchen-Vluyn: Bahn-Friedrich Verlag, 1995.

Urban, Hugh B. "The Torment of Secrecy: Ethical and Epistemological Problems in the Study of Esoteric Traditions." *History of Religions* 37, no. 3 (1998): 209–48.

———. "Fair Game: Secrecy, Security and the Church of Scientology in Cold War America." *Journal of the American Academy of Religion* 74, no. 2 (2006): 356–89.

Urban, Hugh B. *Magia Sexualis: Sex, Magic and Liberation in Modern Western Esotericism*. Berkeley: University of California Press, 2006.

------. *The Secrets of the Kingdom: Religion and Concealment in the Bush Administration*. Lanham, MD: Rowman and Littlefield, 2007.

------. "Secrecy and New Religious Movements: Concealment, Surveillance and Privacy in a New Age of Information." *Religion Compass* 2, no. 1 (2007): 66–83.

------. "The Rundown Truth: Scientology Changes Strategy in War with Media." *Religion Dispatches*, March 17, 2010. http://www.religiondispatches.org/archive/atheologies/2358/the_rundown_truth%3A_scientology_changes_strategy_in_war_with__media_.

------. "The Occult Roots of Scientology? Aleister Crowley, L. Ron Hubbard, and the Origins of a Controversial New Religion." *Nova Religio*, forthcoming (2011).

Wallis, Roy. *The Road to Total Freedom: A Sociological Analysis of Scientology*. New York: Columbia University Press, 1976.

------. "The Moral Career of a Research Project." In *Doing Sociological Research*, ed. Colin Bell and Howard Newby, 148–67. London: Allen and Unwin, 1977.

Whitehead, Harriet. *Renunciation and Reformulation: A Study of Conversion in an American Sect*. Ithaca, NY: Cornell University Press, 1987.

------. "Reasonably Fantastic: Some Perspectives on Scientology, Science Fiction and Occultism." In *Religious Movements in Contemporary America*, ed. I. I. Zaretsky and M. P. Leone. Princeton, NJ: Princeton University Press, 1974.

Whitfield, Stephen J. *The Culture of the Cold War*. Baltimore, MD: Johns Hopkins University Press, 1996.

Williamson, Jack. *Wonder's Child: My Life in Science Fiction*. New York: Bluejay Books, 1984.

Wright, Lawrence. "The Apostate: Paul Haggis v. The Church of Scientology." *New Yorker*, February 11, 2011. http://www.newyorker.com/reporting/2011/02/14/110214fa_fact_wright?currentPage=all.

Zablocki, Benjamin, and Thomas Robbins, eds. *Misunderstanding Cults: Searching for Objectivity in a Controversial Field*. Toronto: University of Toronto Press, 2001.

- INDEX -